Birds, B

'A new Gerald [...] all the qualities that made *My Family and Other Animals* such memorable reading: the humour, the observation, the fine writing and the recurring clashes between the dedicated young naturalist and his long-suffering family. Again we are back in Corfu in that strange household which never refuses admission and attracts a succession of incredible visitors: roistering students, wandering minstrels, a disreputable sea captain and other adventitious humans who are just as exotic and disruptive as the specimens Gerald brings home. Tarantulas, dung beetles, sea horses, water spiders, cuttlefish, owls, and house lizards—they are all his friends, and he makes them as real to to us as they are to himself. This is a book which, I am sure, will be everyone's dish. There is always something to laugh at, but there is much to wonder at also.'

Irish Independent

Birds, Beasts and Relatives

Gerald Durrell

Fontana/Collins

To Theodore Stephanides
in gratitude for laughter
and for learning

First published by Wm. Collins 1969
First issued in Fontana Books 1971
Tenth Impression August 1978

© 1969 Gerald Durrell

Made and printed in Great Britain by
William Collins Sons & Co Ltd, Glasgow

Contents

Conversation

It had been a hard winter and, even when spring was supposed to have taken over, the crocuses—who seemed to have a touching and unshaken faith in the seasons—were having to push their way grimly through a thin crust of snow. The sky was low and grey, liable to discharge another fall of snow at any minute, and a biting wind howled round the house. Taken all round, weather conditions were not ideal for a family reunion, particularly when it was my family.

It was a pity, I felt, that when they had all forgathered in England for the first time since the war, they should be treated to something approaching a blizzard. It did not bring out the best in them; it made them more touchy than usual, quicker to take offence and less likely to lend a sympathetic ear to anyone's point of view but their own.

They were grouped, like a pride of moody lions, round a fire so large and flamboyant that it was in immediate danger of setting fire to the chimney. My sister Margo had just added to it by the simple method of dragging in the carcass of a small tree from the garden and pushing one end into the fireplace, while the remainder of the trunk lay across the hearthrug. My mother was knitting, but you could tell by the slightly vacant look on her face and the way her lips moved occasionally, as if she was in silent prayer, that she was really occupied with the menu for tomorrow's lunch. My brother Leslie was buried behind a large manual on ballistics, while my elder brother Lawrence, clad in a roll-top pullover of the type usually worn by fishermen (several sizes too large for him) was standing by the window sneezing wetly and regularly into a large scarlet handkerchief.

'Really this is a *frightful* country,' he said, turning on us belligerently, as though we were all directly responsible for the climatic conditions prevailing, 'you set foot on shore at Dover and you're met by a positive barrage of cold germs . . . d'you realise that this is the first cold I've had in twelve years? Simply because I had the sense to keep away from Pudding Island.

7

Everyone I've met so far has a cold. The entire population of the British Isles seems to do absolutely nothing from one year's end to another except shuffle round in small circles sneezing voluptuously into each other's faces . . . a sort of merry-go-round of re-infection. What chance of survival has one got?'

'Just because *you've* got a cold you carry on as though the world was coming to an end,' said Margo. 'I can't understand why men always make such a fuss.'

Larry gave her a withering look from watering eyes.

'The trouble with you all is that you like being martyrs. No one free from masochistic tendencies would stay in this . . . this viruses' paradise. You've all stagnated; you *like* wallowing here in a sea of infection. One excuses people who have never known anything else, but you all had a taste of the sun in Greece, you should know better.'

'Yes, dear,' said Mother soothingly, 'but you've just come at a bad time. It can be very nice, you know. In the spring for example.'

Larry glared at her.

'I hate to jolt you out of your Rip Van Winkle-like trance,' he said, 'but this is supposed to be the spring . . . and look at it! You need a team of huskies to go down and post a letter.'

'Half an inch of snow,' snorted Margo. 'You do exaggerate.'

'I agree with Larry,' Leslie said, appearing from behind his book. 'It's bloody cold out. Makes you feel you don't want to do anything. You can't even get any decent shooting.'

'Exactly,' said Larry triumphantly, 'while in a sensible country like Greece one would be having breakfast outside and then going down to the sea for a morning bathe. Here my teeth chattter so much it's only with difficulty that I can eat any breakfast.'

'I do wish you'd stop harping on Greece,' said Leslie irritably. 'It reminds me of that bloody book of Gerry's. It took me ages to live that down.'

'Took *you* ages,' said Larry caustically, 'what about me? You've no idea what damage that Dickens-like caricature did to my literary image.'

'By the way he wrote about *me*, you would think that I

never thought about anything but guns and boats,' said Leslie.

'Well, you never do think about anything but guns and boats.'

'I was the one that suffered most,' said Margo. 'He did nothing but talk about my acne.'

'I thought it was quite an accurate picture of you all,' said Mother, 'but he made me out to be a *positive imbecile*.'

'I wouldn't mind being lampooned in decent prose,' Larry pointed out, blowing his nose vigorously, 'but to be lampooned in bad English is unbearable.'

'The title alone is insulting,' said Margo. '*My Family and Other Animals*. I get sick of people saying "and which other animal are you?" '

'I thought the title was rather funny, dear,' said Mother. 'The only thing I thought was that he hadn't used all the best stories.'

'Yes, I agree,' said Leslie.

'What best stories?' Larry demanded suspiciously.

'Well, what about the time you sailed Max's yacht around the island? That was damned funny.'

'If that story had appeared in print I would have sued him.'

'I don't see why, it was very funny,' said Margo.

'And what about the time you took up spiritualism—supposing he'd written about that? I suppose you'd enjoy that?' enquired Larry caustically.

'No I would not—he couldn't write that!' said Margo in horror.

'Well, there you are,' said Larry in triumph. 'And what about Leslie's court case?'

'I don't see why you have to bring me into it,' said Leslie belligerently.

'You were the one who was going on about him not using the best incidents,' Larry pointed out.

'Yes, I'd forgotten about those stories,' said Mother, chuckling. 'I think they were funnier than the ones you used, Gerry.'

'I'm glad you think that,' I said thoughtfully.

'Why?' asked Larry, glaring at me suspiciously.

'Because I've decided to write another book on Corfu and use all those stories,' I explained innocently.

The uproar was immediate.

'I forbid it,' roared Larry, sneezing violently. 'I absolutely forbid it.'

'You're not to write about my spiritualism,' said Margo loudly. 'Mother, tell him he's not to write about that.'

'Nor my court case,' snarled Leslie. 'I won't have it.'

'And if you so much as mention yachts . . .' Larry began.

'Larry, dear, do keep your voice down,' said Mother.

'Well, forbid him to write a sequel then,' shouted Larry.

'Don't be silly, dear, I can't stop him,' said Mother.

'Do you want it all to happen again?' demanded Larry hoarsely. 'The bank writing to ask you if you will kindly remove your overdraft, the tradesmen looking at you askance, anonymous parcels full of straight-jackets being left on the door step, being cut dead by all the relatives. You are supposed to be head of the family, stop him writing it.'

'You do exaggerate, Larry, dear,' said Mother. 'Anyway, I can't stop him if he wants to write it. I don't think it will do any harm and those stories *are* the best ones. I don't see why he shouldn't write a sequel.'

The family rose in a body and told her loudly and vociferously why I should not write a sequel. I waited for the noise to die down.

'And apart from those stories, there are quite a number of others,' I said reminiscently.

'Which ones, dear?' enquired Mother with interest.

The family, red-faced, bristling, glowered at me in an expectant silence.

'Well,' I said thoughtfully, 'I want to give a description of your love affair with Captain Creech, Mother.'

'What?' squeaked Mother indignantly. 'You'll do no such thing . . . love affair with that disgusting old creature, indeed! I won't have you writing about that.'

'Well, I think that's the best story of the lot,' said Larry unctuously, 'the vibrant passion of the romance, the sweet archaic charm of the leading man . . . the way you led the poor old chap on . . .'

'Oh do be quiet, Larry,' said Mother crossly, 'you make me angry when you talk like that. I don't think it's a good idea for you to write this book, Gerry.'

'I second that,' said Larry, 'if you publish we'll sue you in a body.'

Faced with such a firm and united family, bristling in their resolve to prevent me at all costs, there was only one thing I could do. I sat down and wrote this book.

PART I

London: A Prelude

A BRUSH WITH SPIRITS

*What seest thou else in the dark backward
and abysm of time?*

THE TEMPEST

A Brush with Spirits

It all started when Margo suddenly began to put on weight. Before long, to her horror, she was almost circular. Androuchelli, our doctor, was called in to view this mystery. He uttered a long series of distressed 'Po, po, po's,' as he viewed Margo's obesity. He tried her on several pills and potions and a number of diets, to no effect.

'He says,' Margo confided to us tearfully at lunch one day, 'that he thinks it's glandular.'

'Glandular?' said Mother, alarmed. 'What does he mean, glandular?'

'I don't know,' wailed Margaret.

'Must we always discuss your ailments at mealtimes?' enquired Larry.

'Larry, dear, Androuchelli says it's glandular,' said Mother.

'Rubbish,' said Larry airily. 'It's puppy fat.'

'Puppy fat!' squeaked Margo. 'Do you know how much I weigh?'

'What you want is more exercise,' said Leslie. 'Why don't you take up sailing?'

'Don't think the boat's big enough,' said Larry.

'Beast,' said Margo, bursting into tears. 'You wouldn't say things like that if you knew how I felt.'

'Larry, dear,' said Mother, placatingly, 'that wasn't a very kind thing to say.'

'Well, I can't help it if she's wandering around looking like a water melon covered with spots,' said Larry irritably. 'One would think it was my fault the way you all go on.'

'Something will have to be done,' said Mother. 'I shall see Androuchelli tomorrow.'

But Androuchelli repeated that he thought her condition might be glandular and that in his opinion Margo ought to go to London for treatment. So, after a flurry of cables and letters, Margo was despatched to London and into the tender care of two of the only worthwhile relatives with whom we

15

were still on speaking terms, my Mother's cousin, Prudence, and her mother, Great Aunt Fan.

Apart from a brief letter saying she had arrived safely and that she, Cousin Prue and Aunt Fan had taken up residence at a hotel near Notting Hill Gate and that she had been put in touch with a good doctor, we heard nothing further from Margo for a considerable length of time.

'I do wish she would write,' Mother said.

'Don't fuss, Mother,' said Larry. 'What's she got to write about, anyway, except to give you her new dimensions?'

'Well, I like to know what's going on,' said Mother. 'After all, she's in *London*.'

'What's London got to do with it?' asked Larry.

'In a big city like that anything can happen,' said Mother, darkly. 'You hear all sorts of things about girls in big cities.'

'Really, Mother, you do worry unnecessarily,' said Larry in exasperation. 'What do you think's happened to her, for heaven's sake? Do you think she's being lured into some den of vice? They'd never get her through the door.'

'It's no joking matter, Larry,' said Mother severely.

'But you get yourself into a panic about nothing,' said Larry. 'I ask you, what self-respecting white slaver is going to look at Margo twice? I shouldn't think there's one strong enough to carry her off, anyway.'

'Well, I'm worried,' said Mother pugnaciously, 'and I'm going to send a cable.'

So she sent a cable to Cousin Prudence who replied at length saying that Margo was associating with people she didn't approve of and that she thought it would be a good thing if Mother came to talk some sense into her. Immediately pandemonium reigned. Mother, distraught, despatched Spiro, our self-appointed and indispensable guide, philosopher and friend, to buy tickets and started packing frantically. Then suddenly she remembered me. Feeling it would do more harm than good to leave me in the tender care of my two elder brothers, she decided that I should accompany her. So Spiro was despatched to get more tickets and yet more packing was done. I regarded the whole situation as heaven sent, for I had just acquired a new tutor, Mr Richard Kralefsky, who was endeavouring—with grim determination in the face of my opposition—to instruct me in irregular French verbs, and the trip to England, I thought, would give me a much needed respite.

The journey by train was uneventful, except that Mother was in constant fear of being arrested by the Fascist carabineri. This fear increased a thousandfold when, at Milan, I drew a caricature of Mussolini on the steamy window of the carriage. Mother scrubbed at it for quite ten minutes with her handkerchief, with all the dedication of a washerwoman in a contest, before she was satisfied that it was obliterated.

Coming from the calm, slow, sunlit days of Corfu, our arrival in London, late in the evening, was a shattering experience. So many people were at the station that we did not know, all hurrying to and fro, grey faced and worried. The almost incomprehensible language that the porters spoke, and London glitter with lights and churning with people. The taxi nosing its way through Piccadilly like a beetle through a firework display. The cold air that made your breath float like a web of smoke in front of your mouth as you talked, so that you felt like a character in a cartoon strip.

Eventually the taxi drew up outside the fake, soot-encrusted Corinthian columns of Balaclava Mansions. We got our luggage into the hotel with the aid of an elderly, bow-legged, Irish porter, but there was no one to greet us, so apparently our telegram signalling our arrival had gone astray. The young lady, we were informed by the porter, had gone to her meeting, and Miss Hughes and the old lady had gone to feed the dogs.

'What did he say, dear?' asked Mother when he had left the room, for his accent was so thick that it sounded almost as though he was talking a foreign language. I said that Margo had gone to a meeting and that Cousin Prue and Aunt Fan were feeding the dogs.

'What can he mean?' said Mother, bewildered. 'What meeting has Margo gone to? What dogs is he talking about?'

I said I did not know but, from the little I had seen of London, what it needed was a few more dogs around.

'Well,' said Mother, inexpertly putting a shilling in the meter and lighting the gas fire, 'I suppose we'll just have to make ourselves comfortable and wait until they come back.'

We had waited an hour when suddenly the door burst open and Cousin Prue rushed in, arms outstretched, crying, 'Louie,

Louie, Louie,' like some strange marsh bird. She embraced us both, her sloe dark eyes glowing with love and excitement. Her beautiful face, delicately scented, was soft as a pansy as I kissed her dutifully.

'I began to think that you were never coming,' she said 'Mummy is on her way up. She finds the stairs trying, poor dear. Well now, don't you both look well. You must tell me everything. Do you like this hotel, Louie? It's cheap and convenient, but full of the most peculiar people.'

A gentle wheezing sound made itself heard through the open door.

'Ah, there's Mummy,' cried Prue. 'Mummy! Mummy! Louie's here.'

Through the door appeared my Great Aunt Fan. At first glance she looked, I thought rather uncharitably, like a walking tent. She was enveloped in a rusty-red tweed suit of incredible style and dimensions. On her head she wore a somewhat battered velveteen hat of the style that pixies are reputedly wont to use. Her spectacles, through which her eyes stared owlishly, glittered.

'Louie!' she cried, throwing her arms wide and casting her eyes up as though Mother were some divine apparition. 'Louie and Gerald! You have come!'

Mother and I were kissed and embraced heartily. This was not the feathery, petal-soft embrace of Cousin Prue. This was a hearty, rib-cracking embrace and a firm kiss that left your lips feeling bruised.

'I am so sorry we weren't here to greet you, Louie, dear,' said Prue, 'but we weren't sure when you were arriving and we had the dogs to feed.'

'What dogs?' asked Mother.

'Why, my Bedlington puppies, of course,' said Prue. 'Didn't you know? Mummy and I have become dog breeders.' She gave a coy, tinkling laugh.

'But you had something else last time,' said Mother. 'Goats wasn't it?'

'Oh, we've still got those,' said Aunt Fan. 'And my bees and the chickens. But Prudence here thought it would be a good thing to start dog breeding. She's got such a head for business'

'I really think it's a paying concern, Louie, dear,' said Prue earnestly. 'I bought Tinkerbell and then Lucybell . . .'

18

'And then Tinybell,' interrupted Aunt Fan.

'And Tinybell,' said Prue.

'And then there's Lucybell,' said Aunt Fan.

'Oh, Mummy, do be quiet. I've already said Lucybell.'

'And there's Tinkerbell too,' said Aunt Fan.

'Mummy is a little hard of hearing,' said Prue unnecessarily, and they have all had puppies. I brought them up to London o sell and at the same time we have been keeping an eye on Margo.'

'Yes, where is Margo?' asked Mother.

Prue tiptoed over to the door and closed it softly.

'She's at a *meeting*, dear,' she said.

'I know, but what sort of meeting?' asked Mother.

Prue glanced round nervously.

'A *spiritualist* meeting,' she hissed.

'And then there's Lucybell,' said Aunt Fan.

'Oh, Mummy, do be quiet.'

'Spiritualist meeting?' said Mother. 'What on earth's she one to a spiritualist meeting for?'

'To cure her fatness and her acne,' said Prue. 'But mark my ords, no good will come of it. It's an evil power.'

I could see Mother beginning to get alarmed.

'But I don't understand,' she said. 'I sent Margo home to see at doctor, what's his name?'

'I know you did, dear,' said Prue. 'Then, after she came to is hotel, she fell into the grasp of that evil woman.'

'What evil woman?' said Mother, now considerably armed.

'The goats are well too,' said Aunt Fan, 'but their milk eld is down a little this year.'

'Oh, Mummy, do shut up,' hissed Prue. 'I mean that evil oman, Mrs Haddock.'

'Haddock, haddock,' said Mother bewildered. Her train of ought was always liable to be interrupted if anything culin- y was mentioned.

'She's a medium, my dear,' said Prue, 'and she's got her oks on Margo. She's told Margo that she's got a guide.'

'A guide?' said Mother feebly. 'What sort of guide?'

I could see, in her distraught condition, that she was now ginning to think Margo had taken up mountaineering or me similar occupation.

'A spirit guide,' said Prue. 'It's called Mawake. He's supposed to be a Red Indian.'

'I have got ten hives now,' said Aunt Fan proudly. 'We ge
twice as much honey.'

'Mother, be quiet,' said Prue.

'I don't understand,' said Mother plaintively. 'Why isn't sh
still going to the doctor for her injections?'

'Because Mawake told her not to,' said Prue triumphantl
'Three seances ago, he said—according to Margo, and c
course the whole thing comes through Mrs Haddock so yo
can't trust it for a moment—according to Margo, Mawak
said she was to have no more punctures.'

'Punctures?' said Mother.

'Well, I suppose it's Red Indian for injections,' said Prue.

'It is nice to see you again, Louie,' said Aunt Fan. 'I thir
we ought to have a cup of tea.'

'That's a very good idea,' said Mother faintly.

'I'm not going down there to order tea, Mummy,' sa
Prue, glancing at the door as if, behind it, were all the fien
of hell. 'Not when they're having a meeting.'

'Why, what happens?' asked Mother.

'And some toast would be nice,' said Aunt Fan.

'Oh, Mummy, do be quiet,' said Prue. 'You have no id
what happens at these meetings, Louie. Mrs Haddock go
into a trance, then becomes covered with ectoplasm.'

'Ectoplasm?' said Mother. 'What's ectoplasm?'

'I've got a pot of my own honey in my room,' said Au
Fan. 'I'm sure you will enjoy it, Louie. So much purer th
these synthetic things you buy now.'

'It's a sort of stuff that mediums produce,' said Prue.
looks like . . . Well, it looks like, sort of like—I've nev
actually seen it, but I'm told that it looks like brains. Then th
make trumpets fly about and things. I tell you, my dear ɛ
never go into the lower regions of the hotel when they ɛ
holding a meeting.'

Fascinated though I was by the conversation, I felt t
chance of seeing a woman called Mrs Haddock covered w
brains with a couple of trumpets floating about was too go
to miss, so I volunteered to go down and order tea.

To my disappointment, I saw nothing in the lower regic
of the hotel remotely resembling Cousin Prudence's descr

tion but I did manage to get a tray of tea brought up by the Irish porter. We were sipping this, and I was endeavouring to explain to Aunt Fan what ectoplasm was, when Margo arrived, carrying a large cabbage under one arm, accompanied by a dumpy little woman with protruding blue eyes and wispy hair.

'Mother!' said Margo dramatically. 'You've come!'

'Yes, dear,' said Mother grimly. 'And not a moment too soon, apparently.'

'This is Mrs Haddock,' said Margo. 'She's *absolutely marvellous.*'

It became immediately apparent that Mrs Haddock suffered from a strange affliction. She seemed to be incapable of breathing while talking. The result was that she would gabble, all her words latched together like a daisy chain and would then, when her breath ran out, pause and suck it in, making a noise that sounded like 'Whaaaha'.

Now she said to Mother,

'IamdelightedtomeetyouMrsDurrell. Ofcoursemyspiritguide informedmeofyourcoming.Idohopeyouhadacomfortablejourney . . . . Whaaaha.'

Mother, who had been intending to give Mrs Haddock a very frigid and dignified greeting, was somewhat put off by this strange delivery.

'Oh yes. Did we?' she said nervously, straining her ears to understand what Mrs Haddock was saying.

'Mrs Haddock is a spiritualist, Mother,' said Margo proudly, as though she were introducing Leonardo da Vinci or the inventor of the first aeroplane.

'Really, dear?' said Mother, smiling frostily. 'How very interesting.'

'Itgivesonegreatcomforttoknowthatthosewhohavegonebefore arestillintouchwithone . . . Whaaaha,' said Mrs Haddock earnestly. 'Somanypeopleareunaware . . . Whaaaha . . . ofthe spiritworldthatliessoclose.'

'You should have seen the puppies tonight, Margo,' observed Aunt Fan. 'The little tinkers had torn up all their bedding.'

'Mummy, do be quiet,' said Prue, eyeing Mrs Haddock as though she expected her to grow horns and a tail at any moment.

'Yourdaughterisveryluckyinasmuchasshehas . . . Whaaaha,
. . . managedtoobtainoneofthebetterguides,' said Mrs Haddock,
rather as though Margo had riffled through Debrett before
settling on her spirit counsellor.

'He's called Mawake,' said Margo. 'He's *absolutely marvellous*!'

'He doesn't appear to have done you much good so far,'
said Mother tartly.

'But he has,' said Margo indignantly. 'I've lost three ounces.'

'Ittakestimeandpatienceandimplicitbeliefinthefuturelife . . .
Whaaaha. . . . mydearMrsDurell,' said Mrs Haddock, smiling
at Mother with sickly sweetness.

'Yes, I'm sure,' said Mother, 'but I really would prefer it if
Margo was under a medical practitioner one could see.'

'I don't think they meant it,' said Aunt Fan. 'I think they're
teething. Their gums get sore, you know.'

'Mummy, we are not talking about the puppies,' said Prue.
'We are talking about Margo's guide.'

'That will be nice for her,' said Aunt Fan, beaming fondly at
Margo.

'Thespiritworldissomuchwiserthananyearthlybeing . . . .
Whaaaha,' said Mrs Haddock. 'Youcouldn'thaveyourdaughter
inbetterhands.Mawakewasagreatmedicinemaninhisowntribe.
OneofthemostknowledgeableinthewholeofNorthAmerica . . .
Whaaaha.'

'And he's given me such good advice, Mother,' said Margo.
'Hasn't he, Mrs Haddock?'

'Nomorepunctures.Thewhitegirlmusthavenomorepunctures
. . . Whaaaha,' intoned Mrs Haddock.

'There you are,' hissed Prue triumphantly, 'I told you.'

'Have some honey,' said Aunt Fan, companionably. 'It's
not like that synthetic stuff you buy in the shops nowadays.'

'Mummy, be quiet.'

'I still feel, Mrs Haddock, that I would prefer my daughter
to have sensible medical attention rather than this Mawake.'

'Oh, Mother, you're so narrow-minded and Victorian,' said
Margo in exasperation.

'MydearMrsDurrellyoumustlearntotrustthegreatinfluencesof
thespiritworldthatareafterallonlytryingtohelpandguideus . .
Whaaaha,' said Mrs Haddock. 'Ifeelthatifyoucametooneofou

meetingsyouwouldbeconvincedofthegreatpowersofgoodthatour spiritguideshave . . . Whaaaha.'

'I prefer to be guided by my own spirit, thank you very much,' said Mother, with dignity.

'Honey isn't what it used to be,' said Aunt Fan, who had been giving the matter some thought.

'You are just prejudiced, Mother,' said Margo. 'You're condemning a thing without even trying.'

'IfeelsurethatifyoucouldpersuadeyourMothertoattendoneof ourmeetings . . . Whaaaha,' said Mrs Haddock, 'shewouldfinda wholenewworldopeningupbeforeher.'

'Yes, Mother,' said Margo, 'you must come to a meeting. I'm sure you'd be convinced. The things you see and hear! After all, there are no bricks without fire.'

I could see that Mother was suffering an inward struggle. For many years she had been deeply interested in superstitions, folk magic, witchcraft and similar subjects, and now the temptation to accept Mrs Haddock's offer was very great. I waited breathlessly, hoping that she would accept. There was nothing I wanted more at that moment than to see Mrs Haddock covered with brains and with trumpets flying around her head.

'Well,' said Mother, undecided, 'we'll see. We'll talk about it tomorrow.'

'I'msurethatoncewebreakthroughthebarrierforyouwe'llbeable togiveyoualotofhelpandguidance . . . Whaaaha,' said Mrs Haddock.

'Oh yes,' said Margo. 'Mawake's simply *wonderful*!'

'Wearehavinganothermeetingtomorroweveningherein thehotel . . . Whaaaha,' said Mrs Haddock, 'andIdohopethatbothyou andMargowillattend . . . Whaaaha.'

She gave us a pallid smile as though, reluctantly, forgiving us our sins; patted Margo on the cheek and left.

'Really, Margo,' said Mother, as the door closed behind Mrs Haddock, 'you do make me cross.'

'Oh, Mother, you are so old-fashioned,' said Margo. 'That doctor wasn't doing me any good with his injections anyway, and Mawake is working miracles.'

'Miracles,' snorted Mother scornfully. 'You still look exactly the same size to me.'

'Clover,' said Aunt Fan through a mouthful of toast, 'is supposed to be the best, though I prefer heather myself.'

'I tell you, dear,' said Prue, 'this woman's got a grip on you. She's malignant. Be warned before it's too late.'

'All I ask is that you just simply come to a meeting and see,' said Margo.

'Never,' said Prue, shuddering. 'My nerves wouldn't stand it.'

'It's interesting, too, that they have to have bumble-bees to fertilize the clover,' observed Aunt Fan.

'Well,' said Mother, 'I'm much too tired to discuss it now. We will talk it over in the morning.'

'Can you help me with my cabbage?' asked Margo.

'Do what?' enquired Mother.

'Help me with my cabbage,' said Margo.

'I have often wondered whether one could not cultivate bumble-bees,' said Aunt Fan, thoughtfully.

'What do you do with your cabbage?' enquired Mother.

'She puts it on her face,' hissed Prue. 'Ridiculous!'

'It isn't ridiculous,' said Margo, angrily. 'It's done my acne a world of good.'

'What? Do you mean you boil it or something?' asked Mother.

'No,' said Margo. 'I put the leaves on my face and you tie them on for me. Mawake advised it and it works wonders.'

'It's ridiculous, Louie, dear. You should stop her,' said Prue bristling like a plump kitten. 'It's nothing more than witchcraft.'

'Well, I'm too tired to argue about it,' said Mother. 'I don't suppose it can do you any harm.'

So Margo sat in a chair and held large crinkly cabbage leaves to her face which Mother solemnly fixed to her head with lengths of red twine. I thought she looked like some curious vegetable mummy.

'It's paganism. That's what it is,' said Prue.

'Nonsense, Prue, you do fuss,' said Margo, her voice muffled by cabbage leaves.

'I sometimes wonder,' said Mother, tying the last knot 'whether my family's all there.'

'Is Margo going to a fancy dress ball?' enquired Aunt Fan, who had watched the procedure with interest.

24

'No, Mummy,' roared Prue, 'it's for her spots.'

Margo got up and groped her way to the door.

'Well, I'm going to bed,' she said.

'If you meet anybody on the landing, you'll give them a terrible shock,' said Prue.

'Have a good time,' said Aunt Fan. 'Don't stay out till all hours. I know what you young things are like.'

After Margo had gone, Prue turned to Mother.

'You see, Louie, dear? I didn't exaggerate,' she said. 'That woman is an evil influence. Margo's behaving like a mad thing.'

'Well,' said Mother, whose maxim in life was always defend your young regardless of how much in the wrong they were, 'I think she's being a little unwise.'

'Unwise!' said Prue. 'Cabbage leaves all over her face! Never doing anything that Mawake doesn't tell her! It's not healthy!'

'I shouldn't be a bit surprised if she didn't win first prize,' said Aunt Fan, chuckling. 'I shouldn't think there'll be other people there disguised as a cabbage.'

The argument waxed back and forth, interlaced with Aunt Fan's reminiscences of fancy dress balls she had been to in India. At length Prue and Aunt Fan left us and Mother and I prepared for bed.

'I sometimes think,' said Mother, as she pulled the clothes up and switched off the light, 'I sometimes think that I'm the only sane member of the family.'

The following morning we decided to go shopping since there were a great number of things unobtainable in Corfu that Mother wanted to buy and take back with us. Prue said this would be an excellent plan, since she could drop her Bedlington puppies off with their new owner en route.

So at nine o'clock we assembled on the pavement outside Balaclava Mansions. We must have presented a somewhat curious sight to passers-by. Aunt Fan, presumably to celebrate our arrival, had put on a pixie hat with a large feather in it. She stood on the pavement as entwined as a maypole by the leashes of the eight Bedlington puppies that romped and fought and urinated around her.

'I think we'd better take a taxi,' said Mother, viewing the gambolling puppies with alarm.

'Oh, no, Louie,' said Prue. 'Think of the expense! We can go by tube.'

'With all the puppies?' asked Mother doubtfully.

'Yes, dear,' said Prue. 'Mummy's quite used to handling them.'

Aunt Fan, now bound almost immobile by the puppies' leashes, had to be disentangled before we could walk down the road to the tube station.

'Yeast and maple syrup,' said Margo. 'You mustn't let me forget yeast and maple syrup, Mother. Mawake says it's excellent for acne.'

'If you mention that man once again I shall get seriously angry,' said Mother.

Our progress to the tube station was slow, since the puppies circumnavigated any obstacle in their path in different ways and we had to pause continuously to unwind Aunt Fan from the lamp posts, pillar-boxes and occasional passers-by.

'Little tinkers!' she would exclaim, breathlessly, after each encounter. 'They don't mean any harm.'

When we finally arrived at the ticket office, Prue had a prolonged and acrimonious argument over the price charged for the Bedlingtons.

'But they're only eight weeks old,' she kept protesting. 'You don't charge for *children* under three.'

Eventually, however, the tickets were purchased and we made our way to the escalators to face a blast of warm air from the bowels of the earth, which the puppies appeared to find invigorating. Yapping and snarling in a tangle of leads they forged ahead, dragging Aunt Fan, like a massive galleon behind them. It was only when they saw the escalators that they began to have misgivings about what, hitherto, had appeared an exciting adventure. They did not, it seemed, like to stand on things that moved and they were unanimous in the decision. Before long we were all wedged in a tight knot at the top of the escalator, struggling with the screaming, hysterical puppies.

A queue formed behind us.

'It shouldn't be allowed,' said a frosty-looking man in bowler hat. 'Dogs shouldn't be allowed on the tube.'

'I have paid for them,' panted Prue. 'They have as much right to travel by tube as you have.'

'Bloody 'ell,' observed another man. 'I'm in an 'urry. Can't you let me get by?'

'Little tinkers!' observed Aunt Fan, laughing. 'They're so high spirited at this age.'

'Perhaps if we each picked up a puppy?' suggested Mother, getting increasingly alarmed by the muttering of the mob.

At that moment Aunt Fan stepped backwards on to the first step of the escalator and slipped and fell in a waterfall of tweeds, dragging the shrieking puppies after her.

'Thank God for that,' said the man in the bowler hat. 'Perhaps now we can get on.'

Prue stood at the top of the escalator and peered down. Aunt Fan had now reached the half-way mark and was finding it impossible to rise, owing to the weight of puppies.

'Mummy, Mummy, are you all right?' screamed Prue.

'I'm sure she is, dear,' said Mother soothingly.

'Little tinkers!' said Aunt Fan faintly as she was carried down the escalator.

'Now that your dogs have gone, Madam,' said the man in the bowler hat, 'would it be possible for us, too, to use the amenities of this station?'

Prue turned, bristling to do battle, but Margo and Mother grabbed her and they slid downwards on the staircase towards the heaving heap of tweed and Bedlingtons that was Great Aunt Fan.

We picked her up, dusted her down and disentangled the puppies. Then we made our way along to the platform. The puppies now would have made a suitable subject for an RSPCA poster. Never, at the best of times, a prepossessing breed, Bedlingtons can, in moments of crisis, look more ill-used than any other dog I know. They stood uttering quavering, high-pitched yelps like miniature sea gulls, shivering violently, periodically squatting down bow-legged to decorate the platform with the results of their fear.

'Poor little things,' said a fat woman, commiseratingly, as she passed. 'It's a shame the way some people treat animals.'

'Oh! Did you hear her?' said Prue, belligerently. 'I've a good mind to follow her and give her a piece of my mind.'

Mercifully, at that moment the train arrived with a roar and a blast of hot air, and distracted everybody's attention.

27

The effect on the puppies was immediate. One minute they had been standing there shivering and wailing like a group of half-starved grey lambs, the next they had taken off down the platform like a team of huskies, dragging Aunt Fan in their wake.

'Mummy, Mummy, come back,' screamed Prue as we started off in pursuit.

She had forgotten Aunt Fan's method of leading the dogs, which she had explained to me at great length: Never pull on the lead, because it might hurt their necks. Carrying out this novel method of dog-training, Aunt Fan galloped down the platform with the Bedlingtons streaming before her. We finally caught her and restrained the puppies just as the train doors closed with a self-satisfied hiss and it rumbled out of the station. So we had to wait in a pool of Bedlingtons for the next train to arrive. Once we finally got them into the train the puppies' spirits revived. They fought each other with enjoyment, snarling and screeching. They wound their lead round people's legs and one of them, in a fit of exuberance leapt up and tore a copy of *The Times* from the grasp of a man who looked as though he was the manager of the Bank of England.

We all had headaches by the time we arrived at our destination, with the exception of Aunt Fan who was enchanted by the virility of the puppies. Acting on Mother's advice, we waited until there was a pause in the flow of human traffic before we attempted the escalator. To our surprise, we got the puppies to the top with little or no trouble. They were obviously becoming seasoned travellers.

'Thank goodness that's over,' said Mother as we reached the top.

'I'm afraid the puppies were a little bit trying,' said Prue, flustered. 'But then you see, they are used to the country. In town they think that everything's wrong.'

'Eh?' said Aunt Fan.

'Wrong,' shouted Prue. 'The puppies. They think that everything's wrong.'

'What a pity,' said Aunt Fan, and before we could stop her she had led the puppies on to the other escalator and they disappeared once again into the bowels of the earth.

Once we had got rid of the puppies, in spite of feeling some

28

hat jaded by our experiences, we had a satisfactory morning's
hopping. Mother bought all the things she needed, Margo
ot her yeast and maple syrup and I, while they were pur-
hasing these quite unnecessary items, managed to procure a
eautiful Red Cardinal, a Black Spotted Salamander as fat
nd as shiny as an eiderdown, and a stuffed crocodile.

Satisfied in our own way with our purchases, we re-
urned to Balaclava Mansions.

At Margo's insistence, Mother had decided that she would
ttend the seance that evening.

'Don't do it, Louie, dear,' Cousin Prue said. 'It's dabbling
ith the unknown.'

Mother justified her action with a remarkable piece of
gic.

'I feel I ought to meet this Mawake person,' she said to Prue.
After all, he's giving Margo treatment.'

'Well, dear,' said Prue, seeing that Mother was adamant. 'I
ink it's madness, but I shall have to come with you. I can't
t you attend one of those things on your own.'

I begged to be allowed to go too, for, as I pointed out to
other, I had some little time previously borrowed a book on
e art of exposing fake mediums. I felt my knowledge thus
cquired might come in exceedingly useful.

'I don't think we ought to take Mummy,' said Prue. 'I think
might have a bad effect on her.'

So, at six o'clock that evening, with Prue palpitating in our
idst like a newly-caught bird, we made our way down to
rs Haddock's basement. Here we found quite a collection of
eople. There was Mrs Glut, the manageress of the hotel; a
ll, saturnine Russian with an accent so thick that he sounded
s though he were speaking through a mouthful of cheese; a
oung and very earnest blonde girl and a vapid young man
ho, rumour had it, was studying to be an actor, but whom we
ad never seen do anything more strenuous than doze peace-
lly in the palm-fringed lounge. To my annoyance, Mother
ould not let me search the room before we started for hidden
rds or fake ectoplasm. However, I did manage to tell Mrs
addock about the book I had been reading as I thought that
she was genuine it would be of interest to her. The look she
estowed upon me was anything but benevolent.

We sat in a circle holding hands and got off to a rather in-

auspicious start since, as the lights were switched out, Prue
uttered a piercing scream and leapt out of the chair she had
been sitting in. It was discovered that the handbag which she
had leant against the leg of the chair had slipped and touched
her leg with a leathery clutch. When we had calmed Prue and
assured her that she had not been assaulted by an evil spirit, we
all returned to our chairs and held hands again. The illumina-
tion was from a night light in a saucer that guttered and
blinked and sent shadows rippling down the room and made
everybody's face look as though they were newly arisen from
a very old grave.

'NowIdon'twantanytalkingandImustaskyoualltokeepyour
handsfirmlyclaspedsothatwedon'tloseanyoftheessence . . .
Whaaaha,' said Mrs Haddock. 'Iknowthereareunbelievers
amongstus. NeverthelessIaskyoutomakeyourmindsquietandre-
ceptive.'

'What does she mean?' whispered Prue to Mother. 'I'm
not an unbeliever. My trouble is I believe too much.'

Having given us our instructions, Mrs Haddock then took
up her position in an arm-chair and, with deceptive ease, went
into a trance. I watched her narrowly. I was determined not to
miss the ectoplasm. At first she just sat there with her eye
closed and there was no sound except for the rustle and quiver
of the agitated Prue. Then Mrs Haddock started to breathe
deeply; presently she began to snore richly and vibrantly. I
sounded like a sack of potatoes being emptied across a loft
floor. I was not impressed. Snoring, after all, was one of the
easiest things to fake. Prue's hand clutching mine was moist
with perspiration and I could feel shivers running down
through her arm.

'Ahaaaaa,' said Mrs Haddock suddenly, and Prue leapt in
her chair and uttered a small despairing squeak as though she
had been stabbed.

'Ahaaaaaaaa,' said Mrs Haddock, extracting the full dra-
matic possibilities from this simple utterance.

'I don't like it,' whispered Prue shakily. 'Louie, dear, I
don't like it.'

'Be quiet or you'll spoil it all,' hissed Margo. 'Relax, and
make your mind receptive.'

'I see strangers among us,' said Mrs Haddock suddenly

with such a strong Indian accent that it made me want to giggle. 'Strangers who have come to join our circle. To them I say "welcome".'

The only extraordinary thing about this, as far as I was concerned, was that Mrs Haddock was no longer stringing her words together and uttering that strange inhalation of breath. She mumbled and muttered for a moment or so, incomprehensibly, and then said clearly,

'This is Mawake.'

'Ooo!' said Margo, delighted. 'He's come! There you are, Mother! That's Mawake!'

'I think I'm going to faint,' said Prue.

I stared at Mrs Haddock in the dim, shaky light and could not see any signs of ectoplasm or trumpets.

'Mawake says,' announced Mrs Haddock, 'that the white girl must have no more punctures.'

'There!' said Margo triumphantly.

'Whitegirl must obey Mawake. Must not be influenced by disbelievers.'

I heard Mother snort belligerently in the gloom.

'Mawake says that if white girl trusts him before the coming of two moons she will be cured. Mawake says . . .'

But what Mawake was about to say was never vouchsafed to us, for, at that moment, a cat who had been drifting around the room, cloudlike and unobserved, jumped on to Prue's lap. Her scream was deafening. She leapt to her feet shouting, 'Louie, Louie, Louie!' and blundered like a bedazzled moth round the circle of people, screaming every time she touched anything.

Somebody had the good sense to switch on the lights before Prue, in her chicken-like panic, could do any damage.

'I say, it's a bit much, what?' said the vapid young man.

'You may have done her great harm,' said the girl, glaring at Prue and fanning Mrs Haddock with her handkerchief.

'I was touched by something. It touched me. Got into my lap,' said Prue tearfully. 'Ectoplasm.'

'You spoiled everything,' said Margo angrily. 'Just as Mawake was coming through.'

'I think we have heard quite enough from Mawake,' said Mother. 'It's high time you stopped fooling around with this nonsense.'

Mrs Haddock, who had remained snoring with dignity throughout this scene, suddenly woke up.

'Nonsense,' she said, fixing her protuberant blue eyes on Mother. 'Youaretocallitnonsense . . . ? Whaaaha.'

It was one of the very few occasions when I had seen Mother really annoyed. She drew herself up to her full height of four feet three and a half inches and bristled.

'Charlatan,' she said uncharitably to Mrs Haddock. 'I said it was nonsense and it *is* nonsense. I am not having my family mixed up in any jiggery pokery like this. Come, Margo; come, Gerry; come, Prue. We will leave.'

So astonished were we by this display of determination on the part of the normally placid Mother, that we followed her meekly out of the room, leaving the raging Mrs Haddock and her several disciples.

As soon as we reached the sanctuary of our room, Margo burst into floods of tears.

'You've spoiled it. You've spoiled it,' she said, wringing her hands. 'Mrs Haddock will never talk to us again.'

'And a good job too,' said Mother grimly, pouring out a brandy for the twitching and still distraught Prue.

'Did you have a nice time?' asked Aunt Fan, waking suddenly and beaming at us owlishly.

'No,' said Mother shortly, 'we didn't.'

'I can't get the thought of that ectoplasm out of my mind,' said Prue gulping brandy. 'It was like a sort of . . ., like, . . well, you know, squishy.'

'Just as Mawake was coming through,' howled Margo. 'Just as he was going to tell us something important.'

'I think you are wise to come back early,' said Aunt Fan 'because even at this time of year it gets chilly in the evening.'

'I felt sure it was coming for my throat,' said Prue. 'I felt it going for my throat. It was like a sort of . . ., a kind of . . well, a squishy sort of *hand* thing.'

'And Mawake's the only one that's done me any good.'

'My father used to say that at this time of the year the weather can be very treacherous,' said Aunt Fan.

'Margo, stop behaving so stupidly,' said Mother crossly.

'And, Louie, dear, I could feel these horrible sort of squishy fingers groping up towards my throat,' said Prue, ignoring Margo, busy with the embroidery of her experience.

'My father always used to carry an umbrella, winter and summer,' said Aunt Fan. 'People used to laugh at him, but many's the time, even on quite hot days, when he found he needed it.'

'You always spoil everything,' said Margo. 'You always interfere.'

'The trouble is I don't interfere enough,' said Mother. 'I'm telling you, you're to stop all this nonsense, stop crying, and we are going back to Corfu immediately.'

'If I hadn't leapt up when I did,' said Prue, 'it would have fastened itself in my jugular.'

'There's nothing more useful than a pair of goloshes, my father used to say,' said Aunt Fan.

'I'm not going back to Corfu. I won't. I won't.'

'You will do as you're told.'

'It wound itself round my throat in such an evil way.'

'He never approved of gum-boots, because he said they sent the blood to the head.'

I had ceased listening. My whole being was flooded with excitement. We were going back to Corfu. We were leaving the gritty, soulless absurdity of London. We were going back to the enchanted olive groves and blue sea, to the warmth and laughter of our friends, to the long, golden, gentle days.

PART II

Perama

Here great trees cool-shaded grow, pear,
pomegranate, rich apple, honey-sweet fig and
blossoming olive, forever bearing fruit, winter and
summer never stripped, but ever blowing the western
wind brings fruit to birth and ripens others.
Pear follows pear, apple after apple grows,
fig after fig, and grape yields grape again.

HOMER

The Christening

Corfu lies off the Albanian and Greek coast-lines like a long, rust-eroded scimitar. The hilt of the scimitar is the mountain region of the island, for the most part barren and stony with towering rock cliffs haunted by blue-rock thrushes and peregrine falcons. In the valleys in this mountain region, however, where water gushed plentifully from the red and gold rocks, you would get forests of almond and walnut trees, casting shade as cool as a well, thick battalions of spear-like cypress and silver-trunked fig trees with leaves as large as a salver. The blade of the scimitar is made up of rolling greeny-silver eider-downs of giant olives, some reputedly over five hundred years old and each one unique in its hunched, arthritic shape, its trunk pitted with a hundred holes like pumice stone. Towards the tip of the blade you had Lefkimi with its twinkling, eye-aching sand dunes and great salt marshes, decorated with acres of bamboos that creaked and rustled and whispered to each other surreptitiously.

To go back to Corfu, for me, was to go home. We had first arrived there a year or two before and had quickly settled into a bright crushed-strawberry pink villa with green shutters shaped not unlike a brick. It crouched in a cathedral-like grove of olives that sloped down the hillside to the sea, and was surrounded by a pocket-handkerchief-size garden, the flower beds laid out with a geometrical accuracy so dear to the Victorians, and the whole thing guarded by a tall, thick hedge of fuchsias that rustled mysteriously with birds.

However luxurious our various gardens had been in England they had never provided me with such an assortment of living creatures. I found myself prey to the most curious sensation of unreality. It was rather like being born for the first time. In that brilliant, brittle light I could appreciate the true huntsman's red of a lady-bird's wing case, the magnificent chocolate and amber of an earwig and the deep shining agate of the ants. Then I could feast my eyes on a bewildering number of

creatures unfamiliar to me. The great furry carpenter bees,
which prowled like electric-blue Teddy bears, humming to
themselves, from flower to flower; the sulphur-yellow, black-
striped swallow tail butterflies, with their elegant cut-away
coats, that pirouetted up and down the fuchsia hedge doing
complicated minuets with each other and the Humming Bird
hawk moths that hung, stationary, suspended by a blur of
wings in front of the flowers, while they probed each bloom
with their long, delicate proboscis.

I was exceedingly ignorant as to even the simplest facts
about these creatures and had no books to guide me. All I
could do was to watch them as they went about their business
in the garden or capture them so that I could study them more
carefully at first hand. Very soon my bedroom was filled with
a battalion of jam jars and biscuit tins containing the prizes
that I had found in our tiny garden. These had to be smuggled
surreptitiously into the house for the family, with the possible
exception of Mother, viewed the introduction of fauna into
the villa with considerable alarm.

Each brilliant day brought some new puzzles of behaviour
to underline my ignorance. One of the creatures that intrigued
and irritated me most was the dung beetle. I would lie on my
stomach with Roger, my dog, squatting like a mountain of
black curls, panting, by my side, watching two shiny black
dung beetles, each with a delicately curved rhino horn on its
head, rolling between them (with immense dedication) a
beautifully shaped ball of cow dung. To begin with I wanted
to know how they managed to make the ball so completely
round. I knew from my own experiments with clay and
Plasticine that it was extremely difficult to do, however hard
you rubbed and manipulated the material, yet the dung beetles
with only their spiky legs as instruments, devoid of calipers or
any other aid, managed to produce these lovely balls of dung
as round as the moon. Then there was the second problem.
Why had they made the ball and where were they taking it?

I solved this problem, or part of it, by devoting one entire
morning to a pair of dung beetles, refusing to be diverted
from my task by the other insects in the garden or by the faint
moans and yawns of boredom that came from Roger. Slowly,
on all fours, I followed them foot by laborious foot across the

garden, which was so small to me and yet such a vast world to the beetles. Eventually they came to a small hummock of soft earth under the fuchsia hedge. Rolling the ball of dung uphill was a mammoth task, and several times one or other of the beetles' foot-work was at fault and the ball would break away and roll back to the bottom of the little incline, the beetles hurrying after it and, I liked to imagine, shouting abuse at each other. Eventually, however, they got it to the top of the rise and started down the opposite slope. At the bottom of the slope, I noticed for the first time, was a round hole like a well which had been sunk into the earth, and it was for this that the beetles were heading. When they were within a couple of inches of the hole, one of the beetles hurried ahead and backed into the hole where he sat, gesticulating wildly with his front legs, while the other beetle, with a considerable effort (I could almost convince myself that I could hear him panting) rolled the ball of dung up to the mouth of the burrow. After a time spent in pushing and pulling, the ball slowly disappeared into the depths of the earth and the beetles with it. This annoyed me. After all, they were obviously going to do something with the ball of dung, but if they did it under ground, how could I be expected to see what? Hoping for some enlightenment on this problem, I put it to the family at lunch time. What, I enquired, did dung beetles do with dung? There was a moment's startled silence.

'Well, I expect they find it useful, dear,' said Mother, vaguely.

'I trust you're not hoping to smuggle some into the house?' Larry enquired. 'I refuse to live in a villa whose decor consists of balls of dung all over the floor.'

'No, no, dear, I'm sure he won't,' said Mother peaceably and untruthfully.

'Well, I'm just warning you, that's all,' said Larry. 'As it is, he appears to have all the more dangerous insects out of the garden closeted in his bedroom.'

'They probably want it for warmth,' said Leslie, who had been giving the matter of dung beetles some thought. 'Very warm stuff, dung. Ferments.'

'Should we, at any time, require central heating,' said Larry, 'I'll bear that in mind.'

'They probably eat it,' said Margo.

'Margo, dear,' said Mother. 'Not while we're having lunch.'

As usual my family's lack of biological knowledge had let me down.

'What you want to read,' said Larry, absent-mindedly helping himself to another plateful of stew, which he had just described to Mother as lacking in flavour, 'What you want to read is some Fabre.'

I enquired what or who Fabre was, more out of politeness than anything else, because, as the suggestion had come from Larry, I was convinced that he would turn out to be some obscure medieval poet.

'Naturalist,' said Larry, his mouth full, waving his fork at me. 'Wrote about insects and things. I'll try and get you a copy.'

Overwhelmed by such unlooked-for magnanimity on the part of my elder brother, I was very careful during the next two or three days not to do anything to incur his wrath, but the days passed and no book appeared and eventually I forgot about it and devoted my time to the other insects in the garden.

But the word 'why' pursued and frustrated me on every hand. Why did the carpenter bees cut out little circular pieces from the rose leaves and fly away with them? Why did the ants conduct what appeared to be passionate love affairs with the massed battalions of green fly which infested many of the plants in the garden? What were the strange, amber, transparent insect corpses or shells that I found sticking to grass stalks and to olive trees? They were the empty skins, as fragile as ash, of some creature with a bulbous body, bulbous eyes and a pair of thick, well-barbed forelegs. Why did each of these shells have a split down its back? Had they been attacked and had all their life juices sucked out of them? If so, what had attacked them and what were they? I was a bubbling cauldron of questions which the family were unable to answer.

I was in the kitchen when Spiro arrived one morning some days later showing Mother my latest acquisition, a long, thin caramel-coloured centipede which, I was insisting in spite of her disbelief, glowed with a white light at night. Spiro waddled into the kitchen, sweating profusely, looking, as he always did, truculent and worried.

'I've broughts yours mails,' Mrs Durrells,' he said to Mother, and then, glancing at me, 'Mornings, Masters Gerrys.'

Thinking, in my innocence, that Spiro would share my enthusiasm for my latest pet, I pushed the jam jar under his nose and urged him to feast his eyes upon it. He took one swift look at the centipede, now going round and round in the bottom of the jar like a clockwork train, dropped the mail on the floor and retreated hurriedly behind the kitchen table.

'Gollys, Masters Gerrys,' he said throatily. 'What's you doing with thats?'

I explained it was only a centipede, puzzled at his reaction.

'Those bastards are poisonous, Mrs Durrells,' said Spiro, earnestly, to Mother. 'Honest to Gods Masters Gerrys shouldn't have things like thats.'

'Well, perhaps not,' said Mother vaguely. 'But he's so interested in all these things. Take it outside, dear, where Spiro can't see it.'

'Makes me scarce,' I heard Spiro say, as I left the kitchen with my precious jar. 'Honest to Gods, Mrs Durrells, makes me scarce what that boy finds.'

I managed to get the centipede into my bedroom without meeting any other members of the family and bedded him down in a small dish, tastefully decorated with moss and bits of bark. I was determined that the family should appreciate the fact that I had found a centipede that glowed in the dark. I had planned that night to put on a special pyrotechnic display after dinner. However, all thoughts of the centipede and his phosphorescence were driven from my mind, for in the mail was a fat, brown parcel which Larry, having glanced at, tossed across to me while we were eating lunch.

'Fabre,' he said succinctly.

Forgetting my food, I tore the parcel open and there inside was a squat, green book entitled *The Sacred Beetle and Others* by Jean Henri Fabre. Opening it, I was transported by delight, for the frontispiece was a picture of two dung beetles, and they looked so familiar they might well have been close cousins of my own dung beetles. They were rolling a beautiful ball of dung between them. Enraptured, savouring every moment, I turned the pages slowly. The text was charming. No erudite or confusing tome, this. It was written in such a

simple and straightforward way that even I could understand
it.

'Leave the book till later, dear. Eat your lunch before it gets
cold,' said Mother.

Reluctantly I put the book on my lap and attacked my food
with such speed and ferocity that I had acute indigestion for
the rest of the afternoon. This in no way detracted from the
charm of delving into Fabre for the first time. While the family
had their siesta, I lay in the garden in the shade of the tanger-
ine trees and devoured the book, page by page, until by tea-
time—to my disappointment—I had reached the end. But
nothing could describe my elation. I was now armed with
knowledge. I knew, I felt, everything there was to know about
dung beetles. Now they were not merely mysterious insects
crawling ponderously throughout the olive groves, they were
my intimate friends.

About this time another thing that extended and encouraged my interest in natural history—though I cannot say
that I appreciated it at the time—was the acquisition of my
first tutor, George. George was a friend of Larry's, tall, lanky,
brown bearded and bespectacled, possessed of a quiet and sardonic sense of humour. One morning a week was devoted
exclusively to natural history. This was the only morning that
I would go to meet him. I would amble through the olive
groves half-way to his tiny villa and then Roger and I would
conceal ourselves in a clump of myrtle and await his approach.
Presently he would appear, clad in nothing but a pair of
sandals, faded shorts and a gigantic, tattered straw hat, carrying under one arm a pile of books and swinging a long, slender
walking-stick in the other hand. Roger and I would squat in
the sweet-scented myrtles and lay bets with each other as to
whether or not, on this particular morning, George was going
to fight an olive tree.

George was an expert fencer and had a quantity of cups and
medals to prove it, so the desire to fight something frequently
overcame him. He would be striding along the path, his spectacles glittering, swinging his walking-stick, when suddenly
one olive tree would become an evil and malignant thing that
had to be taught a lesson. Dropping his books and hat by the
side of the path, he would advance cautiously towards the tree,

in question, his walking-stick, now transformed into a sword, held in his right hand at the ready, his left arm held out elegantly behind him. Slowly, stiff-legged, like a terrier approaching a bull mastiff, he would circle the tree, watching with narrowed eyes for its first unfriendly move. Suddenly he would lunge forward and the point of his stick would disappear in one of the holes in the olive tree's trunk. He would utter a pleased 'Ha,' and immediately dodge back out of range, before the tree could retaliate. I noticed that if he succeeded in driving his sword into one of the smaller of the olive tree's holes, this did not constitute a death wound, merely a slight scratch, which apparently had the effect of rousing his antagonist to a fury, for in a second he would be fighting grimly for his life, dancing nimble-footed round the olive tree, lunging and parrying, leaping away with a downward slash of his sword, turning aside the vicious lunge that the olive tree had aimed at him, but so rapidly that I had missed the move. Some olive trees he would finish off quite quickly with a deadly thrust into one of the larger holes, into which his sword disappeared almost up to the hilt, but on several occasions he met with an olive tree that was a match for him and, for perhaps a quarter of an hour, it would be a fight to the death, with George, grim-faced, using every cunning trick he knew to break through the defences of the giant tree. Once he had killed his antagonist, George would wipe the blood off his sword fastidiously, put on his hat, pick up his books and continue, humming to himself, down the path. I always let him get some considerable distance away before joining him for fear that he should realise I had watched his imaginary battle and become embarrassed by it.

George introduced me to someone who was immediately to become the most important person in my life: Dr Theodore Stephanides. To me, Theodore was one of the most remarkable people I had ever met (and thirty-three years later I am still of the same opinion). With his ash-blond hair and beard and his handsome aquiline features, he looked like a Greek god, and certainly he seemed as omniscient as one. Apart from being medically qualified, he was also a biologist, poet, author, translator, astronomer and historian and he found time between those multifarious activities to help run an X-ray laboratory, the only one of its kind, in the town of Corfu. After my first visit to his flat in town, I asked Mother tentatively whether I might ask him to come to tea with us.

'I suppose so, dear,' said Mother. 'I hope he speaks English, though.'

Mother's battle with the Greek language was a losing one. Only the day previously she had spent an exhausting morning preparing a particularly delicious soup for lunch. Having concluded this to her satisfaction, she put it into a soup tureen and handed it to the maid. The maid looked at her enquiringly, whereupon Mother used one of the few Greek words that she had managed to commit to memory. 'Exo,' she had said firmly, waving her arms, 'Exo.' She then went on with her cooking and turned round just in time to see the maid pouring the last of the soup down the sink. This had, not unnaturally, given her a phobia about her linguistic abilities.

I said indignantly that Theodore could speak excellent English: in fact, if anything, better English than we could. Soothed by this, Mother suggested that I write Theodore a note and invite him out for the following Thursday. I spent an agonised two hours hanging about the garden waiting for him to arrive, peering every few minutes through the fuchsia hedge, a prey to the most terrible emotions. Perhaps the note had never reached him? Or perhaps he had put it in his pocket and forgotten about it and was, at this moment, gallivanting eruditely at the southernmost tip of the island? Or perhaps he had heard about the family and just didn't want to come? If that was the case, I vowed, I would not lightly forgive them. But presently I saw him, neatly tweed suited, his Homburg squarely on his head, striding up through the olive trees swinging his stick and humming to himself. Hung over his shoulder was his collecting bag which was as much a part of him as his arms and legs.

To my delight, Theodore was an immediate, uproarious success with the family. He could, with shy urbanity, discuss mythology, Greek poetry and Venetian history with Larry, ballistics and the best hunting areas on the island with Leslie, good slimming diets and acne cures with Margaret; and peasant recipes and detective stories with Mother. The family behaved much in the same way as I had behaved when I went to tea with him. He seemed such an endless mine of information that they ceaselessly bombarded him with questions and Theodore, as effortlessly as a walking encyclopedia, answered them all, adding for good measure a sprinkling of incredibly bad puns and hilarious anecdotes about the island and the islanders.

At one point, to my indignation, Larry said that Theodore ought to desist from encouraging me in my interest in natural history for, as he pointed out, the villa was a small one and already stuffed to capacity with practically every revolting bug and beetle that I could lay my hands on.

'It isn't that,' said Mother, 'that worries me. It's the mess that he gets himself into. Really, Theodore, after he's been out for a walk with Roger he has to change into completely clean clothes. I don't know what he does with them.'

Theodore gave a tiny grunt of amusement.

'I remember once,' he said, popping a piece of cake into his mouth and chewing it methodically, his beard bristling and his eyes kindling happily, 'I was coming to tea with some . . ., um . . ., you know, friends of mine here in Perama. At that time I was in the army and I was rather proud of the fact that I had just been made a captain. So . . ., er . . ., you know . . ., er . . ., to show off I wore my uniform, which included beautifully polished boots and spurs. I was rowed across by the ferry to Perama, and as I was walking through the little marshy bit I saw a plant that was new to me. So I stepped over to collect it. Treading on what . . ., you know . . ., seemed to be firm ground, I suddenly found that I had sunk up to my armpits. Fortunately there was a small tree nearby and I . . ., er . . ., managed to grab hold of it and pull myself out. But now I was covered from the waist downward with stinking black mud. The sea was . . ., er, you know . . ., quite close, so . . ., er . . ., thought it would be better to be wet with clean sea water than covered with mud so I waded out into it and walked up and down. Just at that moment, a bus happened to pass on the road above and as soon as they saw me with my cap on and my uniform coat, walking about in the sea, the bus driver stopped so that all his passengers could . . ., er . . ., get a better view. They all seemed considerably puzzled, but they were even more astonished when I walked out of the sea and they saw that I was wearing boots and spurs as well.'

Solemnly Theodore waited for the laughter to subside.

'I think, you know,' he said meditatively and quite seriously, 'that I definitely undermined their faith in the sanity of the army.'

Ever after that Theodore came out to spend at least one day a week with us, preferably more if we could inveigle him away from his numerous activities.

By this time we had made innumerable friends among the peasant families that lived around us, and so vociferously hospitable were they that even the shortest walk was almost indefinitely prolonged, for every little house we came to we would have to sit down and drink a glass of wine or eat some fruit with its owners and pass the time of day. Indirectly, this was very good for us, for each of these meetings strengthened our rather shaky command over the Greek language so that soon we found that we were fairly proficient in conducting quite complicated conversations with our peasant friends.

Then came the accolade, the gesture that proved to us we had been accepted by the community in general. We were asked to a wedding. It was the wedding of Katerina, the sister of our maid, Maria. She was a voluptuous girl, with wide glittering smile and brown eyes as large and as soft as pansies. Gay, provocative, and melodious as a nightingale, she had been breaking hearts in the district for most of her twenty years. Now she had settled on Stephanos, a sturdy, handsome boy whom the mere sight of Katerina rendered tongue-tied, inarticulate and blushing with love.

When you were invited to a wedding, we soon discovered the thing was not done in half measures. The first festivity was the engagement party when you all went to the bride's house carrying your presents and she thanked you prettily for them and plied you with wine. Having suitably mellowed her guests the future bride and groom would start walking to what was to be their future home, preceded by the village band (two violins, a flute and a guitar) playing sprightly airs, and followed by the guests, all carrying their presents. Katerina's presents were a fairly mixed bag. The most important was a gigantic double brass bed and this led the procession, carried by four of Stephanos's friends. Thereafter followed a string of guests carrying sheets, pillow cases, cushions, a wooden chair, frying pans, large bottles of oil and similar gifts. Having installed the presents in the new cottage, we then drank to the health of the couple and thus warmed their future home for them. We then all retired home, slightly light-headedly, and waited for the next act in the drama, which was the wedding itself.

We had asked, somewhat diffidently, if Theodore might attend the wedding with us and the bride and her parents were enchanted with the idea, since, as they explained with becoming ingenuousness, very few weddings in the district could boast of having a whole English family *and* a genuine doctor as guests.

The great day dawned and, donning our best clothes and collecting Theodore from town, we made our way down to Katerina's parents' house that stood between the olives overlooking the sparkling sea. This was where the ceremony was to take place. When we got there we found it was a hive of activity. Relatives had come on their donkeys from villages as far as ten miles away. All round the house, groups of ancient men and decrepit old women sat engulfing wine in vast quantities, gossiping as ceaselessly and as animatedly as magpies. For them this was a great day, not only because of the wedding, but because, living so far apart, this was perhaps the first opportunity in twenty years that they had had to exchange news and scandal. The village band was in full spate, the violins whining, the guitar rumbling and the flute making periodical squeaks like a neglected puppy, and to this all the younger guests were dancing under the trees, while nearby the carcasses of four lambs were sizzling and bubbling on spits over a great chrysanthemum blaze of charcoal.

'Aha!' said Theodore, his eyes alight with interest, 'now that dance they are doing is the Corfu dance. It and the . . ., er . . ., the originated here in Corfu. There are some authorities, of course, who believe that the dance . . ., that is to say, the *steps* . . ., originated in Crete, but for myself, I believe that it is a . . ., um . . ., an entirely Corfu product.'

The girls in their goldfinch-bright costumes revolved prettily in a half-moon while ahead of them pranced a swarthy young male with a crimson handkerchief, bucking, leaping, twisting and bowing like an exuberant cockerel to his admiring entourage of hens. Katerina and her family came forward to greet us and ushered us to the place of honour, a rickety wooden table that had been spread with a white cloth and at which was already sitting a magnificent old priest who was going to perform the ceremony. He had a girth like a whale and snow-white eyebrows, moustache and beard that were so thick and luxuriant that almost all that could be seen of his face were two twinkling, olive-black eyes and a great, jutting, wine-red nose. On hearing that Theodore was a doctor, he out of the kindness of his heart, described in graphic detail the innumerable symptoms of his several diseases (which God had seen fit to inflict him with) and at the end of the recital laughed uproariously at Theodore's childish diagnosis that a little less wine and a little more exercise might alleviate his ailments.

Larry eyed Katerina, who, clad in her white bridal gown had joined the circle of the dancers. In her tight, white satin, Katerina's stomach was more prominent and noticeable than it would have been otherwise.

'This wedding,' said Larry, 'is taking place not a moment too soon.'

'Do be quiet, dear,' whispered Mother. 'Some of them might speak English.'

'It's a curious fact,' said Theodore, oblivious to Mother's stricture, 'that at a lot of the weddings you will find the bride in . . ., er . . ., um . . ., a similar condition. The peasants here are very Victorian in their outlook. If a young man is . . . er . . ., seriously *courting* a girl, neither family dreams for a moment that he will not marry her. In fact, if he did try and . . ., um . . ., you know . . ., run off, both his family and the bride's family would be after him. This leads to a situation where, when the young man is courting, he is . . ., er . . ., chaffed, that is to say, has his leg pulled by all the young men of the district, who say that they doubt his . . ., um . . ., prowess as a . . ., um . . ., you know . . ., potential father. They get the poor fellow into such a state that he is almost forced to . . ., er . . ., you know . . ., um . . ., *prove* himself.'

'Very unwise, I would have thought,' said Mother.

'No, no,' said Theodore, endeavouring to correct Mother's unscientific approach to the problem 'In fact, it is considered quite a *good* thing for the bride to be pregnant. It proves her . . ., um . . ., fecundity.'

Presently the priest heaved his vast bulk on to his gouty feet and made his way into the main room of the house, which had been prepared for the ceremony. When he was ready

tephanos, perspiring profusely, his suit half a size too small
r him and looking slightly dazed at his good fortune, was
ropelled towards the house by a laughing joking band of
oung men, while a group of shrilly chattering young women
lfilled the same function for Katerina.

The main room of the house was extremely tiny so that by
e time the bulk of the well-larded priest had been inserted
to it, plus all the accoutrements of his trade, there was only
hough room for the happy couple to stand in front of him.
he rest of us had to be content with peering through the door
r through the windows. The service was incredibly long and,
 us, incomprehensible, though I could hear Theodore trans-
ting bits of it to Larry. It seemed to me to involve quite an
nnecessary amount of intoning, accompanied by innumer-
ble signs of the cross and the splashing of tidal waves of holy
ater. Then two little garlands of flowers like twin haloes were
eld over the heads of Katerina and Stephanos, and while the
riest droned on, these were exchanged at intervals. As it had
een some considerable time since the people, who held these
arlands, had been to a wedding, they occasionally misin-
erpreted the priest's instructions and there was, so to speak,
 clash of garlands over the heads of the bridal pair, but at
ong last rings were exchanged and placed upon the brown,
ork-calloused fingers and Katerina and Stephanos were truly
nd, we hoped, irretrievably wed.

The silence during the ceremony had been almost complete,
roken only by the odd drowsy chuckle of a hen or the shrill,
nd instantly repressed, squall of a baby; but now the stern
art of the ceremony was over and the party blossomed once
gain. The band dug down into its repertoire and produced
ayer and more sprightly tunes. Laughter and raucous badin-
ge arose on every side. The wine flowed gurgling from the
ottles and the guests danced round and round and round,
ushed and happy, as inexorably as the hands on a clock face.

The party did not end till well after twelve. All the older
uests had already made their way homewards on drooping
onkeys. The great fires, with the remains of the sheep car-
asses over them, had died in a shroud of grey ash with only a
prinkling of garnet embers winking in it. We took a last glass
f wine with Katerina and Stephanos and then made our way
leepily through the olive groves silvered by a moon as large

49

and as white as a magnolia blossom. The Scops owls chimed mournfully to each other and the odd firefly winked emerald green as we passed. The warm air smelled of the day's sunshine, of dew and of a hundred aromatic leaf scents. Mellow and drugged with wine, walking between the great hunched olives, their trunks striped with cool moonlight, I think we all felt we had arrived, that we had been accepted by the island. We were now, under the quiet bland eye of the moon, christened Corfiots. The night was beautiful and tomorrow, we knew, another tiger-golden day lay ahead of us. It was as though England had never really existed.

The Bay of Olives

As you left the villa and walked down through the olive groves, you eventually reached the road with its thick coating of white dust, soft as silk. If you walked along this for half a mile or so, you came to a goat track which led down a steep slope through the olives and then you reached a small half-moon bay, rimmed with white sands and great piles of dried ribbon weed that had been thrown up by the winter storms and lay along the beach like large, badly made birds' nests. The two arms of the bay were composed of small cliffs, at the base of which were innumerable rock pools, filled with the glint and glitter of sea life.

As soon as George realised that to incarcerate me every morning of the week in the villa impaired my concentration, he instituted the novel educational gambit of 'outdoor lessons'. The sandy beach and the shaggy piles of weed soon became scorching deserts or impenetrable jungles and, with the aid of a reluctant crab or sand-hopper to play the part of Cortez or Marco Polo, we would explore them diligently. Geography lessons done under these circumstances I found had immense charm. We once decided, with the aid of rocks, to do a map of the world along the edge of the sea, so that we had real sea. It was an immensely absorbing task for, to begin with, it was not all that easy to find rocks shaped like Africa or India or South America, and sometimes two or three rocks had to be joined together to give the required shape to the continent. Then, of course, when you were obtaining a rock, you turned it over very carefully and found a host of sea life underneath which would keep us both happily absorbed for a quarter of an hour or so, till George realised with a start that this was not getting on with our map of the world.

This little bay became one of my favourite haunts and early every afternoon while the family were having their siesta, Roger and I would make our way down through the breathless olive groves, vibrating with the cries of the cicadas, and pad our way along the dusty road, Roger sneezing volup-

tuously as his great paws stirred up the dust which went up h
nose like snuff. Once we reached the bay, whose waters in th
afternoon sun were so still and transparent they did not see
to be there at all, we would swim for a while in the shallow
and then each of us would go about his own particular hobbie

For Roger, this consisted of desperate and unsuccessful a
tempts to catch some of the small fish that flicked and trembl
in the shallow water. He would stalk along slowly, mutterin
to himself, his ears cocked, gazing down into the water. The
suddenly, he would plunge his head beneath the surface an
you heard his jaws clop together and he would pull his hea
out, sneeze violently and shake the water off his fur, while th
goby or blenny that he had attempted to catch would flip
couple of yards farther on and squat on a rock pouting at hi
and trembling its tail seductively.

For me the tiny bay was so full of life that I scarcely kne
where to begin my collecting. Under and on top of the roc
were the chalky white tunnels of the tube worms, like son
swirling and complicated pattern of icing sugar on a cake, an
in the slightly deeper water there were stuck in the sand wh
appeared to be lengths of miniature hose pipe. If you stood an
watched carefully, a delicate, feathery, flowerlike cluster
tentacles would appear at the ends of the hose pipes—tentacl
of iridescent blue and red and brown that would turn slow
round and round. These were the bristle worms; a rather ug
name, I felt, for such a beautiful creature. Sometimes the
would be little clusters of them and they looked like a flow
bed whose flowers could move. You had to approach the
with infinite caution, for should you move your feet to
rapidly through the water you would set up currents that tel
graphed your approach and the tentacles would bunch t
gether and dive with incredible speed back into the tube.

Here and there on the sandy floor of the bay were hal
moons of black, shiny ribbon weed looking like dark feath
boas, anchored to the sand, and in these you would find pi
fish, whose heads looked extraordinarily like elongated se
horses, perched on the end of a long, slender body. The pi
fishes would float upright among the ribbon weed which th
resembled so closely that it required a lot of concentrat
searching to find them.

Along the shore, under the rocks, you could find tiny cra

THE BAY OF OLIVES

or beadlet anemones like little scarlet and blue jewelled pin-
cushions, or the snakelocks anemones, their slender, coffee
coloured stalks and long writhing tentacles giving them a hair
style that Medusa might well have envied. Every rock was encrusted with pink, white or green coral, fine forests of minute
sea weeds including a delicate growth of *Acetabularia medi-
terranea* with slender thread-like stalks and perched on the top
of each stalk something that looked like a small green parasol
turned inside out by some submarine wind. Occasionally a
rock would be encrusted with a great black lump of sponge
covered with gaping, protuberant mouths like miniature vol-
canoes. You could pull these sponges off the rocks and split
them open with a razor blade, for sometimes, inside, you
would find curious forms of life; but the sponge, in retaliation,
would coat your hands with a mucus that smelt horribly of
stale garlic and took hours to wear off. Scattered along the
shore and in the rock pools, I would find new shells to add to
my collection and half the delight of collecting these was not
only the beautiful shapes of the shells themselves, but the
extraordinarily evocative names that had been given to them.
A pointed shell like a large winkle, the lip of whose mouth
had been elongated into a series of semi-webbed fingers, was, I
discovered to my delight, called the Pelican's Foot. An almost
circular white, conical limpet-like shell went under the name
of Chinaman's Hat. Then there were the Ark Shells and the
two sides of these strange box-like shells, when separated, did
look (if one used a modicum of imagination) like the hulks of
two little arks. Then there were the Tower Shells, twisted and
pointed as a Narwhal's horn and the Top Shells, gaily striped
with a zig-zag pattern of scarlet, black or blue. Under some of
the bigger rocks, you would find Key-hole Limpets, each one
of which had, as the name implied, a strange key-hole-like
aperture in the top of the shell, through which the creature
breathed. And then, best of all, if you were lucky, you would
find the flattened Ormers, scaly grey with a row of holes along
one side, but if you turned it over and extracted its rightful
occupant, you would find the whole interior of the shell glowing in opalescent, sunset colours, magical in their beauty. I had
at that time no aquarium, so I was forced to construct for
myself, in one corner of the bay, a rock pool some eight feet
long by four feet wide, and into this I would put my various

53

captures so that I could be almost certain of knowing where they would be on the following day.

It was in this bay that I caught my first spider crab. I would have walked right past him thinking him to be a weed-covered rock, if he had not made an incautious movement. His body was about the size and shape of a small flattened pear and at the pointed end it was decorated with a series of spikes, ending in two horn-like protuberances over his eyes. His legs and his pincers were long, slender and spindly. But the thing that intrigued me most was the fact that he was wearing, on his back and on his legs, a complete suit of tiny sea-weeds, which appeared to be growing out of his shell. Enchanted by this weird creature, I carried him triumphantly along the beach to my rock pool and placed him in it. The firm grip with which I had had to hold him (for once having discovered that he was recognised as a crab he made desperate efforts to escape) had rubbed off quite a lot of his sea-weed suit by the time I got him to the pool. I placed him in the shallow, clear water and lying on my stomach, watched him to see what he would do. Standing high on his toes, like a spider in a hurry, he scuttled a foot or so away from where I had put him and then froze. He sat like this for a long time, so long in fact that I was just deciding that he was going to remain immobile for the rest of the morning, recovering from the shock of capture, when he suddenly extended a long, delicate claw and very daintily almost shyly, plucked a tiny piece of sea-weed which was growing on a nearby rock. He put the sea-weed to his mouth and I could see him mumbling at it. At first I thought he was eating it, but I soon realised I was mistaken for, with angular grace, he placed his claw over his back, felt around in a rather fumbling sort of way, and then planted the tiny piece of weed on his carapace. I presumed that he had been making the base of the weed sticky with saliva or some similar substance to make it adhere to his back. As I watched him, he trundled slowly round the pool collecting a variety of sea-weed with the assiduous dedication of a professional botanist in a hitherto unexplored jungle. Within an hour or so his back was covered with such a thick layer of growth that, if he sat still and I took my eyes off him for a moment, I had difficulty in knowing exactly where he was.

Intrigued by this cunning form of camouflage, I searched

the bay carefully until I found another spider crab. For him I built a special small pool with a sandy floor, completely devoid of weed. I put him in and he settled down quite happily. The following day I returned, carrying with me a nail brush (which turned out to be Larry's) and, taking the unfortunate spider crab, scrubbed him vigorously until not an atom of weed remained on his back or legs. Then I dropped into his pool a variety of things; a number of tiny top shells and some broken fragments of coral, some small sea anemones and some minute bits of bottle glass which had been sand-papered by the sea so that they looked like misty jewels. Then I sat down to watch.

The crab, when returned to his pool, sat quite still for several minutes, obviously recovering from the indignity of the scrubbing I had given him. Then, as if he could not quite believe the terrible fate that had overtaken him, he put his two pincers over his head and felt his back with the utmost delicacy, presumably hoping against hope that at least one frond of seaweed remained. But I had done my task well and his back was shining and bare. He walked a few paces tentatively and then squatted down and sulked for half an hour. Then he roused himself out of his gloom, walked over to the edge of the pond and tried to wedge himself under a dark ridge of rock. There he sat brooding miserably over his lack of camouflage until it was time for me to go home.

I returned very early the following morning and, to my delight, saw that the crab had been busy while I had been away. Making the best of a bad job, he had decorated the top of his shell with a number of the ingredients that I had left for him. He looked extremely gaudy and had an air of carnival about him. Striped top shells had been pasted on, interspersed with bits of coral and up near his head he was wearing two beadlet anemones, like an extremely saucy bonnet with ribbons. I thought, as I watched him crawling about the sand, that he looked exceedingly conspicuous, but, curiously enough, when he went over and squatted by his favourite overhang of rock, he turned into what appeared to be a little pile of shell and coral debris, with a couple of anemones perched on top of

To the left of the little bay, a quarter of a mile or so from the shore, lay an island called Pondikonissi, or Mouse Island.

It was shaped not unlike an isosceles triangle and was thick with elderly cypress trees and oleander bushes, that guarded a small snow-white church and the tiny living-quarters adjoining it. This island was inhabited by an elderly and verminous monk, with long black robes and a stove-pipe hat, whose major function appeared to be the ringing of the bell in the match-box-size church at intervals and rowing slowly over to a neighbouring headland in the evening, where there was a small nunnery, inhabited by three ancient nuns. Here he would partake of ouzo and a cup of coffee, discuss, presumably, the state of sin in the world today, and then, as the sun set and turned the calm waters round his island to a multi-coloured sheet of shot silk, he would row back again, like a hunched black crow in his creaking, leaking boat.

Margo, having discovered that constant sunbathing, if anything, inflamed her acne, now decided on another of Mother Nature's cures—sea bathing. Every morning she would get up at about half past five, rout me out of bed and together we would make our way down to the shore and plunge into the clear water, still chilly from the moon's gaze, and then swim slowly and languidly across to Pondikonissi. Here Margo would drape herself on a rock and I would potter happily in the rock pools on the shore. Unfortunately, our visitations to the island seemed to have a detrimental effect upon the monk, for no sooner had Margo landed and arranged herself attractively on a rock than he would come stamping down the long flight of stone steps that led up to the church shaking his fist at her and mouthing incomprehensible Greek from the depths of his long, unkempt beard. Margo would always greet him with a bright smile and a cheerful wave of her hand, and this made him almost apoplectic with rage. He would stamp to and fro, his black robes swishing, pointing one dirty and trembling finger at the heavens and another at Margo. After this had happened on numerous occasions, I managed to commit to memory several of the monk's favourite phrases, for his vocabulary was not an extensive one. I then asked my friend Philemona what they meant. Philemona was convulsed with laughter. He laughed so much that he was almost incapable of explaining to me, but I at length understood that the monk had several derogatory terms that he used for Margo, the mildest of these being 'white witch.'

When I related this to Mother, she was, to my astonishment, considerably shocked.

'Really,' she said, 'we ought to report him to somebody. They'd never be able to carry on like that in the Church of England.'

Eventually, however, the whole thing became a sort of game. When Margo and I swam across, we would take some cigarettes over for the monk. He would come flying down the stone steps, shaking his fist and threatening us with the wrath of God, and then, having done his duty, would hitch up his robes, squat on the wall and with great good humour smoke the cigarettes we had brought him. Occasionally he would even trot back to the church to bring us a handful of figs from his tree or a few almonds, milky and fresh, which we would crack between the smooth stones on the beach.

Between Pondikonissi and my favourite bay, there stretched a whole string of reefs. Most of these were flat-topped, some of them only the size of a table, others of a small garden. The majority of them lay perhaps two inches below the surface of the water, so that if you hauled yourself out and stood on them, from a distance it looked exactly as though you were walking on the surface of the sea. I had long wanted to investigate these reefs, for they contained a lot of sea life that you did not find in the shallow waters of the bay. But this presented insurmountable difficulties for I could not get my equipment out there. I had tried to swim out to one reef with two large jam jars slung round my neck on a string and carrying my net in one hand, but half-way there the jam jars suddenly and maliciously filled with water and their combined weight dragged me under. It was a few seconds before I managed to disentangle myself from them and rise gasping and spluttering to the surface, by which time my jars were lying glinting and rolling in a fathom of water, as irretrievable as though they had been on the moon.

Then, one hot afternoon, I was down in the bay turning over rocks in an effort to find some of the long, multi-coloured ribbon worms that inhabited that sort of terrain. So absorbed was I in my task that the prow of the rowing-boat had crunched and whispered its way into the sandy shore beside me before I was aware of it. Standing in the stern, leaning on his single oar—which he used, as all the fishermen did, twisting it in the water like a fish's tail—was a young man, burnt almost black by the sun. He had a mop of dark, curly hair, eyes as bright and as black as mulberries and his teeth gleamed astonishingly white in his brown face.

'*Yasu*,' he said, 'your health.'

I returned his greeting and watched him as he jumped nimbly out of the boat carrying a small rusty anchor which he wedged firmly behind a great double-bed of drying sea-weed on the beach. He was wearing nothing but a tattered singlet and a pair of trousers which had once been blue, but were now bleached almost white by the sun. He came over, squatted companionably beside me and produced from his pocket a tin containing tobacco and cigarette papers.

'It is hot today,' he said, making a grimace, while his blunt, calloused fingers rolled a cigarette with extraordinary deftness. He stuck it in his mouth and lit it with the aid of a large tin lighter, inhaled deeply and then sighed. He cocked an eyebrow at me, his eyes as bright as a robin's.

'You're one of the strangers that live up on the hill?' he enquired.

By this time my Greek had become reasonably fluent, so I admitted that, yes, I was one of the strangers.

'And the others?' he asked. 'The others in the villa, who are they?'

I had quickly learnt that every Corfiot, particularly the peasants, loved to know all about you and they would in return for this information, vouchsafe to you the most intimate details of their private lives. I explained that the others at the villa were my mother, my two brothers and my sister. He nodded gravely, as though this information were of the utmost importance.

'And your father?' he continued. 'Where is your father?'

I explained that my father was dead.

'Poor thing,' he said, quickly commiserating. 'And your poor mother with four children to bring up.'

He sighed lugubriously at this terrible thought and then brightened.

'Still,' he said philosophically, 'thus is life. What are you looking for here under these stones?'

I explained as best I could, though I always found it ex

THE BAY OF OLIVES

ceedingly difficult to get the peasants to understand why I was so interested in such a variety of creatures that were either obnoxious or not worth worrying about and all of which were inedible.

'What's your name?' he asked.

I said that it was Gerasimos, which was the closest approach to Gerald that one could come to in Greek. But, I explained, my friends called me Gerry.

'I'm Taki,' he said. 'Taki Thanatos. I live at Benitses.'

I asked him what he was doing up here so comparatively far away from his village. He shrugged.

'I have come from Benitses,' he said, 'and I fish on the way. Then I eat and I sleep and when it's night I light my lights and go back to Benitses, fishing again.'

This news excited me, for not long before we had been returning late from town and, standing on the road by the little path that led up to the villa, we had seen a boat passing below us, being rowed very slowly, with a large carbon lamp fixed to the bows. As the fisherman had manoeuvred the boat slowly through the dark, shallow waters, the pool of light cast by his lamp illuminated great patches of sea bed with the utmost vividness, reefs smouldering citron-green, pink, yellow and brown as the boat moved slowly along. I had thought at the time that this must be a fascinating occupation, but I had known no fishermen. Now I began to view Taki with some enthusiasm.

I asked him eagerly what time he intended to start his fishing and whether he meant to go round the reefs that lay scattered between the bay and Pondikonissi.

'I start about ten,' he said. 'I work round the island, then I head towards Benitses.'

I asked him whether it would be possible for me to join him because, as I explained, there were lots of strange creatures living on the reef which I could not obtain without the aid of a boat.

'Why not?' he said. 'I shall be down below Menelaos'. You come at ten. I'll take you round the reefs and then drop you back at Menelaos' before I go to Benitses.'

I assured him fervently that I would be there at ten o'clock. Then, gathering up my net and bottles and whistling for Roger

I beat a hasty retreat before Taki could change his mind. Once I was safely out of earshot, I slowed down and gave considerable thought to how I was going to persuade the family in general and Mother in particular, to let me go out to sea at ten o'clock at night.

Mother, I knew, had always been worried about my refusal to have a siesta during the heat of the day. I had explained to her that this was generally the best time for insects and things like that, but she was not convinced that this was a valid argument. However, the result was that at night, just when something interesting was happening (such as Larry locked in a verbal battle with Leslie) Mother would say, irritatingly,

'It's time you went to bed, dear. After all, remember, you don't have a siesta.'

This I felt might be the answer to the night-fishing. It was scarcely three o'clock and I knew that the family would be lying supine behind closed shutters, only to awake and start to buzz at each other, drowsily, like sun-drugged flies, at about half past five.

I made my way back to the villa with the utmost speed. When I was a hundred yards away, I took off my shirt and wrapped it carefully round my jars full of specimens so that not a chink or a rattle would betray my presence; then cautioning Roger upon pain of death not to utter a sound, we made our way cautiously into the villa and slipped like shadows into my bedroom. Roger squatted panting in the middle of the floor and viewed me with considerable surprise as I took off all my clothes and climbed into bed. He was not at all sure that he approved of this untoward behaviour. As far as he was concerned, the whole afternoon stretched ahead of us, littered with exciting adventures, and here was I preparing to go to sleep. He whined experimentally and I shushed him with such fierceness that his ears drooped and, putting his stumpy tail between his legs, he crept under the bed and curled up with a rueful sigh. I took a book and tried to concentrate on it. The half-closed shutters made the room look like a cool green aquarium, but in fact the air was still and hot and the sweat rolled in rivulets down my ribs. What on earth, I thought shifting uncomfortably on the already sodden sheet, could the family possibly see in a siesta? What good did it do them

n fact, how they managed to sleep at all was a mystery to me.
.t this moment I sank swiftly into oblivion.

I woke at half past five and staggered out, half-asleep, to the
eranda where the family were having tea.

'Good heavens,' said Mother. 'Have you been sleeping?'

I said, as casually as I could, that I thought a siesta a good
ing that afternoon.

'Are you feeling well, dear?' she asked anxiously.

I said, yes, I felt fine. I had decided to have a siesta in order
 prepare myself for that evening.

'Why, what's happening, dear?' asked Mother.

I said, with all the nonchalance I could muster that I was
ing out at ten o'clock with a fisherman who was going to
ke me night-fishing for, as I explained, there were certain
eatures that only came out at night and this was the best
ethod of obtaining them.

'I hope this does not mean,' said Larry ominously, 'that we're
ing to have octopus and conger eels flopping around the
oor. Better stop him, Mother. Before you know where you
re the whole villa will look and smell like Grimsby.'

I replied, somewhat heatedly, that I did not intend to bring
e specimens back to the villa, but to put them straight into
y special rock pool.

'Ten o'clock's rather late, dear,' said Mother. 'What time
ill you be back?'

Lying valiantly, I said I thought I would be back at about
even.

'Well, mind you wrap up warmly,' said Mother, who was
ways convinced that, in spite of the nights being warm and
almy, I would inevitably end up with double pneumonia if I
d not wear a jersey. Promising faithfully to wrap up warmly,
 finished my tea and spent an exciting and satisfying hour or
 marshalling my collecting gear. There was my long-
andled net, a long bamboo with three wire hooks on the end
r pulling interesting clumps of sea-weed nearer to one, eight
ide-mouthed jam jars and several tins and boxes for putting
ch things as crabs or shells in. Making sure that Mother was
ot around, I put on my bathing trunks under my shorts and
d a towel in the bottom of my collecting bag, for I felt sure
at some of the specimens I might have to dive for. Mother's

61

fears of double pneumonia would increase one hundredfold if she thought I was going to do this.

Then, at a quarter to ten, I slung my bag on my back and, taking a torch, made my way down through the olive groves. The moon was a pale, smudged sickle in a starlit sky, shedding only the feeblest light. In the black recesses among the olive roots, glow-worms gleamed like emeralds, and I could hear the Scops owls calling 'toink, toink' to each other from the shadows.

When I reached the beach I found Taki squatting in his boat, smoking. He had already lighted the carbon lamp and it hissed angrily to itself and smelt strongly of garlic as it cast a brilliant circle of white light into the shallow water by the bows. Already I could see that a host of life had been attracted to it. Gobies and blennies had come out of their holes and were sitting on the sea-weed covered rocks pouting and gulping expectantly like an audience in the theatre waiting for the curtain to go up. Shore crabs scuttled to and fro, pausing now and then delicately to pluck some sea-weed and stuff it into their mouths, and everywhere there trundled top shells, dragged by small, choleric-looking hermit crabs, who now occupied the shells in place of their rightful owners.

I arranged my collecting gear in the bottom of the boat and sat down with a contented sigh. Taki pushed off and then, using the oar, punted us along through the shallow water and the beds of ribbon weed that rustled and whispered along the side of the boat. As soon as we were in deeper water, he fixed both his oars, and then rowed, standing up. We progressed very slowly, Taki keeping a careful eye on the nimbus of light that illuminated the sea bottom for some twelve feet in every direction. The oars squeaked musically and Taki hummed to himself. Along one side of the boat lay an eight foot pole ending in a five-pronged, savagely barbed trident. In the bow I could see the little bottle of olive oil, such a necessary accoutrement to the fisherman, for, should a slight wind blow up and ruffle the waters, a sprinkling of oil would have a magically calming effect on the pleated surface of the sea. Slowly and steadily we crept out towards the black triangular silhouette of Pondikonissi to where the reefs lay. When we neared them Taki rested on his oars for a moment and looked at me.

'We'll go round and round for five minutes,' he said, 's

at I may catch what there is. Then after that I will take you
ound to catch the things that you want.'

I readily agreed to this, for I was anxious to see how Taki
shed with his massive trident. Very slowly we edged our
ay round the biggest of the reefs, the light illuminating the
trange submarine cliffs covered with pink and purple sea-
eeds that looked like fluffy oak trees. Peering down into the
ater, one felt as though one were a kestrel, floating smoothly
n outstretched wings over a multi-coloured autumn forest.

Suddenly Taki stopped rowing and dug his oars gently into
e water to act as a brake. The boat came to an almost com-
lete standstill as he picked up the trident.

'Look,' he said, pointing to the sandy bottom under a great
ulwark of submarine cliff. 'Scorpios.'

At first glance I could see nothing, then suddenly I saw what
e meant. Lying on the sand was a fish some two feet long
ith a great filigree of sharp spines, like a dragon's crest along
s back, and enormous petrel fins spread out on the sand.
: had a tremendously wide head with golden eyes and a sulky
outing mouth. But it was the colours that astonished me, for
was decked out in a series of reds ranging from scarlet to
ine, pricked out and accentuated here and there with white. It
oked immensely sure of itself as it lay there, flamboyant, on
e sand, and immensely dangerous too.

'This is good eating,' whispered Taki to my surprise, for the
sh looked highly poisonous.

Slowly and delicately he lowered the trident into the water,
sing the barbed fork inch by inch towards the fish. There
as no sound except the peevish hissing of the lamp. Slowly,
exorably, the trident got closer and closer. I held my breath.
urely that great fish with its gold-flecked eyes must notice its
pproaching doom? A sudden flip of the tail, I thought, a
virl of sand and it would be gone. But no, it just lay there
ulping methodically and pompously to itself. When the
ident was within a foot of it, Taki paused. I saw him gently
ift his grip on the haft. He stood immobile for a second,
though it seemed an interminable time to me, and then
ddenly, so speedily that I did not actually see the movement,
: drove the five prongs swiftly and neatly through the back
: the great fish's head. There was a swirl of sand and blood
d the fish twisted and writhed on the prongs, curling its

63

body so that the spines along its back jabbed at the tride
But Taki had driven the trident home too skilfully and
could not escape. Quickly, hand over hand, he pulled in
pole, and the fish came over the side and into the boat, flapp
and writhing. I came forward to help him get it off the pron
but he pushed me back roughly.

'Take care,' he said, 'the Scorpios is a bad fish.'

I watched while, with the aid of the oar blade, he got
fish off the trident, and, although to all intents and purpose
must have been dead, it still wriggled and flapped and tried
drive the spines on its back into the side of the boat.

'Look, look,' said Taki. 'You see now why we call
Scorpios. If he can stab you with those spines, St Spiridi
what pain you would have. You would have to go to
hospital quickly.'

With the aid of the oar, the trident, and a dexterous bit
juggling, he managed to lift the Scorpion Fish up and drop
into an empty kerosene tin where it could do no harm
wanted to know why, if it was poisonous, it was supposed
be good eating.

'Ah,' said Taki, 'it's only the spines. You cut those off. T
flesh is sweet, sweet as honey. I will give it to you to ta
home with you.'

He bent over his oars once more and we squeaked our w
along the edge of the reef again. Presently he paused on
more. Here the sea bed was sandy with just a few scatter
tufts of young green ribbon weed. Again he slowed the boat
a standstill and picked up his trident.

'Look,' he said. 'Octopus.'

My stomach gave a clutch of excitement, for the on
octopus I had seen had been the dead ones on sale in the tov
and these, I felt sure, bore no resemblance to the living cr
ture. But peer as hard as I could, the sandy bottom appea
to be completely devoid of life.

'There, *there*,' said Taki, lowering the trident gently into
water and pointing. 'Can't you see it? Did you leave yc
eyes behind? There, *there*. Look, I am almost touching it.'

Still I could not see it. He lowered the trident another fo

'Now can you see it, foolish one?' he chuckled. 'Just at
end of the prongs.'

And suddenly I could see it. I had been looking at it all

time, but it was so grey and sand-like that I had mistaken it for part of the sea bed. It squatted on the sand in a nest of tentacles and under its bald domed head its eyes, uncannily human, peered up at us forlornly.

'It's a big one,' said Taki.

He shifted the trident slightly in his grasp, but the movement was incautious. Suddenly the octopus turned from a drab sandy colour to a bright and startling iridescent green. It squirted a jet of water out of its syphon and, projected by this, in a swirl of sand, it shot off the sea bed. Its tentacles trailed out behind it and, as it sped through the water, it looked like a runaway balloon.

'Ah, gammoto!' said Taki.

He threw the trident down and, seizing the oars, rowed swiftly in the wake of the octopus. The octopus obviously possessed a touching faith in its camouflage, for it had come to rest on the sea bed some thirty-five feet away.

Once again, Taki eased the boat up to it and once again lowered the trident carefully into the water. This time he took no risks and made no incautious movements. When the pronged fork was within a foot of the octopus's domed head, Taki strengthened his grip on the pole and plunged it home. Immediately the silver sand boiled up in a cloud as the octopus's tentacles threshed and writhed and wound themselves round the trident. Ink spurted from its body and hung like a trembling curtain of black lace or coiled like smoke across the sand. Taki was chuckling now with pleasure. He hauled the trident up swiftly and as the octopus came into the boat, two of its tentacles seized and adhered to the side. Taki gave a sharp tug and the tentacles were pulled free with a ripping rasping noise which was like the sound of sticking plaster being removed, a thousand times magnified. Swiftly, Taki grabbed the round, slimy body of the octopus and deftly removed it from the prongs. Then, to my astonishment, he lifted this writhing Medusa head and put it to his face so that the tentacles wound round his forehead, his cheeks and his neck, the suckers leaving white impressions against his dark skin. Choosing his spot carefully, he suddenly buried his teeth in the very core of the creature with a snap and a sideways jerk, reminiscent of a terrier breaking the back of a rat. He had obviously bitten through some vital nerve centre, for immediately the ten-

tacles released their grip on his head and fell limply, only the
very extremities twitching and curling slightly. Taki thre
the octopus into the tin with the Scorpion Fish, spat over th
side of the boat and then, reaching over, cupped a handful o
sea water and swilled his mouth out with it.

'You have brought me luck,' he said, grinning and wipin
his mouth. 'It is not many nights that I get an octopus an
a Scorpios.'

But apparently Taki's luck stopped short at the octopus, fo
although we circled the reef several times, we caught nothin
more. We did see the head of a Moray Eel sticking out of i
hole in the reef, an extremely vicious-looking head the size of
small dog's. But when Taki lowered the trident, the Mora
Eel, smoothly and with much dignity, retreated with flui
grace into the depths of the reef and we did not see him agai
For myself, I was quite glad, for I imagined he must hav
been about six feet long and to wrestle about in a dimly l
boat with a six-foot Moray Eel was an experience that eve
I, ardent naturalist though I was, felt I could do without.

'Ah, well,' said Taki philosophically. 'Now let's go and d
your fishing.'

He rowed me out to the largest of the reefs and landed m
with my gear on its flat top. Armed with my net, I prowle
along the edges of the reef while Taki rowed the boat some si
feet behind me, illuminating the smouldering beauty of th
rocks. There was so much life that I despaired of being abl
to capture it all.

There were fragile blennies, decked out in gold and scarlet
tiny fish half the size of a match stick with great black eye
and pillar-box red bodies and others, the same size, whos
colouring was a combination of deep Prussian and pal
powder-blue. There were blood-red star fish and purple britt
star fish, their long, slender, spiky arms for ever coiling an
uncoiling. These had to be lifted in the net with the utmos
delicacy, for the slightest shock and they would, with ga
abandon, lavishly shed all their arms. There were slippe
limpets that, when you turned them over, you found had ha
the underside covered by a neat flange of shell, so that th
whole thing did look rather like a baggy, shapeless carpe
slipper designed for a gouty foot. Then there were cowrie
some as white as snow and delicately ribbed, others a pal

cream, heavily blotched and smudged with purple-black markings. There were the coat-of-mail shells, or chitons, some two and a half inches long, that clung to crannies in the rocks looking like gigantic wood lice. I saw a baby cuttlefish the size of a match box and almost fell off the edge of the reef in my efforts to capture him, but, to my immense chagrin, he escaped. After only half an hour's collecting I found that my jars, tins and boxes were crammed to overflowing with life, and I knew that, albeit reluctantly, I would have to stop.

Taki, very good humouredly, rowed me over to my favourite bay and stood watching amusedly while I carefully emptied my jars of specimens into my rock pool. Then he rowed me back to the jetty below Menelaos'. Here he strung a cord through the gills of the now dead Scorpion Fish and handed it to me.

'Tell your mother,' he said, 'to cook it with hot paprika and oil and potatoes and little marrows. It is very sweet.'

I thanked him for this and for the fact that he had been so patient with me.

'Come fishing again,' he said. 'I shall be up here next week. Probably Wednesday or Thursday. I'll send a message to you when I arrive.'

I thanked him and said I would look forward to it. He pushed the boat off and poled his way through the shallow waters heading in the direction of Benitses.

I shouted 'Be happy,' after him.

'*Pasto calo*,' he answered. 'Go to the good.'

I turned and trudged my way wearily up the hill. To my horror I discovered that it was half past two and I knew Mother would by now have convinced herself that I had been drowned or eaten by a shark or overtaken by some similar fate. However, I hoped that the Scorpion Fish would placate her.

The Myrtle Forests

About half a mile north of the villa the olive grove thinned
out and there was a flat basin, fifty or sixty acres in extent, on
which no olives grew. Here was only a great green forest of
myrtle bushes, interspersed with dry stony grassland, decorated
with the strange candlebras of the thistles, glowing a vivid
electric blue, and the huge flaky bulbs of squills. This was one
of my favourite hunting-grounds, for it contained a remarkable selection of insect life. Roger and I would squat in the
heavily scented shade of the myrtle bushes and watch the array
of creatures that passed us, and at certain times of the day
the branches were as busy as the main street of a town.

The myrtle forests were full of mantis some three inches
long, with vivid green wings. They would sway through the
myrtle branches on their slender legs, their wickedly barbed
front arms held up in an attitude of hypocritical prayer, their
little pointed faces with their bulbous straw-coloured eyes
turning this way and that, missing nothing, like angular, em-
bittered spinsters at a cocktail party. Should a Cabbage White
or a Fritillary land on the glossy myrtle leaves, the mantis
would approach them with the utmost caution, moving almost imperceptibly, pausing now and then to sway gently to
and fro on their legs, beseeching the butterfly to believe they
were really wind-ruffled leaves.

I once saw a mantis stalk and finally launch himself at a
large Swallow Tail which was sitting in the sun gently moving
his wings and meditating. At the last minute, however, the
mantis missed its footing and instead of catching the Swallow
Tail by the body, as it had intended to do, caught it by one
wing. The Swallow Tail came out of its trance with a start
and flapped its wings so vigorously that it succeeded in lifting
the forequarters of the mantis off the leaves. A few more
vigorous flappings and, to the mantis's annoyance, the Swallow
Tail flew lopsidedly away with a large section missing from
one wing. The mantis philosophically sat down and ate the
piece of wing that it had retained in its claws.

Under the rocks that littered the ground among the thistles there lived a surprising variety of creatures, in spite of the fact that the earth was baked rock-hard by the sun and was almost hot enough to poach an egg on. Here lived beasts which always gave me the creeps. They were flattened centipedes some two inches long, with a thick fringe of long spiky legs along each side of their body. They were so flat that they could get into the most minute crevice and they moved with tremendous speed, seeming more to glide over the ground than run, as smoothly as a flat pebble skims across ice. They were called *Scutigeridae*, and I could think of no other name which would be so apt in conjuring up this creature's particularly obnoxious form of locomotion.

Scattered among the rocks, you would find holes that had been driven into the hard ground, each the size of a half-crown or larger. They were silk-lined and with a web spread to a three inch circle around the mouth of the burrow. These were the lairs of the tarantulas, great fat, chocolate-coloured spiders with fawn and cinnamon markings. With their legs spread out, they covered an area perhaps about the size of a coffee saucer and their bodies of half a small walnut. They were immensely powerful, quick and cruel in their hunting and displaying a remarkable sort of inimical intelligence. For the most part, they hunted at night, but occasionally you would see them during the day, striding swiftly through the thistles on their long legs, in search of their prey. Generally, as soon as they saw you, they would scuttle off and soon be lost among the myrtles, but one day I saw one who was so completely absorbed that he let me approach quite close.

He was some six or seven feet away from his burrow and was standing half way up a blue thistle, waving his front legs and peering about him, reminding me irresistibly of a hunter who had climbed a tree in order to see if there is any game about. He continued to do this for about five minutes while I squatted on my haunches and watched him. Presently he climbed carefully down the thistle and set off in a very determined manner. It was almost as though he had seen something from his lofty perch, but searching the ground, I could see no sign of life, and in any case I was not at all sure that a tarantula's eyesight was as good as all that. But he marched along in a determined fashion until he came to a large clump of Job's Tears; a fine trembling grass whose seed heads look like little white plaited rolls of bread. Going closer to this, I suddenly realised what the tarantula appeared to be after, for under the delicate fountain of white grass there was a lark's nest. It had four eggs in it. One of them had just hatched, and the tiny, pink, downy offspring was still struggling feebly in the remains of the shell.

Before I could do anything sensible to save it, the tarantula had marched over the edge of the nest. He loomed there for a moment, monstrous and terrifying, and then swiftly drew the quivering baby to him and sank his long, curved mandibles into its back. The baby gave two minute, almost inaudible squeaks and opened its mouth wide as it writhed briefly in the hairy embrace of the spider. Then the poison took effect; it went rigid for a brief moment and then hung limply. The spider waited, immobile, till he was certain the poison had done its work and then turned and marched off, the baby hanging limply from his jaws. He looked like some strange, leggy retriever, bringing in his first grouse of the season. Without a pause, he hurried back to his burrow and disappeared inside it carrying the limp, pathetic little body of the fledgeling.

I was amazed by this encounter for two reasons: firstly because I did not realise that tarantulas would tackle anything the size of a baby bird, and secondly because I could not see how he knew the nest was there, and he obviously *did* know, for he walked, unhesitatingly, straight to it. The distance from the thistle to the nest was about thirty-five feet, as I found out by pacing it, and I was positive that no spider had the eyesight to be able to spot such a well-camouflaged nest and the fledgeling from that distance. This left only smell, and here again, although I knew animals could smell subtle scents which our blunted nostrils could not pick up, I felt that on a breathlessly still day at thirty-five feet it would take a remarkable olfactory sense to be able to pin-point the baby lark. The only solution I could come to was that the spider had, during his perambulations, discovered the nest and kept checking on it periodically to see whether the young had hatched. But this did not satisfy me as an explanation, for it attributed a thought process to an insect which I was pretty certain it did not possess. Even my oracle, Theodore, could not explain this puzzle.

satisfactorily. All I knew was that that particular pair of larks did not succeed in rearing a single young one that year.

Other creatures in the myrtle forests that fascinated me greatly were the ant lion larvae. Adult ant lions come in a variety of sizes and, for the most part, rather drab colouring. They look like extremely untidy and demented dragonflies. They have wings that seem to be out of all proportion to their bodies and these they flap with a desperate air, as though it required the maximum amount of energy to prevent them from crashing to the earth. They are a good natured, bumbling sort of beast, and do no harm to anybody. But the same could not be said of their larvae. What the rapacious dragonfly larva was to the pond, the ant lion was to the dry, sandy areas that lay between the myrtle bushes. The only sign that there were ant lion larvae about was a series of curious, cone-shaped depressions in areas where the soil was fine and soft enough to be dug. The first time I discovered these cones, I was greatly puzzled as to what had made them. I wondered if perhaps some mice had been excavating for roots or something similar, and I was unaware that at the base of each cone was the architect, waiting taut and ready on the sand, as dangerous as a hidden man-trap. Then I saw one of these cones in action and realised for the first time that it was not only the larva's home, but also a gigantic trap.

An ant would come trotting along (and I always felt they hummed to themselves as they went about their work), he might be one of the little busy black variety or one of the large red solitary ants which staggered about the countryside with their red abdomens pointing to the sky like anti-aircraft guns. Whichever species it was, if it happened to walk over the edge of one of the little pits, it immediately found that the sloping sides shifted so that it started to slide down towards the base of the cone. It would then turn and try and climb out of the pit, but the earth or sand would shift in little avalanches under its feet. As soon as one of these avalanches had trickled down to the base of the cone, it would be the signal for the larva to come into action. Suddenly the ant would find itself bombarded with a rapid machine-gun fire of sand or earth, projected up from the bottom of the pit with incredible speed by the head of the larva. With the shifting ground under foot and bombarded with earth or sand, the ant would miss its foothold and roll ignominiously down to the bottom of the pit. Out of the sand, with utmost speed, would appear the head of the ant lion larva, a flattened, ant-like head, with a pair of enormous curved jaws, like sickles. These would be plunged into the unfortunate ant's body and the larva would sink back beneath the sand, dragging the kicking and struggling ant with it to its grave. As I felt the ant lion larvae took an unfair advantage over the dim-witted and rather earnest ants, I had no compunction in digging them up when I found them and taking them home and making them hatch out eventually in little muslin cages, so that if they were a species new to me, I could add them to my collection.

One day we had one of those freak storms when the sky turned blue-black and the lightning fretted a silver filigree across it. And then had come the rain; great, fat, heavy drops, as warm as blood. When the storm had passed, the sky had been washed to the clear blue of a hedge sparrow's egg The damp earth sent out wonderfully rich, almost gastronomic smells like fruit cake or plum puddings, and the olive trunks steamed as the rain was dried off them by the sun, each trunk looking as thought it was on fire. Roger and I liked these summer storms. It was fun to be able to splash through the puddles and feel your clothes getting wetter and wetter in the warm rain. In addition to this, Roger derived considerable amusement from barking at the lightning. When the rain ceased we were passing the myrtle forests and I called in on the off-chance that the storm might have brought out some creatures that would normally be sheltering from the heat of the day. Sure enough, on a myrtle branch there were two fat honey and amber coloured snails gliding smoothly toward each other, their horns waving provocatively. Normally, knew, in the height of the summer, these snails would aestivate They would attach themselves to a convenient branch, construct a thin, paper-like front door over the mouth of the shell and then retreat deep into its convolutions in order to husband the moisture in their bodies from the fierce heat of the sun. This freak storm had obviously woken them up and made them feel gay and romantic. As I watched them the glided up to each other until their horns touched. Then the

aused and gazed long and earnestly into each other's eyes.
ne of them shifted his position slightly so that he could glide
longside the other one. When he was alongside, something
appened that made me doubt the evidence of my own eyes.
rom his side, and almost simultaneously from the side of the
ther snail, there shot what appeared to be two minute, fragile
hite darts, each attached to a slender white cord. The dart
om one snail pierced the side of snail two and disappeared,
hile the dart from snail two did the same on snail one. So
ere they were, side by side, attached to each other by the
vo little white cords. And there they sat like two curious
ailing ships roped together. This was amazing enough, but
ranger things were to follow. The cords gradually appeared
▸ get shorter and shorter and drew the two snails together.
eering at them so closely that my nose was almost touching
nem, I came to the incredulous conclusion that each snail, by
ome mechanism in its body, was winching its rope in, thus
auling the other snail alongside, until presently their bodies
ere pressed tightly together. I knew they must be mating,
ut their bodies had become so amalgamated that I could not
ee the precise nature of the act. They stayed rapturously side
y side for some fifteen minutes and then, without so much
s a nod or a thank-you, glided away in opposite directions,
either one displaying any signs of darts or ropes, nor indeed
ny enthusiasm at having culminated their love affair so suc-
essfully.

I was so intrigued by this piece of behaviour that I could
ardly wait until the following Thursday, when Theodore came
▸ tea, to tell him about it. Theodore listened, rocking gently
n his toes and nodding gravely while I graphically described
hat I had witnessed.

'Aha, yes,' he said when I had finished. 'You were . . ., um
. ., you know . . ., um . . ., extremely lucky to see that. I
ave watched any number of snails and I have never seen it.'

I asked whether I had imagined the little darts and the ropes.

'No, no,' said Theodore. 'That's quite correct. The darts
re formed of a sort of . . ., um . . ., calcium-like substance
nd once they have penetrated the snail, they, you know,
isappear, . . ., dissolve. It seems there is some evidence to
hink that the darts cause a *tingling* sensation which the snails
. ., um, . . ., apparently find pleasant.'

I asked whether I was right in assuming that each snail had winched its rope in.

'Yes, yes, that's quite correct,' said Theodore. 'They apparently have some, . . ., um, . . ., sort of mechanism inside which can pull the rope back again.'

I said I thought it was one of the most remarkable things I had ever seen.

'Yes, indeed. Extremely curious,' said Theodore, and then added a bombshell that took my breath away. 'Once they are alongside, the, . . ., um, . . ., male half of one snail mates with the, um, . . ., female half of the other snail, and, . . ., um vice versa as it were.'

It took me a moment or so to absorb this astonishing information. Was I correct in assuming, I enquired cautiously, that each snail was both male and female?

'Um. Yes,' said Theodore. 'Hermaphrodite.'

His eyes twinkled at me and he rasped the side of his beard with his thumb. Larry, who had been wearing the pained expression he normally wore when Theodore and I discussed natural history, was equally astonished by this amazing revelation of the snails' sex life.

'Surely you're joking, Theodore?' he protested. 'You mean to say that each snail is both a male and a female?'

'Yes indeed,' said Theodore, adding with masterly understatement, 'It's very curious.'

'Good God,' said Larry explosively. 'I think it's unfair. All those damned slimy things wandering about seducing each other like mad all over the bushes, and having the pleasures of both sensations. Why couldn't such a gift be given to the human race? That's what I want to know.'

'Aha, yes. But then you would have to lay eggs,' Theodore pointed out.

'True,' said Larry, 'but what a marvellous way of getting out of cocktail parties—"I'm terribly sorry I can't come," you would say, "I've got to sit on my eggs".'

Theodore gave a little snort of laughter.

'But snails don't sit on their eggs,' he explained. 'They bury them in damp earth and leave them.'

'The ideal way of bringing up a family,' said Mother, unexpectedly but with immense conviction. 'I wish I'd been able to bury you all in some damp earth and leave you.'

'That's an extremely harsh and ungrateful thing to say,' said Larry. 'You've probably given Gerry a complex for the rest of his life.'

But if the conversation had given me a complex, it was one about snails, for I was already planning vast snail-hunting expeditions with Roger, so that I could bring dozens of them back to the villa and keep them in tins, where I could observe them shooting their love darts at each other to my heart's content. But, in spite of the fact that I caught hundreds of snails during the next few weeks, kept them incarcerated in tins and lavished every care and attention on them (even gave them simulated thunder-storms with the aid of a watering can), I could not get them to mate.

The only other time I saw snails indulging in this curious love play was when I succeeded in obtaining a pair of the giant Roman or Apple Snails which lived on the stony outcrops of the Mountain of the Ten Saints, and the only reason I was able to get up there and capture these snails was because, on my birthday, Mother had purchased for me my heart's desire, a sturdy, baby donkey.

Although, ever since we arrived in Corfu, I had been aware that there were vast quantities of donkeys there—indeed the entire agricultural economy of the island depended on them—I had not really concentrated on them until we had gone to Katerina's wedding. Here a great number of the donkeys had brought their babies, many of them only a few days old. I was enchanted by their bulbous knees, their great ears and their wobbling, uncertain walk and I had determined then, come what might, that I would possess a donkey of my own.

As I explained to Mother, while trying to argue her into agreeing to this, if I had a donkey to carry me and my equipment, I could go so much farther afield. Why couldn't I have it for Christmas, I asked? Because, Mother replied, firstly they were too expensive and secondly there were not any babies available at that precise time. But if they were too expensive, I argued, why couldn't I have one as a Christmas and birthday present? I would willingly forgo all other presents in lieu of a donkey. Mother said she would see, which I knew from bitter experience generally meant that she would forget about the matter as rapidly and as comprehensively as possible. As it

75

got near to my birthday, I once again reiterated all the arguments in favour of having a donkey. Mother just repeated that we would see.

Then, one day, Costas, the brother of our maid, made his appearance in the olive grove just outside our little garden carrying on his shoulders a great bundle of tall bamboos. Whistling happily to himself he proceeded to dig holes in the ground and set the bamboos upright so that they formed a small square. Peering at him through the fuchsia hedge I wondered what on earth he was doing, so whistling Roger, I went round to see.

'I am building,' said Costas, 'a house for your mother.'

I was astonished. What on earth could Mother want a bamboo house for? Had she, perhaps, decided to sleep out of doors? I felt this was unlikely. What, I enquired of Costas did Mother want with a bamboo house?

He gazed at me wall-eyed.

'Who knows?' he said shrugging. 'Perhaps she wants to keep plants in it or store sweet potatoes for the winter.'

I thought this was extremely unlikely as well, but having watched Costas for half an hour I grew bored and went off for a walk with Roger.

By the next day the framework of the bamboo hut had been finished and Costas was now busy twining bundles of reeds in between the bamboos to form solid walls and the roof. Another day, and it was completed, looking exactly like one of Robinson Crusoe's earlier attempts at house-building. When enquired of Mother what she intended to use the house for, she said that she was not quite sure, but felt it would come in useful. With that vague information I had to be content.

The day before my birthday, everybody started acting in a slightly more eccentric manner than usual. Larry, for some reason best known to himself, went about the house shouting 'Tantivy!' and 'Tally-ho' and similar hunting slogans. As he was fairly frequently afflicted in this way, I did not take much notice.

Margo kept dodging about the house carrying mysterious bundles under her arm and at one point I came face to face with her in the hall and noted, with astonishment, that he arms were full of multi-coloured decorations left over from Christmas. On seeing me, she uttered a squeak of dismay and rushed into her bedroom in such a guilty and furtive manner that I was left staring after her with open mouth.

Even Leslie and Spiro were afflicted, it seemed, and they kept going into mysterious huddles in the garden. From the snippets of their conversation that I heard, I could not make head or tail of what they were planning.

'In the backs seats,' Spiro said, scowling. 'Honest to Gods, Masters Leslies, I have dones it befores.'

'Well, if you're sure, Spiro,' Leslie replied doubtfully, 'but we don't want any broken legs or anything.'

Then Leslie saw me undisguisedly eavesdropping and asked me truculently what the hell I thought I was doing, eavesdropping on people's private conversations? Why didn't I go down to the nearest cliff and jump off? Feeling that the family were in no mood to be amicable, I took Roger off into the olive groves and for the rest of the day we ineffectually chased green lizards.

That night I had just turned down the lamp and snuggled into bed when I heard sounds of raucous singing, accompanied by gales of laughter coming through the olive groves. As the uproar got closer, I could recognise Leslie's and Larry's voices combined with Spiro's, each of them appearing to be singing a different song. It seemed as though they had been somewhere and celebrated too well. From the indignant whispering and shuffling going on in the corridor, I could tell that Margo and Mother had reached the same conclusion.

They burst into the villa, laughing hysterically at some witticism that Larry had produced and were shushed fiercely by Margo and Mother.

'Do be quiet,' said Mother. 'You'll wake Gerry. What have you been drinking?'

'Wine,' said Larry in a dignified tone. Then he hiccuped.

'Wine,' said Leslie. 'And then we danced and Spiro danced, and I danced, and Larry danced. And Spiro danced and then Larry danced and then I danced.'

'I think you had better go to bed,' said Mother.

'And then Spiro danced again,' said Leslie, 'and then Larry danced.'

'All right, dear, all right,' said Mother. 'Go to *bed* fo heaven's sake. Really, Spiro, I do feel that you shouldn't hav let them drink so much.'

'Spiro danced,' said Leslie, driving the point home.

'I'll take him to bed,' said Larry. 'I'm the only sober membe of the party.'

There was the sound of lurching feet on the tiles as Lesli and Larry, clasped in each other's arms, staggered down th corridor.

'I'm now dancing with *you*,' came Leslie's voice as Larr dragged him into his bedroom and put him to bed.

'I am sorrys, Mrs Durrells,' said Spiro, his deep voic thickened with wine, 'but I couldn't stops thems.'

'Did you get it?' said Margo.

'Yes, Missy Margos. Don'ts you worrys,' said Spiro. 'I down with Costas.'

Eventually Spiro left and I heard Mother and Marg going to bed. It made a fittingly mysterious end to what ha been a highly confusing day. But I soon forgot about th family's behaviour, as, lying in the dark wondering what m presents were going to be, I drifted off to sleep.

The following morning I woke and lay for a moment wo dering what was so special about that day. Then I remembere It was my birthday. I lay there savouring the feeling of havi a whole day to myself when people would give me presen and the family would be forced to accede to any reasonab requests. I was just about to get out of bed and go and s what my presents were, when a curious uproar broke out the hall.

'Hold its head. Hold its *head*,' came Leslie's voice.

'Look out, you're spoiling the decorations,' wailed Marg

'Damn the bloody decorations,' said Leslie. 'Hold its *hea*

'Now, now, dears,' said Mother. 'Don't quarrel.'

'Dear God,' said Larry in disgust, 'dung all over the floo

The whole of this mysterious conversation was accompani by a strange pitta-pattering noise, as though someone we bouncing ping-pong balls on the tile floor of the hall. What earth, I wondered, were the family up to now? Normally, this time they were still lying, semi-conscious, groping blea eyed for their early morning cups of tea. I sat up in bed, p paratory to going into the hall to join in whatever fun w

oot, when my bedroom door burst open and a donkey, clad
festoons of coloured crêpe paper, Christmas decorations
d with three enormous feathers attached skilfully between its
rge ears, came galloping into the bedroom, Leslie hanging
imly on to its tail shouting 'Woa, you bastard!'

'Language, dear,' said Mother, looking flustered in the door-
ay.

'You're spoiling the decorations,' screamed Margo.

'The sooner that animal gets out of here,' said Larry, 'the
etter. There's dung all over the hall now.'

'You frightened it,' said Margo.

'I didn't do anything,' said Larry indignantly. 'I just gave it
little push.'

The donkey skidded to a halt by my bedside and gazed at
e out of enormous brown eyes. It seemed rather surprised. It
ook itself vigorously so that the feathers between its ears fell
f and then, very dexterously, hacked Leslie on the shin with
s hind leg.

'Jesus!' roared Leslie, hopping around on one leg. 'It's
roken my bloody leg.'

'Leslie, dear, there is no need to swear so much,' said
Iother. 'Remember Gerry.'

'The sooner you get it out of that bedroom the better,'
aid Larry, 'otherwise the whole place will smell like a
idden.'

'You've simply ruined its decorations,' said Margo, 'and it
ook me hours to put them on.'

But I was taking no notice of the family. The donkey had
pproached the edge of my bed, stared at me inquisitively for
moment and had then given a little throaty chuckle and
rust in my outstretched hands a grey muzzle as soft as every-
ing soft I could think of—silk worm cocoons, newly-born
uppies, sea pebbles, or the velvety feel of a tree frog. Leslie
ad now removed his trousers and was examining the bruise
n his shin, cursing fluently.

'Do you like it, dear?' asked Mother.

Like it! I was speechless.

The donkey was a rich dark brown, almost a plum colour,
ith enormous ears like arum lilies, white socks over tiny
olished hoofs as neat as a tap dancer's shoes. Running along
er back was the broad black cross that denotes so proudly

79

that her race carried Christ into Jerusalem (and has continu
to be one of the most maligned domestic animals ever sinc
and round each great shining eye she had a neat white circ
which denoted that she came from the village of Gastouri.

'You remember Katerina's donkey that you liked so much,'
said Margo. 'Well, this is her baby.'

This, of course, made the donkey even more special. Th
donkey stood there looking like a refugee from a circus, che
ing a piece of tinsel meditatively, while I scrambled out of be
and flung on my clothes. Where, I enquired breathlessly
Mother, was I to keep her? Obviously I couldn't keep her
the villa in view of the fact that Larry had just pointed out
Mother that she could, if she so wished, grow a good crop
potatoes in the hall.

'That's what the house Costas built is for,' said Mother.

I was beside myself with delight. What a noble, kind
benevolent family I had! How cunningly they had kept th
secret from me! How hard they had worked to deck th
donkey out in its finery! Slowly and gently, as though she w
some fragile piece of china, I led my steed out through th
garden and round into the olive grove, opened the door of th
little bamboo hut and took her inside. I thought I ought to t
her for size, because Costas was a notoriously bad workma
The little house was splendid. Just big enough for her. I too
her out again and tethered her to an olive tree on a long leng
of rope, then stayed for half an hour in a dream-like tran
admiring her from every angle while she grazed placidl
Eventually I heard Mother calling me in to breakfast and
sighed with satisfaction. I had decided that, without any dou
whatsoever, and without wishing in any way to be partisa
this donkey was the finest donkey in the whole of the isla
of Corfu. For no reason that I could think of, I decided to c
her Sally. I gave her a quick kiss on her silken muzzle and the
went in to breakfast.

After breakfast, to my astonishment, Larry, with a ma
nanimous air, said that if I liked he would teach me to rid
I said that I didn't know he could ride.

'Of course,' said Larry, airily. 'When we were in India I w
always galloping about on ponies and things. I used to groo
them and feed them and so forth. Have to know what you
doing, of course.'

So, armed with a blanket and a large piece of webbing, we
went out into the olive grove, placed the blanket on Sally's
back and tied it in position. She viewed these preparations
with interest but a lack of enthusiasm. With a certain amount
of difficulty, for Sally would persist in walking round and
round in a tight circle, Larry succeeded in getting me on to her
back. He then exchanged her tether for a rope halter and rope
reins.

'Now,' he said, 'you just steer her as though she's a boat.
When you want her to go faster, kick her in the ribs with your
heels.'

If that was all there was to riding, I felt, it was going to be
simplicity itself. I jerked on the reins and dug my heels into
Sally's ribs. It was unfortunate that my fall was broken by a
large and exceptionally luxuriant bramble-bush. Sally peered
at me as I extricated myself, with a look of astonishment on
her face.

'Perhaps,' said Larry, 'you ought to have a stick so then
you can use your legs for gripping on to her and you won't fall
off.'

He cut me a short stick and once again I mounted Sally.
This time I wrapped my legs tightly round her barrel body
and gave her a sharp tap with my switch. She bucked several
times, indignantly, but I clung on like a limpet and to my
delight, within half an hour, I had her trotting to and fro
between the olive trees, responding neatly to tugs on the rein.
Larry had been lying under the olives smoking and watching
my progress. Now, as I appeared to have mastered the eques-
trian art, he rose to his feet and took a pen-knife out of his
pocket.

'Now,' he said, as I dismounted, 'I'll show you how to look
after her. First of all, you must brush her down every morning.
We'll get a brush for you in town. Then you must make sure
that her hooves are clean. You must do that every day.'

I enquired, puzzled, how did one clean donkeys' hooves?

'I'll show you,' said Larry nonchalantly.

He walked up to Sally, bent down and picked up her hind
leg.

'In here,' he said, pointing with the blade of the knife at
Sally's hoof, 'an awful lot of muck gets trapped. This can lead

to all sorts of things, foot rot and so forth. It's very important
to keep them clean.'

So saying, he dug his pen-knife blade into Sally's hoof.
What Larry had not realised was that donkeys in Corfu were
unshod and that a baby donkey's hoof is still, comparatively
speaking, soft and very delicate. So, not unnaturally, Sally
reacted as though Larry had jabbed her with a red-hot skewer.
She wrenched her hoof out of his hands and, as he straightened
up and turned in astonishment, she did a pretty pirouette and
kicked him neatly in the pit of the stomach with both hind
legs. Larry sat down heavily, his face went white and he
doubled up, clasping his stomach and making strange rattling
noises. The alarm I felt was not for Larry but for Sally, for I
was quite sure that he would exact the most terrible retribution
when he recovered. Hastily I undid Sally's rope, flicked her
on the rump with the stick and watched her canter off into
the olives. Then I ran into the house and informed Mother that
Larry had an accident. The entire family, including Spiro
who had just arrived, came running out into the olive grove
where Larry was still writhing about uttering great sobbing
wheezing noises.

'Larry, dear,' said Mother distraught, 'what have you been
doing?'

'Attacked,' gasped Larry in between wheezes. 'Unprovoked
. . . Creature mad . . . Probably rabies . . . Ruptured appen-
dix.'

With Leslie on one side of him and Spiro on the other they
carted Larry slowly back to the villa, with Mother and Margo
fluttering commiseratingly and ineffectually around him. In a
crisis of this magnitude involving my family, one had to keep
one's wits about one or all was lost. I ran swiftly round to the
kitchen door where, panting but innocent, I informed our maid
that I was going to spend the day out and could she give me
some food to eat. She put half a loaf of bread, some onions,
some olives and a hunk of cold meat into a paper bag and gave
it to me. Fruit I knew I could obtain from any of my peasant
friends. Then I raced through the olive groves, carrying the
provender, in search of Sally.

I eventually found her half a mile away, grazing on a succulent patch of grass. After several ineffectual attempts, I managed to scramble up on to her back and then, belabouring her

behind with a stick, I urged her to a brisk trot as far away from the villa as possible.

I had to return to the villa for tea because Theodore was coming. When I got back I found Larry, swathed in blankets, lying on the sofa giving Theodore a graphic description of the incident.

'And then, absolutely unprovoked, it suddenly turned on me with slavering jaws, like the charge of the Light Brigade.' He broke off to glare at me as I entered the room. 'Oh, so you decided to come back. And what may I enquire have you done with that equine menace?'

I replied that Sally was safely bedded down in her stable and had, fortunately, suffered no ill effects from the incident. Larry glared at me.

'Well, I'm delighted to hear that,' he said caustically. 'The fact that I am lying here with my spleen ruptured in three places is apparently of little or no moment.'

'I have brought you . . ., um . . ., a little, you know . . ., a, . . ., gift,' said Theodore and presented me with a replica of his own collecting box, complete with tubes and a fine muslin net. I could not have asked for anything nicer and thanked him volubly.

'You had better go and thank Katerina too, dear,' said Mother. 'She didn't really want to part with Sally, you know.'

'I am surprised,' said Larry. 'I'd have thought she'd have been only too glad to get rid of her.'

'You'd better not go and see Katerina now,' said Margo. 'She's getting near her time.'

Intrigued by this unusual phrase, I asked what 'getting near her time' meant.

'She's going to have a baby, dear,' said Mother.

'The wonder of it is,' said Larry, 'as I thought when we went to the wedding, she didn't have it in the vestry.'

'Larry, dear,' said Mother. 'Not in front of Gerry.'

'Well, it's true,' said Larry. 'I've never seen such a pregnant bride in white.'

I said I thought it would be a good idea if I went to thank Katerina before she had the baby because after she had it she would probably be very busy. Reluctantly, Mother agreed and so the following morning I mounted Sally and rode off through the olive trees in the direction of Gastouri, Roger

PERAMA

trotting behind and indulging in a game which he and Sally
had invented between them, which consisted of Roger darting
in at intervals and nibbling her heels gently, growling furiously,
whereupon Sally would give a skittish little buck and attempt
to kick him in the ribs.

Presently we came to the low white house with the flattened
area outside its front door neatly ringed with rusty cans filled
with flowers. To my astonishment I saw that we were not the
only visitors that day. There were several elderly gentlemen
sitting round a small table, hunched over glasses of wine, their
enormous swooping, nicotine-stained moustaches flapping up
and down as they talked. Clustered in the doorway of the
house and peering eagerly through the one small window that
illuminated its interior, there was a solid wedge of female
relatives, all chattering and gesticulating at once.

From inside the house came a series of piercing shrieks
interspersed with cries for help from the Almighty, the Virgin
Mary and Saint Spiridion. I gathered from all this uproar and
activity that I had arrived in the middle of a family row. The
inter-family warfare was quite a common thing among the
peasants and something I always found very enjoyable, for any
quarrel, however trivial, was carried on with grim determination until it was sucked dry of the very last juices of drama,
with people shouting abuse at one another through the olive
trees and the men periodically chasing each other with bamboos.

I tethered Sally and made my way to the front door of the
house, wondering, as I did so, what this particular row was
about. The last one in this area that I remembered had lasted
for a prodigious length of time (three weeks) and had all been
started by a small boy who told his cousin that his grandfather
cheated at cards. I wriggled and pushed my way determined
through the knot of people who blocked the doorway and
finally got inside, only to find the entire room seemed to be
filled with Katerina's relatives, packed shoulder to shoulder
like a football crowd. I had, quite early in life, discovered that
the only way of dealing with a situation like this was to get
down on your hands and knees and crawl. This I did and by
this means successfully achieved the front row in the circle of
relatives that surrounded the great double bed.

Now I could see that something much more interesting

84

than a family row was taking place. Katerina was lying on the
bed with her cheap print frock rolled right up above her great,
swollen breasts. Her hands were tightly clasping the head of the
big brass bedstead, her white mound of a stomach quivered
and strained with what appeared to be a life of its own and she
kept drawing her legs up and screaming, rolling her head from
side to side, the sweat pouring down her face. Near her by the
bedside, and obviously in charge of the proceedings, was a
tiny, dirty, wizened little witch of a woman holding in one
hand a bucket full of well water. Periodically she would dip a
bundle of filthy rags into this and mop Katerina's face and her
thighs with it. On the table by the bedstead a jug full of wine
and a glass stood, and every time the old crone had finished
the ablutions, she would put a drop of wine in the glass and
force it into Katerina's mouth. Then she would fill the glass
and drain it herself, for presumably, in her capacity as midwife, she needed to keep up her strength as much as Katerina.

I congratulated myself warmly on the fact that I had not
been diverted on my ride up to Katerina's house by several
interesting things I had seen. If, for example, I had stopped to
climb up to what I was pretty certain was a magpie's nest, I
would probably have missed this whole exciting scene. Curiously enough, I was so used to the shrill indignation of the
peasants over the most trivial circumstances that I did not
consciously associate Katerina's falsetto screams with pain. Her
face was white, crumpled and old-looking, but I automatically
subtracted ninety per cent of the screaming as exaggeration.
Now and then, when she uttered a particularly loud scream
and implored Saint Spiridion for his aid, all the relatives would
scream in sympathy and also implore the saint's intervention.
The resulting cacophony in that tiny space had to be heard
to be believed.

Suddenly Katerina clasped the bed head still more tightly,
the muscles in her brown arms showing taut. She writhed,
drew up her legs and spread them wide apart.

'It is coming. It is coming. Praised be Saint Spiridion,'
shouted all the relatives in chorus and I noticed in the middle
of the tangled, matted mass of Katerina's pubic hairs a round
white object appear, rather like the top of an egg. There was a
moment's pause and Katerina strained again and uttered a
moaning gasp. Then, to my entranced delight, the baby's head

suddenly popped out of her like a rabbit out of a hat, to be
quickly followed by its pink, twitching body. Its face and its
limbs were as crumpled and as delicate as a rose's petals. But
it was its minuteness and the fact that it was so perfectly
formed that intrigued me. The midwife shuffled forward shouting prayers and instructions to Katerina and seized the baby
from between her blood-stained thighs. At that moment, to
my intense annoyance, the ring of relatives all moved forward
a pace in their eagerness to see the sex of the child, so that
I missed the next piece of the drama, for all I could see were
the large and extremely well-padded rumps of two of Katerina's larger aunts.

By the time I had burrowed between their legs and voluminous skirts and got to the front of the circle again, the midwife—to shouts of delight from everybody—had declared th
baby to be a boy and severed the umbilical cord with a larg
and very ancient pen-knife which she had extracted from
pocket in her skirt. One of the aunts surged forward and to
gether she and the midwife tied the cord. Then, while the aur
held the squalling, twitching pink blob of life, the midwif
dipped her bundle of rags into the bucket and proceeded t
swab the baby down. This done, she filled a glass with win
gave a couple of sips to Katerina and then filled her mout
with wine and proceeded to spit it from her toothless gums a
over the baby's head, making the sign of the cross over i
little body as she did so. Then she clasped the baby to he
bosom and turned fiercely on the crowd of relatives.

'Come now, come now,' she shrilled. 'It is done. He ha
arrived. Go now, go now.'

Laughing and chattering excitedly, the relatives poured ou
of the little house and immediately started drinking wir
and congratulating each other as though they had all perso
ally been responsible for the successful birth of the baby. I
the airless little room, smelling so strongly of sweat and garli
Katerina lay exhausted on the bed, making feeble attempts t
pull her dress down to cover her nakedness. I went to th
edge of the bed and looked down at her.

'Yasu, Gerry mine,' she said and sketched a white traves
of her normal brilliant smile. She looked incredibly old, lyi
there. I congratulated her politely on the birth of her first s
and then thanked her for the donkey. She smiled again.

'Go outside,' she said. 'They will give you some wine.'

I left the little room and hurried after the midwife, for I as anxious to see what the next stage was in her treatment of e baby. Out at the back of the house she had spread a white nen cloth over a small table and placed the child on it. Then e picked up great rolls of previously prepared cloth, like ery wide bandage, and with the aid of one of the more mble and sober aunts, proceeded to wind this round and und the baby's tiny body, pausing frequently to make sure s arms lay flat by its sides and its legs were together. Slowly nd methodically she bound it up as straight as a guardsman. lay there with only its head sticking out from this cocoon of ebbing. Greatly intrigued, I asked the midwife why she was nding the baby up.

'Why? Why?' she said, her grizzled grey eyebrows flapping ver her eyes, milky with cataracts, that peered at me fiercely. ecause, if you don't bind up the baby, its limbs won't grow raight, Its bones are as soft as an egg. If you don't bind it up s limbs will grow crooked or when it kicks and waves its rms about, it will break its bones, like little sticks of char- al.'

I knew that babies in England were not bound up in this ay and wondered whether this was because the British were some way tougher boned. Otherwise, it seemed to me, there ould have been an awful lot of deformities inhabiting the ritish Isles. I made a mental note to discuss this medical roblem with Theodore at the first available opportunity.

After I had drunk several glasses of wine to honour the baby nd eaten a large bunch of grapes, I got on Sally's back and de slowly home. I would not have missed that morning for nything, I decided. But, thinking about it as we jogged rough the dappled shade of the olives, the thing that amazed e was that anything so perfect and so beautiful should have atured and come forth from the interior of what, to me, was n old woman. It was like, I reflected, breaking open the old, own, prickly husk of a chestnut and finding the lovely gleam- g trophy inside.

PART III

Kontokali

Hospitality is, indeed, now no less than in classical times, a sacred duty in these islands, and it is a duty most conscientiously performed.

PROF. ANSTEAD

The Pygmy Jungle

It was a warm spring day, as blue as a jay's wing, and I waited impatiently for Theodore to arrive, for we were going to take a picnic and walk two or three miles to a small lake which was one of our happiest hunting-grounds. These days spent with Theodore, these 'excursions' as he called them, were of absorbing interest to me, but they must have been very exhausting for Theodore for, from the moment of his arrival till his departure, I would ply him with a ceaseless string of questions.

Eventually, Theodore's cab clopped and tinkled its way up the drive and Theodore dismounted, clad, as always, in the most unsuitable outfit for collecting: a neat tweed suit, respectable highly-polished boots and a grey Homburg perched squarely on his head. The only ungracious note in this city gentleman's outfit was his collecting box, full of tubes and bottles, slung over one shoulder and a small net with a bottle dangling from the end, attached to the end of his walking-stick.

'Ah um,' he said, shaking me gravely by the hand. 'How are you? I see that we have got, um . . ., a nice day for our excursion.'

As at that time of year one got weeks upon end of nice days, this was scarcely surprising, but Theodore always insisted on mentioning it as though it was some special privilege that had been granted us by the gods of collecting. Quickly we gathered up the bag of food and the little stone bottles of ginger beer Mother had prepared for us and slung these on our backs, together with my collecting equipment, which was slightly more extensive than Theodore's, since everything was grist to my mill and I had to be prepared for any eventuality.

Then, whistling for Roger, we went off through the sunlit olive groves, striped with shade, the whole island, spring-fresh and brilliant, lying before us. At this time of the year the olive groves would be full of flowers. Pale anemones with the tips of their petals dyed red as though they had been sipping wine, pyramid orchids that looked as though they had been made

out of pink icing sugar and yellow crocuses so fat, glossy and
waxy-looking you felt they would light like a candle if you
set a match to their stamens. We would tramp along the rough
stone paths among the olives, then for a mile or so follow the
road lined with tall and ancient cypresses, each covered in a
layer of white dust, like a hundred dark paint brushes loaded
with chalk-white. Presently, we would strike off from the
road and make our way over the crest of a small hill and there,
lying below us, would be the lake, perhaps four acres in extent
its rim shaggy with reeds and its water green with plants.

On this particular day, as we made our way down the hillside towards the lake, I was walking a little ahead of Theodore
when I suddenly came to an abrupt halt and stared with amaze
ment at the path ahead of me. Alongside the edge of the path
was the bed of a tiny stream which meandered down to join
the lake. The stream was such a tiny one that even the early
spring sun had succeeded in drying it up so that there was only
the smallest trickle of water. Through the bed of the stream
and then up across the path and into the stream again, lay wha
at first sight appeared to be a thick cable mysteriously pos
sessed a life of its own. When I looked closely I could se
that the cable was made up of what looked like hundreds o
small dusty snakes. I shouted eagerly to Theodore and whe
he came I pointed this phenomenon out to him.

'Aha!' he said, his beard bristling and a keen light of in
terest in his eyes. 'Um. yes. Very interesting. Elvers.'

What kind of snake was an elver I enquired and why wer
they all travelling in a procession?

'No, no,' said Theodore. 'They are not snakes. They ar
baby eels and they appear to be, um . . ., you know, makin
their way down to the lake.'

Fascinated, I crouched over the long column of baby eel
wriggling determinedly through the stone and grass an
prickly thistles, their skins dry and dusty. There seemed to l
millions of them. Who, in this dry dusty place, would expe
to find eels wriggling about?

'The whole, um . . ., history of the eel,' said Theodor
putting his collecting box on the ground and seating himself o
a convenient rock, 'is very curious. You see, at certain tim
the adult eels leave the ponds or rivers where they have bee

living and, er . . ., make their way down to the sea. All the
European eels do this and so do the North American. Where
they went to was, for a long time, a mystery. The only thing,
um . . ., you know . . ., scientists knew was that they never
came *back*, but that eventually these baby eels would return
and repopulate the same rivers and streams. It was not until
after quite a number of years that people discovered what
really happened.'

He paused and scratched his beard thoughtfully.

'All the eels made their way down to the sea and then swam
through the Mediterranean, across the Atlantic, until they
reached the Sargasso Sea, which is, as you know, just off the
coast of South America. The . . ., um . . ., North American
eels, of course, didn't have so far to travel, but they made
their way to the same place. Here they mated, laid their eggs
and died. The eel larva, when it hatches out, is a very curious,
um . . ., you know . . ., leaf shaped creature and transparent,
so unlike the adult eel that, for a long time, it was classified in
a separate genera. Well, these larvae make their way slowly
back to the place where their parents have come from and by
the time they reach the Mediterranean or the North American
shore, they look like these.'

Here Theodore paused, rasped his beard again and delicately inserted the end of his cane into the moving column of
elvers so that they writhed indignantly.

'They seem to have a very . . ., um . . ., you know . . .,
strong homing instinct,' said Theodore. 'We must be some
two miles from the sea I suppose, and yet all these little elvers
are making their way across this countryside in order to get
back to the same lake that their parents left.'

He paused, glanced about him keenly and then pointed with
his stick.

'It's quite a hazardous journey,' he observed, and I saw what
I meant for a kestrel was flying like a little black cross just
above the line of baby eels and as we watched he swooped
and flew away, his claws firmly gripping a writhing mass of
them.

As we walked on, following the line of eels, since they were
going in the same direction, we saw other predators at work.
Groups of magpies and jackdaws and a couple of jays flew up

at our approach and we caught out of the corner of our e
the red glint of a fox disappearing into the myrtle bushes.

When we reached the lake side, we had a set pattern
behaviour. First we would discuss under which olive tree
would be best to put our equipment and food, which one wo
cast the deepest and the best shade at noon. Having decided
this we would make a little pile of our possessions under
and then, armed with our nets and collecting boxes, wo
approach the lake. Here we would potter happily for the
of the morning, pacing with the slow concentration of a p
of fishing herons, dipping our nets into the weed-filigr
water. Here Theodore came into his own more than anywh
else. From the depths of the lake, as he stood there with
big scarlet dragonflies zooming like arrows around him,
would extract magic that Merlin would have envied.

Here in the still, wine-gold waters, lay a pygmy jungle.
the lake bottom prowled the deadly dragonfly larvae,
cunning predators as the tiger, inching their way through
debris of a million last year's leaves. Here the black tadpo
sleek and shiny as licorice drops, disported in the shallows
plump herds of hippo in some African river. Through gr
forests of weed the multi-coloured herds of microsco
creatures twitched and fluttered like flocks of exotic bi
whilst among the roots of the forests the newts and the leec
uncoiled like great snakes in the gloom, stretching out
seechingly, ever hungry. And here the caddis larvae in th
shaggy coats of twigs and debris crawled dimly like be
fresh from hibernation across the sun-ringed hills and vall
of soft black mud.

'Aha, now, this is rather interesting. You see this, um .
little maggot-like thing? Now this is the larvae of the Chi
mark Moth. I think, as a matter of fact, you have got on
your collection. What? Well, they're called Chinamark Mo
because of the markings on the wing which are said to
semble very closely marks that potters put on the base of
. . ., you know, very *good* china. Spode and so forth. Now
Chinamark is interesting because it is one of the few mo
which have aquatic larvae. The larvae live under water u
they are . . ., um . . ., ready to pupate. The interesting th
about this particular species is that they have, er . . ., um .

you know, two forms of female. The male, of course, is fully winged and flies about when it hatches and er . . ., so does one of the females. But the other female when it hatches out has, um . . ., no wings and continues to live under the water, using its legs to swim with.'

Theodore paced a little farther along the bank on the mud that was already dried and jigsawed by the spring sun. A kingfisher exploded like a blue firework from the small willow, and out on the centre of the lake a tern swooped and glided on graceful, sickle-shaped wings. Theodore dipped his net into the weedy water, sweeping it to and fro gently, as though he were stroking a cat. Then the net was lifted and held aloft, while the tiny bottle that dangled from it would be subjected to a minute scrutiny through a magnifying glass.

'Um, yes. Some cyclops. Two mosquito larvae. Aha, that's interesting. You see this caddis larva has made his case entirely out of baby rams-horn snail shells. It is . . ., you know . . ., remarkably pretty. Ah now! Here we have, I think, yes, yes, here we have some rotifers.'

In a desperate attempt to keep pace with this flood of knowledge, I asked what rotifers were and peered into the little bottle through the magnifying glass at the twitching, wriggling creatures, as Theodore told me.

'The early naturalists used to call them wheel animalcules, because of their curious limbs, you know. They wave them about in a very curious fashion, so that they almost look like, an . . ., you know, um . . ., er . . ., like the wheels of a watch. When you next come to see me I'll put some of these under the microscope for you. They are really extraordinarily beautiful creatures. These are, of course, all females.'

I asked why, of course, they should be females.

'This is one of the interesting things about the rotifer. The females produce virgin eggs. Um . . ., that is to say they produce eggs without having come into contact with a male. Um . . ., er . . ., somewhat like a chicken you know. But the difference is that the *rotifer* eggs hatch out into other females which in turn are capable of laying more eggs which . . ., um . . ., again hatch out into females. But at certain times, the females lay *smaller* eggs which hatch out into males. Now, as you will see when I put these under the microscope, the female

has a—how shall one say?—a quite *complex* body, an ali
mentary tract and so on. The male has nothing at all. He i
really just, er . . ., um . . ., a swimming bag of sperm.'

I was bereft of speech at the complexities of the privat
life of the rotifer.

'Another curious thing about them,' Theodore continue
happily piling miracle upon miracle, 'is that at certain times,
. . ., you know, if it is a hot summer or something like th
and the pond is liable to dry up, they go down to the botto
and form a sort of hard shell round themselves. It's a sort
suspended animation, for the pond can dry up for, er . . ., u
. . ., let us say seven or eight years, and they will just lie the
in the dust. But as soon as the first rain falls and fills the pon
they come to life again.'

Again we moved forward, sweeping our nets through t
balloon-like masses of frogs' spawn and the trailing necklac
like strings of the toad spawn.

'Here is, er . . ., if you just take the glass a minute and lo
. . ., an exceptionally fine hydra.'

Through the glass there sprang to life a tiny fragment
weed to which was attached a long slender coffee-colour
column, at the top of which was a writhing mass of elega
tentacles. As I watched, a rotund and earnest cyclops carryi
two large and apparently heavy sacks containing pink eg
swam in a series of breathless jerks too close to the writhi
arms of the hydra. In a moment it was engulfed. It gave
couple of violent twitches before it was stung to death. I kne
if you watched long enough, you could see the cyclops bei
slowly and steadily engulfed and passing, in the shape of
bulge, down the column of the hydra.

Presently the height and the heat of the sun would tell
that it was lunch time and we would make our way back
our olive trees and sit there eating our food and drinking
ginger beer to the accompaniment of the sleep zithering
the first-hatched cicadas of the year and the gentle, question
coos of the collared doves.

'In Greek,' Theodore said, munching his sandwich metho
cally, 'the name for collared dove is *dekaoctura*, eighteen
you know. The story goes that when Christ was . . ., um .
carrying the cross to Calvary, a Roman soldier seeing that

as exhausted, took pity on Him. By the side of the road there as an old woman selling . . ., um . . ., you know . . ., *milk* id so the Roman soldier went to her and asked her how much cupful would cost. She replied that it would cost eighteen ins. But the soldier only had seventeen. He . . ., er . . ., you how . . ., pleaded with the woman to let him have a cupful milk for Christ for seventeen coins, but the woman avarici- isly stuck out for eighteen. So, when Christ was crucified e old woman was turned into a collared dove and con- emned to go about the rest of her days repeating *dekaocto, kaocto,* eighteen, eighteen. If ever she agrees to say *dekaepta,* venteen, she will regain her human form. If, out of obstin- y, she says *dekaennaea,* nineteen, the world will come to end.'

In the cool olive shade the tiny ants, black and shiny as viare, would be foraging for our left-overs among last year's scarded olive leaves that the past summer's sun had dried id coloured a nut-brown and banana yellow. They lay there curled and as crisp as brandy-snaps. On the hillside behind a herd of goats passed, the leader's bell clonking mournfully. e could hear the tearing sound of their jaws as they e, indiscriminately, any foliage which came within their ach. The leader paced up to us and gazed for a minute with leful yellow eyes, snorting clouds of thyme-laden breath us.

'They should not, er . . ., you know, be left unattended,' id Theodore, prodding the goat gently with his stick. 'Goats more damage to the countryside than practically anything se.'

The leader uttered a short sardonic 'bah' and moved away, s destructive troop following him.

We would lie for an hour or so, drowsing and digesting our od, staring up through the tangled olive branches at a sky at was patterned with tiny white clouds like a child's finger- ints on a blue, frosty winter window.

'Well,' Theodore would say at last, getting to his feet, 'I ink perhaps we ought to . . ., you know . . ., just see what e *other* side of the lake has to offer.'

So once more we would commence our slow pacing of the m of the shore. Steadily our test tubes, bottles and jars would

fill with a shimmer of microscopic life and my boxes and ti
and bags would be stuffed with frogs, baby terrapins and
host of beetles.

'I suppose,' Theodore would say at last, reluctantly, glanci
up at the sinking sun, 'I suppose . , ., you know . . ., we oug
to be getting along home.'

And so we would laboriously hoist our now extremely hea
collecting boxes on to our shoulders and trudge homeward
weary feet, Roger, his tongue hanging out like a pink fla
trotting soberly ahead of us. Reaching the villa, our catch
would be moved to more capacious quarters; then Theodo
and I would relax and discuss the day's work, drinking gallo
of hot, stimulating tea and gorging ourselves on golden scon
bubbling with butter, fresh from Mother's oven.

It was when I paid a visit to this lake without Theodore th
I caught, quite by chance, a creature that I had long wanted
meet. As I drew my net up out of the waters and examined tl
tangled weed mass, I found crouching there, of all unlike
things, a spider. I was delighted for I had read about tl
curious beast, which must be one of the most unusual speci
of spider in the world, for it lives a very strange aquatic exi
ence. It was about half an inch long and marked, in a vag
sort of way, with silver and brown. I put it triumphantly in
one of my collecting tins and carried it home tenderly.

Here I set up an aquarium with a sandy floor and decorat
it with some small dead branches and fronds of water wee
Putting the spider on one of the twigs that stuck up above tl
water level, I watched to see what it would do. It immediate
ran down the twig and plunged into the water where it turn
a bright and beautiful silver, owing to the numerous minu
air bubbles trapped in the hairs on its body. It spent fi
minutes or so running about below the surface of the wat
investigating all the twigs and water weed before it final
settled on a spot in which to construct its home.

Now the water spider was the original inventor of the divi
bell and, sitting absorbed in front of the aquarium, I watch
how it was done. First the spider attached several lengtl
strands of silk from the weeds to the twigs. These were to a
as guy ropes. Then, taking up a position roughly in the centr
it proceeded to spin an irregular oval shaped, flat web of
more or less conventional type but of a finer mesh, so that

oked more like a cobweb. This occupied the greater part of
vo hours. Having got the structure of its home built to its
.tisfaction, it now had to give it an air supply. This it did by
aking numerous trips to the surface of the water and into
.e air. When it returned to the water its body would be
lvery with air bubbles. It would then run down and take up
s position underneath the web and, by stroking itself with
s legs, rid itself of the air bubbles which rose and were im-
ediately trapped underneath the web. After doing this five or
x times, all the tiny bubbles under the web had amalgamated
.to one big bubble. As the spider added more and more
r to this bubble and it grew bigger and bigger, its strength
arted to push the web up until eventually the spider had
:hieved success. Firmly anchored by the guy ropes between
.e weed and the twigs was suspended a bell-shaped structure
ill of air. This was now the spider's home in which it could
ve quite comfortably without having to pay frequent visits
> the surface, for the air in the bell would, I knew, be re-
lenished by the oxygen given up by the weeds, and the car-
on dioxide given out by the spider would soak through the
lky walls of its house.

Sitting and watching this miraculous piece of craftsmanship,
wondered how on earth the very first water spider (who
anted to *become* a water spider) had managed to work out
is ingenious method of living below the surface. But the
abit of living in its own home-made submarine is not the
nly peculiar thing about this spider. Unlike the great majority
f species the male is about twice the size of the female
nd once they have mated the male is not devoured by his
ife, as happens so frequently in the married life of the spider.
could tell from her size that my spider was a female and I
lought that her abdomen looked rather swollen. It seemed to
le she might be expecting a happy event, so I took great
ains to make sure that she got plenty of good food. She liked
at green daphnia, which she was extraordinarily adept at
atching as they swam past, but probably her favourite food of
ll was the tiny, newly hatched newt eft which, although a
ulky prey for her, she never hesitated to tackle. Having cap-
ared whatever titbit happened to be passing, she would carry
up into her bell and eat it there in comfort.

Then came the great day when I saw that she was adding

99

an extension to the bell. She did not hurry over this and it took
her two days to complete. Then one morning, on peering into
her tank, I saw to my delight that the nursery contained a
round ball of eggs. In due course these hatched out into
miniature replicas of the mother. I soon had more water
spiders than I knew what to do with and found, to my annoyance, that the mother, with complete lack of parental feeling,
was happily feeding off her own progeny. So I was forced to
move the babies into another aquarium, but as they grew they
took to feeding upon each other and so in the end I just kept
the two most intelligent looking ones and took all the rest
down to the lake and let them go.

It was at this time, when I was deeply involved with the
water spiders, that Sven Olson at last turned up. Larry had, to
Mother's consternation, developed the habit of inviting hordes
of painters, poets and authors to stay without any reference to
her. Sven Olson was a sculptor and we had had some warning
of his impending arrival, for he had been bombarding us for
weeks with contradictory telegrams about his movements.
These had driven Mother to distraction, because she kept
having to make and unmake his bed. Mother and I were
having a quiet cup of tea on the veranda when a cab made its
appearance, wound its way up the drive and came to a stop
in front of the house. In the back was seated an enormous man
who bore a remarkable facial resemblance to the reconstruc-
tions of Neanderthal Man. He was clad in a white singlet, a
pair of voluminous brightly checked plus fours and sandals.
On his massive head was a broad-brimmed straw hat. The two
holes situated one each side of the crown argued that this hat
had been designed for the use of a horse. He got ponderously
out of the cab carrying a very large and battered Gladstone bag
and an accordion. Mother and I went down to greet him. As
he saw us approaching, he swept off his hat and bowed, re-
vealing that his enormous cranium was completely devoid of
hair except for a strange, grey, tattered duck's tail on the nape
of his neck.

'Mrs Durrell?' he enquired, fixing Mother with large and
child-like blue eyes. 'I am enchanted to meet you. My name is
Sven.'

His English was impeccable with scarcely any trace of an
accent, but his voice was quite extraordinary for it wavered

tween a deep rich baritone and a quavering falsetto, as
ough, in spite of his age, his voice was only just breaking.
 extended a very large, white, spade-shaped hand to Mother
d bowed once again.

Well, I am glad you have managed to get here at last,' said
other, brightly and untruthfully. 'Do come in and have
ne tea.'

I carried his accordion and his Gladstone bag and we all
nt and sat on the balcony and drank tea and stared at each
ier. There was a long, long silence while Sven munched a
ce of toast and occasionally smiled lovingly at Mother,
ile she smiled back and desperately searched her mind for
table intellectual topics of conversation. Sven swallowed a
ce of toast and coughed violently. His eyes filled with tears.
I love toast,' he gasped. 'I simply love it. But it always does
s to me.'

We plied him with more tea and presently his paroxysms of
ughing died away. He sat forward, his huge hands folded in
 lap, showing white as marble against the hideous pattern
his plus fours, and fixed Mother with an enquiring eye.

'Are you,' he enquired wistfully, 'are you, by any chance,
isically inclined?'

'Well,' said Mother, startled, and obviously suffering from
 hideous suspicion that if she said 'Yes' Sven might ask her
 sing, 'I like music, of course, but I, um . . ., can't play
ything.'

I suppose,' said Sven diffidently, 'you wouldn't like me to
iy something for you?'

'Oh, er, yes by all means,' said Mother. 'That would be
ightful.'

Sven beamed lovingly at her, picked up his accordion and
strapped it. He extended it like a caterpillar and it produced
ioise like the tail end of a donkey's bray.

She,' said Sven, lovingly patting the accordion, 'has got
ne sea air in her.'

He settled his accordion more comfortably against his broad
st, arranged his sausage-like fingers carefully on the keys,
sed his eyes and began to play. It was a very complicated
i extraordinary tune. Sven was wearing such an expression
 rapture upon his ugly face that I was dying to laugh and
ving to bite the insides of my cheeks to prevent it. Mother

101

sat there with a face of frozen politeness like a world-famo
conductor being forced to listen to somebody giving a reci
on a penny whistle. Eventually the tune came to a harsh, d
cordant end. Sven heaved a sigh of pure delight, opened l
eyes and smiled at Mother.

'Bach is so beautiful,' he said.

'Oh yes,' said Mother with well-simulated enthusiasm.

'I'm glad you like it,' said Sven. 'I'll play you some mor

So for the next hour Mother and I sat there, trapped, wh
Sven played piece after piece. Every time Mother made so
move to seek an escape, Sven would hold up one of his hu
hands, as though arresting a line of imaginary traffic, and sa
'Just one more,' archly, and Mother, with a tremulous sm
would sit back in her chair.

It was with considerable relief that we greeted the rest of t
family when they arrived back from town. Larry and Sv
danced round each other, roaring like a couple of bulls a
exchanging passionate embraces and then Larry dragged Sv
off to his room and they were closeted there for hours, t
sound of gales of laughter occasionally drifting down to

'What's he like?' asked Margo.

'Well, I don't really know, dear,' said Mother. 'He's be
playing to us ever since he arrived.'

'Playing?' said Leslie. 'Playing what?'

'His barrel organ, or whatever you call it,' said Mother.

'My God,' said Leslie. 'I can't stand those things. I hope
isn't going to play it all over the house.'

'No, no, dear. I'm sure he won't,' said Mother, hastily, l
her tone lacked conviction.

Just at that moment Larry appeared on the veranda aga

'Where's Sven's accordion?' he asked. 'He wants to pl
me something.'

'Oh God,' said Leslie. 'There you are. I told you.'

'I hope he isn't going to play that accordion all the tin
dear,' said Mother. 'We've already had an hour of it and
given me a splitting headache.'

'Of course he won't play it all the time,' said Larry irritab
picking up the accordion. 'He just wants to play me one tu
What was he playing to you, anyway?'

'The most weird music,' said Mother. 'By some man
you know the one—something to do with trees.'

The rest of the day was, to say the least, harrowing. Sven's
pertoire was apparently inexhaustible and when, during
nner, he insisted on giving us an impression of meal-time in
Scottish fortress by marching round and round the table
aying one of the more untuneful Scottish reels, I could see
e defences of the family crumbling. Even Larry was
eginning to look a little pensive. Roger, who was uninhibited
d straightforward in his dealings with human beings,
mmed up his opinion of Sven's performance by throwing
ck his head and howling dismally, a thing he normally
d only when he heard the National Anthem.

But by the time Sven had been with us three days, we had
come more or less inured to his accordion and Sven himself
armed us all. He exuded a sort of innocent goodness, so
at whatever he did one could not be annoyed with him, any
ore than you could be annoyed with a baby for wetting its
appy. He quickly endeared himself to Mother for, she dis-
vered, he was an ardent cook himself and carried round an
ormous leather-bound note book in which he jotted down
cipes. He and Mother spent hours in the kitchen teaching
ch other how to cook their favourite dishes and the results
ere meals of such bulk and splendour that all of us began
feel liverish and out of sorts.

It was about a week after his arrival that Sven wandered one
orning into the room I proudly called my study. In that
assive villa we had such a superfluity of rooms that I had
cceeded in getting Mother to give me a special one of my
wn in which I could keep all my creatures.

My menagerie at this time was pretty extensive. There was
lysses, the Scop's Owl, who spent all day sitting on the
elmet above the window imitating a decaying olive stump,
d occasionally, with a look of great disdain, regurgitating a
ellet on to the newspaper spread below him. The dog con-
ngent had been increased to three by a couple of young
ongrels given to me for my birthday by a peasant family
ho, because of their completely undisciplined behaviour, had
een christened Widdle and Puke. There were rows and rows
jam jars, some containing specimens in methylated spirits,
hers microscopic life. And then there were six aquariums
hich housed a variety of newts, frogs, snakes and toads.
les of glass-topped boxes contained my collections of butter-

flies, beetles and dragonflies. Sven, to my astonishment, ⸱
played a deep and almost reverent interest in my collecti⸱
Delighted to have somebody showing enthusiasm for ⸱
cherished menagerie, I took him on a carefully conducted t⸱
and exhibited everything, even, after swearing him to secre⸱
my family of tiny chocolate-coloured scorpions that I h⸱
smuggled into the house unbeknownst to the family. One ⸱
the things that impressed Sven most was the underwater b⸱
of the spider and he stood quite silently in front of it, his gr⸱
blue eyes fixed on it intensely, watching the spider as ⸱
caught her food and carried it up into the little dome. Sv⸱
displayed such enthusiasm that I suggested to him, rather te⸱
tatively, that he might like to spend a little time in the ol⸱
groves with me, so that I could show him some of th⸱
creatures in their natural haunts.

'But how kind of you,' he said, his great, ugly face lighti⸱
up delightedly. 'Are you sure I won't be interfering?'

No, I assured him, he would not be interfering.

'Then I would be delighted,' said Sven. 'Absolutely ⸱
lighted.'

So, for the rest of his stay, we would disappear from ⸱
villa after breakfast and spend a couple of hours in the ol⸱
groves.

On Sven's last day—he was leaving on the evening boat⸱
we held a little farewell lunch party for him and invit⸱
Theodore. Delighted at having a new audience, Sven i⸱
mediately gave Theodore a half-hour recital of Bach on ⸱
accordion.

'Um,' said Theodore, when Sven had finished, 'do yo⸱
know, er . . ., know any other tunes?'

'Just name it, Doctor,' said Sven spreading out his han⸱
expansively, 'I will play it for you.'

Theodore rocked thoughtfully for a moment on his to⸱

'You don't by any chance, I suppose, er . . ., happen ⸱
know a song called "There is a Tavern in the Town"?'
enquired shyly.

'Of course!' said Sven and immediately crashed into t⸱
opening bars of the song.

Theodore sang vigorously, his beard bristling, his eyes brig⸱
and when we had come to the end, Sven, without pau⸱
switched into 'Clementine.' Emboldened by Theodore's Phil⸱

ine attitude towards Bach, Mother asked Sven whether he
ould play 'If I were a Blackbird' and 'The Spinning Wheel
song' which he promptly executed in a masterly fashion.

Then the cab arrived to take him down to the docks and he
mbraced each one of us fondly, his eyes full of tears. He
limbed into the back of the cab with his Gladstone bag beside
im and his precious accordion on his lap and waved to us
xtravagantly as the cab disappeared down the drive.

'Such a *manly* man,' said Mother with satisfaction, as we
vent inside. 'Quite one of the old school.'

'You should have told him that,' said Larry, stretching him-
elf out on the sofa and picking up his book. 'There's nothing
omos like better than to be told they are virile and manly.'

'What ever do you mean?' asked Mother, putting on her
pectacles and glaring at Larry suspiciously.

Larry lowered his book and looked at her puzzled.

'Homosexuals like to be told they are virile and manly,' he
aid at length, patiently and with the air of one explaining a
imple problem to a backward child.

Mother continued to glare at him, trying to assess whether
r not it was one of Larry's elaborate leg pulls.

'You are not trying to tell me,' she said at last, 'that that man
s a—is a—is one of *those*?'

'Dear God, Mother, of course he is,' said Larry, irritably.
He's a rampaging old queer—the only reason he's gone rush-
ng back to Athens is because he's living with a ravishing
eventeen-year-old Cypriot boy and he doesn't trust him.'

'Do you mean to say,' asked Margo, her eyes wide, 'that
hey get jealous of each other?'

'Of course they do,' said Larry, and, dismissing the subject,
eturned to his book.

'How extraordinary,' said Margo. 'Did you hear that,
Mother? They actually get jealous——'

'Margo!' said Mother quellingly, 'we won't go into that.
Vhat I want to know, Larry, is why you invited him here if
ou knew he was, er, that way inclined?'

'Why not?' Larry enquired, simply.

'Well, you might at least have thought of Gerry,' said
Mother, bristling.

'Gerry?' asked Larry in surprise. 'Gerry? What's he got to
o with it?'

105

'What's he got to do with it? Really, Larry, you do ma[ke]
me cross. That man could have been a bad influence on t[he]
boy if he had had much to do with him.'

Larry sat back on the sofa and looked at Mother. He gave [a]
small exasperated sigh and put his book down.

'For the last three mornings,' he said, 'Gerry's been givi[ng]
Sven natural history lessons in the olive groves. It does[n't]
appear to have done either of them irretrievable harm.'

'What?' squeaked Mother. 'What?'

I felt it was time to intervene. After all, I liked Sven. I e[x-]
plained how, early in his stay he had wandered into my roo[m]
and had become immediately absorbed and fascinated by n[y]
collection of creatures. Feeling that one convert was wor[th]
half a dozen saints, I had offered to take him into the oli[ve]
groves and show him all my favourite haunts. So every mor[n-]
ing we would set off into the olives and Sven would spe[nd]
hours lying on his stomach peering at the busy lines of ar[ts]
carrying their grass seeds or watching the bulbous-bodi[ed]
female mantis laying her frothy egg case on a stone, or peeri[ng]
down the burrows of trap door spiders, murmuring, 'Wonde[r-]
ful! Wonderful!' to himself, in such an ecstatic tone of voi[ce]
that it warmed my heart.

'Well, dear,' said Mother, 'I think, in future, if you want [to]
take one of Larry's friends for walks you should tell me firs[t.]

Cuttlefish and Crabs

Each morning when I awoke, the bedroom would be tiger-striped by the sun peering through the shutters. As usual, I would find that the dogs had managed to crawl on to the bed without my realising it and would now be occupying more than their fair share, sleeping deeply and peacefully. Ulysses would be sitting by the window, staring at the bars of golden sunlight, his eyes slit into malevolent disapproval. Outside one could hear the hoarse, jeering crow of a cockerel and the soft murmuring of the hens (a sound soothing as bubbling porridge) as they fed under the orange and lemon trees, the distant clonk of goat bells, sharp chittering of sparrows in the eaves and the sudden outburst of wheezing, imploring cries that showed one of the parent swallows had brought a mouthful of food to their brood in the nest beneath my window. I would throw back the sheet and turf the dogs out on to the floor, where they would shake and stretch and yawn, their pink tongues curled like exotic leaves, and then I would go over to the window and throw back the shutters. Leaning out over the sill, the morning sun warm on my naked body, I would scratch thoughtfully at the little pink seals the dogs' fleas had left on my skin, while I got my eyes adjusted to the light. Then I would peer down over the silver olive tops to the beach and the blue sea which lay half a mile away. It was on this beach that, periodically, the fishermen would pull in their nets and when they did so this was always a special occasion for me, since the net dragged to shore from the depths of the blue bay would contain a host of fascinating sea life which was otherwise beyond my reach.

If I saw the little fishing-boats bobbing on the water I would get dressed hurriedly and, taking my collecting gear, would run through the olive trees down to the road and along it until I reached the beach. I knew most of the fishermen by name, but here was one who was my special friend, a tall powerful young man with a mop of auburn hair. Inevitably, he was called Spiro after Saint Spiridion, so in order to distinguish

him from all the other Spiros I knew, I called him Kokino, o
red. Kokino took a great delight in obtaining specimens fo
me and, although he was not a bit interested in the creature
himself, he got much pleasure from my obvious delight

One day I went down to the beach when the net was half
way in. The fishermen, brown as walnuts, were hauling on th
dripping lines, their toes spreading wide in the sand as the
pulled the massive bag of the net nearer and nearer to th
shore.

'Your health, *kyrié* Gerry,' Kokino cried to me, waving
large freckled hand in greeting, his mop of hair glinting in th
sun like a bonfire. 'Today, we should get some fine animal
for you, for we put the net down in a new place.'

I squatted on the sand and waited patiently while the fisher
men, chattering and joking, hauled away steadily. Presentl
the top of the net was visible in the shallow waters and as
broke surface you could see the glitter and wink of the trappe
fish inside it. Hauled out on to the sand it seemed as though th
net was alive, pulsating with the fish inside it, and there wa
the steady, staccato purring noise of their tails, flappin
futilely against each other. The baskets were fetched and th
fish picked out of the net and cast into them. Red fish, whit
fish, fish with wine-coloured stripes, scorpion fish like flam
boyant tapestries. Sometimes there would be an octopus c
a cuttlefish leering up from inside the net with a look o
alarm in its human eyes. Once all the edible contents of th
net had been safely stowed away in the baskets, it was m
turn.

In the bottom of the net would be a great heap of stone
and sea-weed and it was among this that my trophies lay
Once I found a round flat stone from which grew a perfec
coraline tree, pure white. It looked like a young beech tree i
winter, its branches bare of leaves and covered with a layer o
snow. Sometimes there would be cushion star fish, as thick a
a sponge cake and almost as large, the edges not formin
pointed arms as with normal star fish, but rounded scallop
These star fish would be of pale fawn with a bright pattern o
scarlet blotches. Once I got two incredible crabs whose pincer
and legs when pulled in tight fitted with immaculate precisio
the sides of their oval shells. These crabs were white with
rusty red pattern on the back which looked not unlike a

iental face. It was hardly what I would call protective
louration and I imagine they must have had few enemies to
able to move about the sea bed wearing such a conspicuous
ery.

On this particular morning, I was picking over a great pile
weed when Kokino, having stowed away the last of the fish
the baskets, came over to help me. There were the usual
sortment of squids the size of a match box, pipe fish, spider
abs and a variety of tiny fish which, in spite of their size,
d been unable to escape through the mesh of the net. Sud-
nly Kokino gave a little grunt half surprise and half amuse-
ent, picked something out of a tangled skein of sea-weed
d held it out to me on the calloused palm of his hand. I
uld hardly believe my eyes, for it was a sea horse. Browny
een, carefully jointed, looking like some weird chess man, it
y on Kokino's hand, its strange protruding mouth gasping
d its tail coiling and uncoiling frantically. Hurriedly I
atched it from him and plunged it into a jar full of sea water,
tering a mental prayer to Saint Spiridion that I would be in
ne to save it. To my delight it righted itself, then hung sus-
nded in the jar, the tiny fins on each side of its horse's head
ttering themselves into a blur. Pausing only to make sure
at it really was all right, I scrabbled through the rest of the
ed with the fervour of a gold prospector panning a river bed
ere he had found a nugget. My diligence was rewarded for
a few minutes I had six sea horses of various sizes hanging
spended in the jar. Enraptured by my good luck, I bid
okino and the other fisherman a hasty farewell and raced
ck to the villa.

Here I unceremoniously foreclosed on fourteen slow worms
d usurped their aquarium to house my new catches. I knew
at the oxygen in the jar in which the sea horses were im-
isoned would not last for long and if I wanted to keep them
ve I would have to move quickly. Carrying the aquarium
raced down to the sea again, washed it out carefully, filled
e bottom with sand and dashed back to the villa with it; then
ad to run down to the sea again three times with buckets to
l it up with the required amount of water. By the time I had
ured the last bucket into it, I was so hot and sweaty I began
wonder whether the sea horses were worth it. But as soon as
ipped them into the aquarium I knew that they were. I had

placed a small twiggy dead olive branch in the aquariu
which I had anchored to the sand and as the sea hors
plopped out of the jar they righted themselves and then, like
group of ponies freshly released in a field, they sped rou
and round the aquarium, their fins moving so fast that y
could not see them and each one gave the appearance
being driven by some small internal motor. Having, as it we
galloped round their new territory, they all made for the oli
branch, entwined their tails round it lovingly and stood the
gravely at attention.

The sea horses were an instant success. They were about t
only animal that I had introduced to the villa that earned t
family's unanimous approval. Even Larry used to pay furti
visits to my study in order to watch them zooming and bol
ing to and fro in their tank. They took up a considera
amount of my time, for I found that the sea water soon gr
rancid and in order to keep it clear and fresh I had to go do
to the sea with buckets four or five times a day. This w
an exhausting process, but I was glad that I kept it up f
otherwise I would not have witnessed a very extraordina
sight.

One of the sea horses, who was obviously an old specim
since he was nearly black, had a very well-developed paun
This I merely attributed to age; then I noticed one morni
there was a line along the paunch, almost as though it h
been slit with a razor blade. I was watching this and wonderi
whether the sea horses had been fighting and if so what th
used as a weapon (for they seemed so defenceless) when to
complete and utter astonishment the slit opened a little wi
and out swam a minute and fragile replica of the sea horse
could hardly believe my eyes, but as soon as the first baby v
clear of the pouch and hanging in the clear water, another c
joined it and then another and another until there were twe
microscopic sea horses floating round their giant parent lik
little cloud of smoke. Terrified lest the other adult sea hor
eat the babies, I hurriedly set up another aquarium and pla
what I fondly imagined to be the mother and her offspring
it. Keeping two aquariums going with fresh water was
even more Herculean task and I began to feel like a pit-po
but I was determined to continue until Thursday, wl

Theodore came to tea, so that I could show him my acquisitions.

'Aha,' he said, peering into the tanks with professional zeal, 'these are really most interesting. Sea horses are, of course, according to the books, supposed to be found here, but I myself have er . . ., you know . . ., never seen them previously.'

I showed Theodore the mother with her swarm of tiny babies.

'No, no,' said Theodore. 'That's not the mother, that's the father.'

At first I thought that Theodore was pulling my leg, but he went on to explain that, when the female laid the eggs and they had been fertilized by the male, they were taken into this special brood pouch by the male and there they matured and hatched. What I had thought was a proud mother was in reality a proud father.

Soon the strain of keeping my stable of sea horses with a supply of microscopic sea food and fresh water became too great and so with the utmost reluctance I had to take them down to the sea and release them.

It was Kokino who, as well as contributing specimens from his nets to my collection, showed me one of the most novel fishing methods I had ever come across.

I met him one day down by the shore putting a kerosene tin full of sea water into his rickety little boat. Reposing in the bottom of the tin was a large and soulful looking cuttlefish. Kokino had tied a string round it where the head met the great egg-shaped body. I asked him where he was going and he said he was going to fish for cuttlefish. I was puzzled because his boat did not contain any lines or nets or even a trident. How then did he propose to catch cuttlefish?

'With love,' said Kokino mysteriously.

I felt it was my duty, as a naturalist, to investigate every method of capturing animals, so I asked Kokino whether it was possible for me to accompany him. We rowed the boat out into the blue bay until she hung over a couple of fathoms of crystal clear water. Here Kokino took the end of the long string that was attached to the cuttlefish and tied it carefully round his big toe. Then he picked up the cuttlefish and dropped

111

it over the side of the boat. It floated in the water for a bri
moment, looking up at us with what seemed to be an incred
lous expression, and then, squirting out jets of water, shot c
in a series of jerks, trailing the string behind it and soon di
appearing into the blue depths. The string trailed gradual
over the side of the boat then tautened against Kokino's to
He lit a cigarette and rumpled his flaming hair.

'Now,' he said, grinning at me, 'we will see what love ca
do.'

He bent to his oars and rowed the boat slowly and gent
along the surface of the bay, with frequent pauses during whi
he stared with intense concentration at the string fastened
his toe. Suddenly he gave a little grunt, let the oars fold to th
side of the boat like the wings of a moth and, grasping th
line, started to pull it in. I leant over the side staring down in
the clear water, my eyes straining towards the end of the ta
black line. Presently in the depths, a dim blur appeared
Kokino hauled more quickly on the line and the cuttlefi
came into sight. As it got closer, I saw, to my astonishment,
was not one cuttlefish but two, locked together in a passiona
embrace. Swiftly Kokino hauled them alongside and with
quick flip of the line landed them in the bottom of the boat.
engrossed was the male cuttlefish with his lady love that n
even the sudden transition from his watery home to the op
air seemed to worry him in the slightest. He was clasping t
female so tightly that it took Kokino some time to prise hi
loose and drop him into the tin of sea water.

The novelty of this form of fishing greatly appealed to n
although I had the sneaking feeling that perhaps it was a lit
unsporting. It was rather like catching dogs by walking arou
with a bitch in season on the end of a long leash. Within
hour we had caught five male cuttlefish in a comparativ
small area of the bay. It amazed me that there should be
dense a population, for they were a creature that you rar
saw unless you went fishing at night. The female cuttlefi
throughout this time, played her part with a sort of stoi
indifference, but even so I felt that she should be rewarded.
I prevailed upon Kokino to let her go, which he did wi
obvious reluctance.

I asked him how he knew that the female was ready
attract the males, and he shrugged.

112

'It is the time,' he said.

Could you then at this time, I enquired, put any female on the end of a string and obtain results?

'Yes,' said Kokino. 'But of course, some females, like some women, are more attractive than others and so you get better results with those.'

My mind boggled at the thought of having to work out the comparative merits of two female cuttlefish. I felt it was a great pity that this method could not be employed with other creatures. The idea, for example, of dropping a female sea horse over the side on a length of cotton and then pulling her up in a tangled entourage of passionate males was very appealing. Kokino was, as far as I knew, the only exponent of this peculiar brand of fishing for I never saw any other fisherman employ it and, indeed, the ones I mentioned it to had never even heard of it and were inclined to treat my story with raucous disbelief.

This tattered coastline near the villa was particularly rich in sea life and, as the water was comparatively shallow, it made it easier for me to capture things. I had succeeded in inveigling Leslie into making me a boat which greatly facilitated my investigations. This craft, almost circular, flat-bottomed and with a heavy list to starboard, had been christened the Bootlebumtrinket and, next to my donkey, was my most cherished possession. Filling the bottom with jars, tins and nets and taking a large parcel of food with me, I would set sail in the Bootlebumtrinket accompanied by my crew of Widdle, Puke, Roger and, occasionally, Ulysses my owl, should he feel so inclined. We would spend the hot, breathless days exploring remote little bays and rocky and weed-encrusted archipelagos. We had many curious adventures on these expeditions of ours. Once we found a whole acre of sea-bed covered with a great swarm of sea hares, their royal purple, egg-shaped bodies with a neat pleated frill along the edge and two strange protuberances on the head which did in fact look extraordinarily like the long ears of a hare. There were hundreds of them gliding over the rocks and across the sand, all heading towards the south of the island. They did not touch or display any interest in each other, so I assumed it was not a mating gathering, but some form of migration.

On another occasion, a group of languid, portly and good-

natured dolphins discovered us riding at anchor in a small bay
and, presumably attracted by the friendly colour scheme of
orange and white in which the Bootlebumtrinket was painted
disported themselves around us, leaping and splashing, coming
up alongside the boat with their grinning faces and breathing
deep, passionate sighs at us from their blow holes. A young
one, more daring than the adults, even dived under the boat
and we felt his back scrape along the Bootlebumtrinket's flat
bottom. My attention was equally divided between enjoying
this delightful sight and trying to quell mutiny on the part of
my crew who had all reacted to the arrival of the dolphins in
their individual ways. Widdle, never a staunch warrior, had
lived up to his name copiously and then crouched shivering in
the bows, whining to himself. Puke had decided that the only
way to save his life was to abandon ship and swim for the
shore and had to be restrained forcibly, as did Roger who was
convinced that, if he was only allowed to jump into the sea
with the dolphins, he would be able to kill them all, single
handed, in a matter of moments.

It was during one of these expeditions that I came across
magnificent trophy which was, indirectly, to be responsible for
leading Leslie into court. The family had all gone into town
with the exception of Leslie who was recovering from a very
severe attack of dysentery. It was his first day's convalescence
and he lay on the sofa in the drawing-room as weak as
kitten, sipping iced tea and reading a large manual on ballistics.
He had informed me, in no uncertain terms, that he did not
want me hanging around making a nuisance of myself and so
as I did not want to go into the town, I had taken the dogs out
in Bootlebumtrinket.

As I rowed along, I discerned on the smooth waters of the
bay what I took to be a large patch of yellow sea-weed. Sea-
weed was always worth investigating as it invariably contained
a host of small life and sometimes, if you were lucky, quite
large creatures, so I rowed towards it. But as I got closer,
saw that it was not sea-weed, but what appeared to be
yellowish-coloured rock. But what sort of rock could it be that
floated in some twenty feet of water? As I looked closer,
saw, to my incredulous delight, that it was a fairly large turtle.
Shipping the oars and urging the dogs to silence I poised myself
in the bows and waited, tense with excitement as the Bootl

umtrinket drifted closer and closer. The turtle, outspread, appeared to be floating on the surface of the sea, soundly asleep. My problem was to capture him before he woke up. The nets and various other equipment I had in the boat had not been designed for the capture of a turtle measuring some three feet in length, so the only way I felt I could achieve success was by diving in, grabbing him and somehow getting him into the boat before he woke up. In my excitement it never occurred to me that the strength possessed by a turtle of this size was considerable and it was unlikely that he was going to give up without a struggle. When the boat was some six feet away I held my breath and dived. I decided to dive under him so as to cut off his retreat, as it were, and as I plunged into the lukewarm water I uttered a brief prayer that the splash I made would not awaken him and that, even if it did, he would still be too dozy to execute a rapid retreat. I had dived deep and now I turned on my back and there, suspended above me like an enormous golden guinea, was the turtle. I shot up under him and grabbed him firmly by his front flippers which curved like horny sickles from out of his shell. To my surprise even this action did not wake him and when I rose, gasping, to the surface, still retaining my grasp on his flippers, and shook the water from my eyes, I discovered the reason. The turtle had been dead for a fair length of time, as my nose and the host of tiny fish nibbling at his scaly limbs told me.

Disappointing though this was, a dead turtle was better than no turtle at all and so I laboriously towed his body alongside the Bootlebumtrinket and made it fast by one flipper to the side of the boat. The dogs were greatly intrigued, under the impression that this was some exotic and edible delicacy I had procured for their special benefit. The Bootlebumtrinket, owing to her shape, had never been the easiest of craft to steer, and now, with the dead weight of the turtle lashed to one side of her, she showed a tendency to turn in circles. However, after an hour's strenuous rowing, we arrived safely at the jetty and having tied the boat up I hauled the turtle's carcass up on to the shore where I could examine it. It was a Hawksbill turtle, the kind whose shell is used for the manufacture of spectacle frames and whose stuffed carcass you occasionally see in opticians' windows. His head was massive, with a great wrinkled jowl of yellow skin and a swooping beak of a nose that did give him an extraordinarily hawk-like look. The shell was battered in places, presumably by ocean storms or by the snap of a passing shark, and here and there it was decorated with little snow-white clusters of baby barnacles. His underside of pale daffodil-yellow was soft and pliable like thick damp cardboard.

I had recently conducted a long and fascinating dissection of a dead terrapin that I had found and I felt this would be an ideal opportunity to compare the turtle's internal anatomy with that of his fresh-water brother, so I went up the hill, borrowed the gardener's wheel-barrow, transported my prize up to the house and laid it out in state on the front veranda.

I knew there would be repercussions if I performed my dissection of the turtle inside the house, but I felt that nobody in their right mind would object to the dissection on the front veranda. With my note book at the ready and my row of saws, scalpels and razor blades neatly laid out as though in an operating theatre, I set to work.

I found that the soft yellow plastern came away quite easily compared with the underside of the terrapin which had taken me three-quarters of an hour to saw through. When the plastern was free, I lifted it off like a cover off a dish and there underneath, were all the delicious mysteries of the turtle's internal organs displayed, multi-coloured and odoriferous to a degree. So consumed with curiosity was I that I did not even notice the smell. The dogs, however, who normally considered fresh cow dung to be the ideal scent to add piquancy to their love life, disappeared in a disapproving body, sneezing violently. I discovered, to my delight, that the turtle was a female and had a large quantity of half-formed eggs in her. They were about the size of ping-pong balls, soft, round and as orange as a nasturtium. There were fourteen of them and I removed them carefully and laid them in a gleaming, glutinous row on the flagstones. The turtle appeared to have a prodigious quantity of gut, and I decided that I should enter the exact length of this astonishing apparatus in my already blood-stained note book. With the aid of a scalpel I detached the gut from the rear exit of the turtle and then proceeded to pull out. It seemed never-ending, but before long I had it all laid out carefully across the veranda in a series of loops and twists like a drunken railway line. One section of it was composed of

e stomach, a hideous greyish bag like a water-filled balloon.
his obviously was full of the turtle's last meal and I felt, in
e interest of science, that I ought to check on what it had
een eating just prior to its demise. I stuck a scalpel in the
eat wobbling mound and slashed experimentally. Imme-
ately the whole stomach bag deflated with a ghastly sigh-
g noise and a stench arose from its interior which made all
e other smells pale into insignificance. Even I, fascinated as
was by my investigations, reeled back and had to retreat
ughing to wait for the smell to subside.

I knew I could get the veranda cleaned up before the family
t back from town, but in my excitement, I had completely
erlooked the fact that Leslie was convalescing in the draw-
g-room. The scent of the turtle's interior, so pungent that it
emed almost solid, floated in through the french windows
d enveloped the couch on which he lay. My first intimation
 this catastrophe was a blood-curdling roar from inside
e drawing-room. Before I could do anything sensible, Leslie,
vathed in blankets appeared in the french windows.

'What's that bloody awful stink?' he enquired throatily.
en, as his glance fell upon the dismembered turtle and its
ettily arranged internal organs spread across the flagstones,
s eyes bulged and his face took on a heliotrope tinge. 'What
e hell's that?'

I explained, somewhat diffidently, that it was a turtle that I
as dissecting. It was a female, I went on hurriedly, hoping to
stract Leslie by detail. Here he could see the fascinating eggs
at I had extracted from her interior.

'Damn her eggs,' shouted Leslie, making it sound like some
ange medieval oath. 'Get the bloody thing away from here.
s stinking the place out.'

I said that I had almost reached the end of my dissection
d that I had then planned to bury all the soft parts and
erely keep the skeleton and shell to add to my collection.

'You're doing nothing of the sort,' shouted Leslie. 'You're
 take the whole bloody thing and bury it. Then you can
me back and scrub the veranda.'

Lugaretzia, our cook, attracted by the uproar, appeared in
e french window next to Leslie. She opened her mouth to
quire into the nature of this family quarrel when she was
uck amidships by the smell of the turtle. Lugaretzia always

117

had fifteen or sixteen ailments worrying her at any giv
moment, which she cherished with the loving care that oth
peolpe devote to window-boxes or a Pekinese. At this partic
lar time it was her stomach that was causing her the mo
trouble. In consequence she gasped two or three times feebl
like a fish, uttered a strangled 'Saint Spiridion!' and fell in
Leslie's arms in a well-simulated faint.

Just at that moment, to my horror, the car containing th
rest of the family swept up the drive and came to a halt belo
the veranda.

'Hello, dear,' said Mother, getting out of the car an
coming up the steps. 'Did you have a nice morning?'

Before I could say anything, the turtle, as it were, got
before me. Mother uttered a couple of strange hiccuping cri
pulled out her handkerchief and clapped it to her nose.

'What,' she demanded indistinctly, 'is that terrible smell

'It's that bloody boy,' roared Leslie from the french wi
dows, making ineffectual attempts to prop the moaning Luga
etzia against the door jamb.

Larry and Margo had now followed Mother up the ste
and caught sight of the butchered turtle.

'What . . . ?' began Larry and then he too was seized wi
a convulsive fit of coughing.

'It's that damned boy,' he said gasping.

'Yes, dear,' said Mother through her handkerchief. 'Lesli
just told me.'

'It's disgusting,' wailed Margo, fanning herself with h
handkerchief. 'It looks like a railway accident.'

'What is it, dear?' Mother asked me.

I explained that it was an exceedingly interesting Hawksb
turtle, female, containing eggs.

'Surely you don't have to chop it up on the veranda?' sa
Mother.

'The boy's mad,' said Larry with conviction. 'The who
place smells like a bloody whaling ship.'

'I really think you'll have to take it somewhere else, dea
said Mother. 'We can't have this smell on the front veranda

'Tell him to bury the damned thing,' said Leslie clasping
blankets more firmly about him.

'Why don't you get him adopted by a family of Eskimos

118

CUTTLEFISH AND CRABS

nquired Larry. 'They like eating blubber and maggots and
ings.'

'Larry, don't be disgusting,' said Margo. 'They can't eat
nything like this. The very thought of it makes me feel
ick.'

'I think we ought to go inside,' said Mother faintly. 'Per-
aps it won't smell as much in there.'

'If anything, it smells worse in here,' shouted Leslie from the
rench windows.

'Gerry, dear, you must clean this up,' said Mother as she
icked her way delicately over the turtle's entrails, 'and disin-
ect the flagstones.'

The family went inside and I set about the task of clearing
p the turtle from the front veranda. Their voices arguing
erociously drifted out to me.

'Bloody menace,' said Leslie. 'Lying here peacefully reading,
nd I was suddenly seized by the throat.'

'Disgusting,' said Margo. 'I don't wonder Lugaretzia
ainted.'

'High time he had another tutor,' said Larry. 'You leave the
ouse for five minutes and come back and find him disem-
owelling Moby Dick on the front porch.'

'I'm sure he didn't mean any harm,' said Mother soothingly,
ut it was rather silly of him to do it on the veranda.'

'Silly!' said Larry caustically. 'We'll be blundering round
e house with gas masks for the next six months.'

I piled the remains of the turtle into the wheel-barrow and
ok it up to the top of the hill behind the villa. Here I dug a
ole, buried all the soft parts and then placed the shell and the
one structure near the nest of some friendly ants who had,
n previous occasions, helped me considerably by picking
keletons clean. The most they had ever tackled had been a
ery large green lizard, so I was interested to see what they
ould make of the turtle. They ran towards it, their antennae
aving eagerly, stopped, thought about it for a bit, held a
ttle consultation and then retreated in a body. Apparently
ven the ants were against me. I returned dispiritedly to the
illa.

Here I found that a thin, whining little man, obviously made
elligerent by wine, was arguing with Lugaretzia on the still
doriferous veranda. I enquired what the man wanted.

119

'He says,' said Lugaretzia, with fine scorn, 'that Roger h
been killing his chickens.'

'Turkeys,' corrected the man. 'Turkeys.'

'Well, turkeys then,' said Lugaretzia, conceding the poi

My heart sank. One calamity was being succeeded by a
other. Roger, we knew, had the most reprehensible habit
killing chickens. He derived a lot of innocent amusement
the spring and summer by chasing swallows. They would dri
him into an apoplectic fury by zooming past his nose and th
flying along the ground just ahead of him while he chas
them, bristling with rage, uttering roars of fury. The peasa
chickens used to hide in the myrtle bushes and then, just
Roger was passing, they would leap out with a great flutt
of wings and insane hysterical cackling right into his pat
Roger, I was sure, was convinced that these chickens were
sort of ungainly swallow that he could get to grips with a
so, in spite of yells of protest on our part, he would leap
them and kill them with one swift bite, all his hatred of t
teasing summer swallows showing in his action. No punishme
had any effect on him. He was normally an extremely obedie
dog, except about this one thing. All we could do was p
recompense to the owners, but only on condition that t
corpse of the chicken was produced as evidence.

Reluctantly I went in to tell the family that Roger h
been at it again.

'Christ!' said Leslie, getting laboriously to his feet. 'You a
your sodding animals.'

'Now, now, dear,' said Mother placatingly. 'Gerry ca
help it if Roger kills chickens.'

'Turkeys,' said Leslie. 'I bet he'll want a hell of a lot f
those.'

'Have you cleaned up the veranda, dear?' enquired Moth

Larry removed a large handkerchief, drenched in eau-d
Cologne, which he had spread over his face. 'Does it smell
though he's cleaned up the veranda?' he enquired.

I said hastily that I was just about to do it and follow
Leslie to see the outcome of his conversation with the turk
owner.

'Well,' said Leslie belligerently, striding out on to t
veranda, 'what do you want?'

The man cringed, humble, servile and altogether repulsiv

'Be happy, *kyrié*, be happy,' he greeted Leslie.

'Be happy,' Leslie replied gruffly, in the tone of voice that implied that he hoped the man would be anything but. 'What do you wish to see me about?'

'My turkeys, *kyrié*,' said the man deprecatingly. 'I apologise for troubling you, but your dog, you see, he's been killing my turkeys.'

'Well,' said Leslie, 'how many has he killed?'

'Five, *kyrié*,' said the man, shaking his head sorrowfully. 'Five of my best turkeys. I am a poor man, *kyrié*, otherwise I wouldn't have dreamt . . .'

'Five!' said Leslie startled, and turned an enquiring eye on me.

I said I thought it was quite possible. If five hysterical turkeys had leapt out of a myrtle bush I could well believe that Roger would have killed them all. For such a benign and friendly dog, he was a ruthless killer when he got started.

'Roger is a good dog,' said Lugaretzia belligerently.

She had joined us on the veranda and she obviously viewed the turkey owner with the same dislike as myself. Apart from this, in her eyes Roger could do no wrong.

'Well,' said Leslie, making the best of a bad job, 'if he's killed five turkeys, he's killed five turkeys. Such is life. Where are the bodies?'

There was a moment of silence.

'The bodies, *kyrié*?' queried the turkey owner tentatively.

'The bodies, the bodies,' said Leslie impatiently. 'You know, the bodies of the turkeys. You know we can't pay until you produce the bodies.'

'But that's not possible,' said the turkey owner nervously.

'What do you mean, not possible?' enquired Leslie.

'Well, it's not possible to bring the bodies, *kyrié*,' said the turkey owner with a flash of inspiration, 'because your dog has eaten them.'

The explosion that this statement provoked was considerable. We all knew that Roger was, if anything, slightly overfed, and that he was of a most fastidious nature. Though he would kill a chicken, nothing would induce him to feed upon the carcass.

'Lies! Lies!' shrilled Lugaretzia, her eyes swimming with tears of emotion. 'He's a good dog.'

'He's never eaten anything in his life that he's kille
shouted Leslie. 'Never.'

'But five of my turkeys!' said the little man. 'Five of th
he's eaten!'

'When did he kill them?' roared Leslie.

'This morning, *kyrié*, this morning,' said the man, crossi
himself. 'I saw it myself, and he ate them all.'

I interrupted to say that Roger had been out that morni
in the Bootlebumtrinket with me and, intelligent dog thou
he was, I did not see how he could be consuming the prod
ious quantity of five turkeys on this man's farm and out in
boat with me at the same time.

Leslie had had a trying morning. All he had wanted was
lie peacefully on the sofa with his manual of ballistics, t
first he had been almost asphyxiated by my investigations in
the internal anatomy of the turtle and now he was being fac
by a drunken little man, trying to swindle us out of the pr
of five turkeys. His temper, never under the best of contr
bubbled over.

'You're a two-faced liar and a cheat,' he snarled. The lit
man backed away and his face went white.

'*You* are the liar and the cheat,' he said with drunken b
ligerence. '*You* are the liar and the cheat. You let your dog I
everybody's chickens and turkeys and then when they come
you for payment, you refuse. *You* are the liar and the che

Even at that stage, I think that sanity could have prevail
but the little man made a fatal mistake. He spat copiously a
wetly at Leslie's feet. Lugaretzia uttered a shrill wail of hor
and grabbed hold of Leslie's arm. Knowing his temper
grabbed hold of the other one. The little man, appalled into
moment of sobriety, backed away. Leslie quivered like a v
cano and Lugaretzia and I hung on like grim death.

'Excreta of a pig,' roared Leslie. 'Illegitimate son of a
eased whore . . .'

The fine Greek oaths rolled out, rich, vulgar and biologic
and the little man turned from white to pink and from pink
red. He had obviously been unaware of the fact that Le
had such a command over the fruitier of the Greek insults

'You'll be sorry,' he quavered. 'You'll be sorry.'

He spat once more with a pathetic sort of defiance and th
turned and scuttled down the drive.

It took the combined efforts of the family and Lugaretzia three-quarters of an hour to calm Leslie down, with the aid of several large brandies.

'Don't you worry about him, *kyrié* Leslie,' was Lugaretzia's final summing up. 'He's well known in the village as a bad character. Don't you worry about him.'

But we were forced to worry about him, for the next thing we knew, he had sued Leslie for not paying his debts and for defamation of character.

Spiro, when told the news was furious.

'Gollys, Mrs Durrells,' he said, his face red with wrath. 'Why don'ts yous lets Masters Leslies shoot the son of a bitch?'

'I don't think that would really solve anything, Spiro,' said Mother. 'What we want to know now is whether this man has any chance of winning his case.'

'Winnings!' said Spiro with fine scorn. 'That bastard won't wins anything. You just leaves it to me. I'll fixes it.'

'Now, don't go and do anything rash, Spiro,' said Mother. 'It'll only make matters worse.'

'I won'ts do anythings rash, Mrs Durrells. But I'll fixes that bastard.'

For several days he went about with an air of conspiratorial gloom, his bushy eyebrows tangled in a frown of immense concentration, only answering our questions monosyllabically. Then, one day, a fortnight or so before the case was due to be heard, we were all in town on a shopping spree. Eventually, weighed down by our purchases, we made our way to the broad, tree-lined Esplanade and sat there having a drink and passing the time of day with our numerous acquaintances who passed. Presently, Spiro, who had been glaring furtively about him with the air of a man who had many enemies, suddenly stiffened. He hitched his great belly up and leant across the table.

'Master Leslies, you sees that mans over there, that one with the white hair?'

He pointed a sausage-like finger at a small neat little man who was placidly sipping a cup of coffee under the trees.

'Well, what about him?' enquired Leslie.

'He's the judges,' said Spiro.

'What judge?' said Leslie bewildered.

123

'The judges who is going to tries your case,' said Spiro
'I wants you go to over there and talks to him.'

'Do you think that's wise?' said Larry. 'He might thin
you're trying to muck about with the course of justice and giv
you ten years in prison or something.'

'Gollys, nos,' said Spiro aghast at such a thought: 'H
wouldn't puts Master Leslies in prison. He knows betters then
to do thats while I ams here.'

'But even so, Spiro, don't you think he'll think it a littl
funny if Leslie suddenly starts talking to him?' asked Mothe
worriedly.

'Gollys nos,' said Spiro. He glanced about him to make sur
that we weren't overheard, leant forward and whispered. 'H
collects stamps.'

The family looked bewildered.

'You mean he's a philatelist?' said Larry at length.

'No, no, Master Larrys,' said Spiro. 'He's not one of them
He's a married man and he's gots two childrens.'

The whole conversation seemed to be getting even more in
volved than the normal ones that we had with Spiro.

'What,' said Leslie patiently, 'has his collecting stamps go
to do with it?'

'I will takes you over there,' said Spiro, laying bare fo
the first time the Machiavellian intricacies of his plot, 'an
yous tells hims that you will get him some stamps from
England.'

'But that's bribery,' said Margo shocked.

'It isn't bribery, Misses Margos,' said Spiro, 'he collect
stamps. He *wants* stamps.'

'I should think if you tried to bribe him with stamps he'
give you about five hundred years penal servitude,' said Larr
to Leslie, judiciously.

I asked eagerly whether, if Leslie was condemned, he woul
be sent to Vido, the convict settlement on a small island tha
lay in the sparkling sea half a mile or so away from the tow

'No, no, dear,' said Mother, getting increasingly flustere
'Leslie won't be sent to Vido.'

I felt this was rather a pity. I already had one convict frien
serving a sentence for the murder of his wife, who lived o
Vido. He was a 'trusty' and so had been allowed to build hi
own boat and row home for the weekends. He had given me

onstrous black-backed gull which tyrannized all my pets and
e family. I felt that, exciting though it was to have a real
urderer as a friend, it would have been better to have Leslie
carcerated on Vido so that he too could come home for the
eekends. To have a convict brother would, I felt, be rather
otic.

'I don't see that if I just go and talk to him it can do any
rm,' said Leslie.

'I wouldn't,' said Margo. 'Remember, there's many a slip
thout a stitch.'

'I do think you ought to be careful, dear,' said Mother.

'I can see it all,' said Larry with relish. 'Leslie with a ball
d chain; Spiro too, probably, as an accessory. Margo knitting
em warm socks for the winter, Mother sending them food
rcels and anti-lice ointment.'

'Oh, do stop it, Larry,' said Mother crossly. 'This is no
ughing matter.'

'All you've gots to dos is to talks to him, Master Leslies,'
d Spiro earnestly. 'Honest to Gods you've got to, otherwise
an't fixes it.'

Spiro had, prior to this, never let us down. His advice had
vays been sound and, even if it hadn't been legal, we had
ver so far come to grief.

'All right,' said Leslie, 'let's give it a bash.'

'Do be careful, dear,' said Mother as Leslie and Spiro rose
d walked over to where the judge was sitting.

The judge greeted them charmingly and for half an hour
slie and Spiro sat at his table sipping coffee while Leslie
ked to him in voluble, but inaccurate Greek. Presently the
lge rose and left them with much hand-shaking and bowing.
ey returned to our table where we waited agog for the
ws.

'Charming old boy,' said Leslie. 'Couldn't have been nicer.
promised to get him some stamps. Who do we know in
gland who collects them?'

'Well, your father used to,' said Mother. 'He was a very
en philatelist when he was alive.'

'Gollys, don't says that, Mrs Durrells,' said Spiro, in genuine
guish.

A short pause ensued while the family explained to him the
aning of the word philatelist.

'I still don't see how this is going to help the case,' sa
Larry. 'Even if you inundate him with penny blacks.'

'Never yous minds, Masters Larrys,' said Spiro, darkly.
said I'd fixes it and I will. You just leaves it to me.'

For the next few days Leslie, convinced that Spiro cou
obstruct the course of justice, wrote to everybody he cou
think of in England and demanded stamps. The result was th
our mail increased three-fold and practically every free spa
in the villa was taken up by piles of stamps which, wheneve
wind blew, would drift like autumn leaves across the room
the vociferous, snarling delight of the dogs. Many of t
stamps began to look slightly the worse for wear.

'You're not going to give him *those* are you?' said Larry d
dainfully surveying a pile of mangled, semi-masticated stam
that Leslie had rescued from the jaws of Roger half an ho
previously.

'Well, stamps are supposed to be old, aren't they?' s
Leslie belligerently.

'Old, perhaps,' said Larry, 'but surely not covered w
enough spittle to give him hydrophobia.'

'Well, if you can think of a better bloody plan, why do
you suggest it?' enquired Leslie.

'My dear fellow, I don't mind,' said Larry. 'When the jud
is running around biting all his colleagues and you are la
guishing in a Greek prison, don't blame me.'

'All I ask is that you mind your own bloody business,' s
Leslie loudly.

'Now, now, dear, Larry's only trying to be helpful,' s
Mother.

'Helpful,' snarled Leslie, making a grab at a group of stam
that were being blown off the table. 'He's just interfering
usual.'

'Well, dear,' said Mother adjusting her spectacles, 'I
think he may be right, you know. After all, some of th
stamps do look a little, well, you know, second-hand.'

'He wants stamps and he's bloody well going to get stam
said Leslie.

And stamps the poor judge got, in a bewildering variety
sizes, shapes, colours and stages of disintegration.

Then another thing happened that increased Leslie's co

126

dence in winning the case one hundredfold. We discovered
that the turkey man, whom Larry constantly referred to as
Trippenopoulos, had been unwise enough to subpoena Lugaretzia, as a witness for the prosecution. Lugaretzia, furious,
wanted to refuse until it was explained to her that she could
not.

'Imagine that man calling me as a witness to help him,' she
said. 'Well, don't you worry, *kyrié* Leslie, I'll tell the court
how he forced you to swear at him and call him . . .'

The family rose in a body and vociferously informed
Lugaretzia that she was not to do anything of the sort. It took
us half an hour to impress upon her what she should and
should not say. At the end of it, since Lugaretzia, like most
Corfiots, was not very strong on logic, we felt somewhat
jaded.

'Well, with her as witness for the prosecution,' said Larry,
'I should think you'll probably get the death sentence.'

'Larry, dear, don't say things like that,' said Mother. 'It's
not funny even in a joke.'

'I'm not joking,' said Larry.

'Rubbish,' said Leslie uneasily. 'I'm sure she'll be all right.'

'I think it would be much safer to disguise Margo as Lugaretzia,' said Larry, judicially. 'With her sweeping command over
the Greek language she would probably do you considerably
less harm.'

'Yes,' said Margo excitedly, struck for the first time by
Larry's perspicacity, 'Why can't I be a witness?'

'Don't be damned silly,' said Leslie. 'You weren't there.
How can you be a witness?'

'I was almost there,' said Margo. 'I was in the kitchen.'

'That's all you need,' said Larry to Leslie. 'Margo and
Lugaretzia in the witness box and you won't even need a
judge. You'll probably be lynched by the mob.'

When the day of the case dawned, Mother rallied the family.

'It's ridiculous for us all to go,' said Larry. 'If Leslie wants
to get himself into prison, that's his affair. I don't see why
we should be dragged into it. Besides, I wanted to do some
writing this morning.'

'It's our duty to go,' said Mother firmly. 'We must put on a
bold front. After all, I don't want people to think that I'm
rearing a family of gaol birds.'

127

So we all put on our best clothes and sat waiting patien
until Spiro came to collect us.

'Now, don'ts yous worries, Master Leslies,' he scowled, w
the air of a warder in the condemned cell. 'Everything's goi
to be O.K.s.'

But in spite of this prophecy, Larry insisted on reciting T
Ballad of Reading Gaol as we drove into town, much
Leslie's annoyance.

The court-room was a bustle of unco-ordinated activi
People sipped little cups of coffee, other people shuffl
through piles of papers in an aimless but dedicated way a
there was lots of chatter and laughter. Crippenopoulos w
there in his best suit, but avoided our eye. Lugaretzia, f
some reason best known to herself, was clad entirely in bla
It was, as Larry pointed out, a premature move. Surely s
should have reserved her mourning for after the trial.

'Now, Master Leslies,' said Spiro, 'You stands there, and
stands there and translates for you.'

'What for?' enquired Leslie, bewildered.

'Because you don'ts speaks Greeks,' said Spiro.

'Really, Spiro,' protested Larry, 'I admit his Greek is n
Homeric, but it is surely perfectly adequate?'

'Masters Larrys,' said Spiro scowling earnestly, 'Mas
Leslies mustn'ts speaks Greeks.'

Before we could enquire more deeply into this, there wa
general scuffling and the judge came in. He took his seat a
his eyes roved round the court and then, catching sight
Leslie, he beamed and bowed.

'Hanging judges always smile like that,' said Larry.

'Larry, dear, do stop it,' said Mother. 'You're making
nervous.'

There was a long pause while what was presumably
Clerk of the Court read out the indictment. Then Cripp
opoulos was called to give his evidence. He put on a lov
performance, at once servile and indignant, placating
belligerent. The judge was obviously impressed and I began
get quite excited. Perhaps I would have a convict for a broth
after all. Then it was Leslie's turn.

'You are accused,' said the judge, 'Of having used
famatory and insulting language to this man and endeavour

128

deprive him of rightful payment for the loss of five turkeys,
led by your dog.'

Leslie stared blank-faced at the judge.

'What's he say?' he enquired of Spiro.

Spiro hitched his stomach up.

'He says, Masters Leslies,' and his voice was so pitched that
rumbled through the court-room like thunder, 'He says that
ou insults this mans and that you tries to swindle him out of
oneys for his turkeys.'

'That's ridiculous,' said Leslie firmly.

He was about to go on when Spiro held up a hand like a
m and stopped him. He turned to the judge.

'The *kyrios* denies the charge,' he said. 'It would be im-
ossible for him to be guilty anyway, because he doesn't speak
reek.'

'Christ!' groaned Larry sepulchrally. 'I hope Spiro knows
at he's doing.'

'What's he saying? What's he doing?' said Mother ner-
usly.

'As far as I can see, putting a noose round Leslie's neck,' said
arry.

The judge, who had had so many coffees with Leslie, who
d received so many stamps from him, and who had had so
any conversations in Greek with him, stared at Leslie im-
ssively. Even if the judge had not known Leslie personally
would have been impossible for him not to know that
slie had some command over the Greek language. Nothing
yone did in Corfu was sacrosanct and if you were a for-
gner, of course, the interest in and the knowledge of your
ivate affairs was that much greater. We waited with bated
eath for the judge's reactions. Spiro had his massive head
ghtly lowered like a bull about to charge.

'I see,' said the judge dryly.

He shuffled some papers aimlessly for a moment and then
anced up.

'I understand,' he said, 'that the prosecution have a witness.
suppose we had better hear her.'

It was Lugaretzia's big moment. She rose to her feet, folded
r arms and stared majestically at the judge, her normally pale
ce pink with excitement, her soulful eyes glowing.

'You are Lugaretzia Condos, and you are employed by th‸ people as a cook?' enquired the judge.

'Yes,' said Lugaretzia, 'and a kinder, more generous fam‸ you could not wish to meet. Why, only the other day th‸ gave me a frock for myself and for my daughter and it w‸ only a month or two ago that I asked the *kyrios* . . .'

'Yes,' interrupted the judge, 'I see. Well, this has not ‸ much relevance to the case. I understand that you were th‸ when this man called to see about his turkeys. Now tell me‸ your own words what happened.'

Larry groaned.

'If she tells him in her own words, they'll get Leslie ‸ sure,' he said.

'Well,' said Lugaretzia, glancing round the court to ma‸ sure she had everybody's attention. 'The *kyrios* had been v‸ ill, very ill indeed. At times we despaired for his life. I k‸ suggesting cupping to his mother, but she wouldn't hear ‸ it . . .'

'Would you mind getting to the point?' said the judge.

'Well,' said Lugaretzia reluctantly abandoning the subject‸ illness, which was always a favourite topic with her, 'it w‸ the *kyrios*'s first day up and he was very weak. Then this ma‸ she said, pointing a scornful finger at Crippenopoulos, 'arri‸ dead drunk and said that their dog had killed five of his t‸ keys. Now the dog wouldn't do that, *kyrié* judge. A swee‸ kinder, nobler dog was never seen in Corfu.'

'The dog is not on trial,' said the judge.

'Well,' said Lugaretzia, 'when the *kyrios* said, quite righ‸ that he would have to see the corpses before he paid the m‸ the man said he couldn't show them because the dog had ea‸ them. This is ridiculous, as you can well imagine, *kyrié* jud‸ as no dog could eat five turkeys.'

'You are supposed to be a witness for the prosecution, are‸ you?' said the judge. 'I ask only because your story doe‸ tally with the complainant's.'

'Him,' said Lugaretzia, 'you don't want to trust him. He'‸ drunkard and a liar and it is well known in the village that ‸ has got two wives.'

'So you are telling me,' said the judge, endeavouring to s‸ out this confusion, 'that the *kyrios* didn't swear at him ‸ Greek and refuse payment for the turkeys.'

'Of course he didn't,' said Lugaretzia. 'A kinder, finer, more upstanding *kyrios* . . .'

'Yes, yes, all right,' said the judge.

He sat pondering for some time while we all waited in suspense, then he glanced up and looked at Crippenopoulos.

'I can see no evidence,' he said, 'that the Englishman has behaved in the way you have suggested. Firstly he does not speak Greek.'

'He does speak Greek,' shouted Crippenopoulos wrathfully. 'He called me a . . .'

'Will you be quiet,' said the judge coldly. 'Firstly, as I was saying he does not speak Greek. Secondly, your own witness denies all knowledge of the incident. It seems to me clear that you endeavoured to extract payment for turkeys which had not, in fact, been killed and eaten by the defendant's dog. However, you are not on trial here for that, so I will merely find the defendant not guilty, and you will have to pay the costs.'

Immediately pandemonium reigned. Crippenopoulos was on his feet, purple with rage, shouting at the top of his voice and calling on Saint Spiridion's aid. Spiro, bellowing like a bull, embraced Leslie, kissed him on both cheeks and was followed by the weeping Lugaretzia who did likewise. It was some time before we managed to extricate ourselves from the court and jubilantly we went down to the Esplanade and sat at a table under the trees to celebrate.

Presently the judge came past and we rose in a body to thank him and invite him to sit and have a drink with us. He refused the drink shyly and then fixed Leslie with a penetrating eye.

'I wouldn't like you to think,' he said, 'that justice in Corfu is always dispensed like that, but I had a long conversation with Spiro about the case and after some deliberation I decided that your crime was not as bad as the man's. I hoped it might teach him not to swindle foreigners in future.'

'Well, I really am most grateful to you,' said Leslie.

The judge gave a little bow. He glanced at his watch.

'Well, I must be going,' he said. 'By the way, thank you so much for those stamps you sent me yesterday. Among them were two quite rare ones which were new to my collection.'

Raising his hat he trotted off across the Esplanade.

The Olive Merry-Go-Round

By May the olive-picking had been in progress for some time.
The fruit had plumped and ripened throughout the ho[t]
summer days and now it fell and lay shining in the grass like
a harvest of black pearls. The peasant women appeared in
droves carrying tins and baskets on their heads. They would
crouch in circles round the base of the olive tree chattering as
shrilly as sparrows as they picked up the fruit and placed it in
the containers. Some of the olive trees had been producing
crops like this for five hundred years and for five hundre[d]
years the peasants had been gathering the olives in precisel[y]
the same way.

It was a great time for gossip and for laughter. I used t[o]
move from tree to tree joining the different groups, squatting
on my haunches, helping them pick up the glossy olive[s]
hearing gossip about all the relatives and friends of the oliv[e]
pickers and occasionally joining them as they ate under th[e]
trees, wolfing down the sour black bread and the little fla[t]
cakes wrapped in vine leaves that were made out of la[st]
season's dried figs. Songs would be sung and it was curiou[s]
that the peasants' voices, so sour and raucous in speech, coul[d]
be plaintively sweet when raised in harmony together. At tha[t]
time of year with the yellow, waxy crocuses just starting t[o]
bubble up amongst the olive roots and the banks purple wit[h]
campanulas, the peasants gathered under the trees looked lik[e]
a moving flower bed and the songs would echo down the nav[e]
between the ancient olives, the sound as melancholy and [as]
sweet as goat bells.

When the containers were piled high with the fruit, the[y]
would be hoisted up and we would carry them down to th[e]
olive press in a long chattering line. The olive press, a gaun[t]
gloomy building, was down in a valley through which ran [a]
tiny, glittering stream. The press was presided over by Pap[a]
Demetrios, a tough old man, as twisted and bent as the oliv[e]
trees themselves, with a completely bald head and an enormo[us]

moustache, snow-white except where it was stained yellow by nicotine, and reputed to be the biggest moustache in the whole of Corfu. Papa Demetrios was a gruff, bad-tempered old man, but for some reason he took a fancy to me and we got along splendidly. He even allowed me into the holy of holies itself, the olive press.

Here was a great circular trough like an ornamental fish pond and mounted in it a gigantic grindstone with a central strut of wood jutting from it. This strut was harnessed to Papa Demetrios's ancient horse who, with a sack over its head so that it did not get giddy, would circle the trough, thus rolling the great grindstone round and round so that it could crush the olives as they were poured into it in a glinting cascade. As the olives were crushed, a sharp, sour smell rose in the air. The only sounds were the solid ploddings of the horse's hooves, the rumbling of the great grindstone and the steady drip, drip of the oil trickling out of the vents of the trough, golden as distilled sunlight.

In one corner of the press was a huge black crumbling mound which was the residue from the grinding; the crushed seeds, pulp and skin of the olives forming black crusty cakes, like coarse peat. It had a rich, sweet-sour smell that almost convinced you it was good to eat. It was in fact fed to the cattle and horses with their winter food and it was also used as a remarkably efficient, if somewhat over-pungent, fuel.

Papa Demetrios, because of his bad temper, was left severely alone by the peasants who would deliver their olives and depart from the press with all speed. For you were never certain whether anybody like Papa Demetrios might not have the evil eye. In consequence, the old man was lonely and so he welcomed my intrusion into his domain. From me he would get all the local gossip; who had given birth and whether it was a boy or a girl, who was courting who, and sometimes a more juicy item such as that Pepe Condos had been arrested for smuggling tobacco. In return for my acting as a sort of newspaper for him, Papa Demetrios would catch specimens for me. Sometimes it would be a pale pink gulping gecko, or a praying mantis, or the caterpillar of an Oleander Hawk Moth, striped like a Persian carpet, pink and silver and green. It was Papa Demetrios who got me one of the most charming pets that I had at that time, a spade-footed toad whom I christened Augustus Tickletummy.

I had been down in the olive groves helping the peasants and I started to feel hungry. I knew that Papa Demetrios always kept a good supply of food at the olive press, so I went down to visit him. It was a sparkling day with a rumbustious, laughing wind that thrummed through the olive grove like a harp. There was a nip in the air and so I ran all the way with the dogs leaping and barking about me, and arrived flushed and panting to find Papa Demetrios crouched over a fire that he had constructed out of slabs of olive 'cake'.

'Ah!' he said glaring at me fiercely. 'So you've come, have you. Where have you been? I haven't seen you for two days. I suppose now spring is here you've got no time for an old man like me.'

I explained that I had been busy with a variety of things such as making a new cage for my magpies since they had just raided Larry's room and stood in peril of their lives if they were not incarcerated.

'Hum,' said Papa Demetrios. 'Ah, well. Do you want some corn?'

I said, as nonchalantly as I could, that there was nothing would like better than corn.

He got up, strutted bow-legged to the olive press and reappeared carrying a large frying-pan, a sheet of tin, a bottle of oil and five golden-brown cobs of dried maize, like bars of bullion. He put the frying-pan on the fire and scattered a small quantity of oil into it, then waited until the heat of the fire made the oil purr and twinkle and smoke gently in the bottom of the pan. Then he seized a cob of maize and twisted it rapidly between his arthritic hands so that the golden beads of corn pattered into the pan with a sound of rain on a roof. He put the flat sheet of tin over the top, gave a little grunt and sat back, lighting a cigarette

'Have you heard about Andreas Papoyakis?' he asked, running his fingers through his luxurious moustache.

No, I said, I had not heard.

'Ah,' he said with relish. 'He's in hospital, that foolish one!

I said I was sorry to hear it, because I liked Andreas. He was a gay, kind hearted, exuberant boy who inevitably managed to do the wrong things. They said of him in the village that he

ould ride a donkey backwards if he could. What, I enquired,
as his affliction?

'Dynamite,' said Papa Demetrios, waiting to see my reac-
on.

I gave a slow whistle of horror and nodded my head slowly.
apa Demetrios, now assured of my undivided attention,
ettled himself more comfortably.

'This was how it happened,' he said. 'He's a foolish boy,
ndreas is, you know. His head is as empty as a winter
wallow's nest. But he's a good boy though. He's never done
nybody any harm. Well, he went dynamite fishing. You know
nat little bay down near Benitses? Ah well, he took his boat
nere because he had been told that the country policeman had
one farther down the coast for the day. Of course, foolish
oy, he never thought to check and make sure that the police-
nan *was* farther down the coast.'

I clicked my tongue sorrowfully. The penalty for dynamite
shing was five years in prison and a heavy fine.

'Now,' said Papa Demetrios, 'he got into his boat and was
owing slowly along when he saw ahead of him, in the shallow
ater, a big shoal of barbouni. He stopped rowing and lit the
use on his stick of dynamite.'

Papa Demetrios paused dramatically, peered at the corn to
ee how it was doing and lit another cigarette.

'That would have been all right,' he went on, 'but, just as he
as about to throw the dynamite, the fish swam away and
hat do you think that idiot of a boy did? Still holding the
ynamite he rowed after them. Bang!'

I said I thought that there could not be very much left of
ndreas.

'Oh yes,' said Papa Demetrios scornfully. 'He can't even
ynamite properly. It was such a tiny stick all it did was blow
ff his right hand. But even so, he owes his life to the police-
an, who hadn't gone farther down the coast. Andreas man-
ged to row to the shore and there he fainted from loss of
lood and he would undoubtedly have died if the policeman,
aving heard the bang, had not come down to the shore to see
ho was dynamiting. Luckily the bus was just passing and the
oliceman stopped it and they got Andreas into it and into the
ospital.'

I said I thought it was a great pity that it should happen to

anybody as nice as Andreas, but he was lucky to be alive.
presumed that when he was better he would be arrested ar
sent to Vido for five years.

'No, no,' said Papa Demetrios. 'The policeman said l
thought Andreas had been punished quite enough, so he to'
the hospital that Andreas had caught his hand in some machin
ery.'

The corn had now started to explode, banging on to th
top of the tin like the explosions of miniature cannons. Pap
Demetrios lifted the pan off the fire and took the lid off. Ther
was each grain of corn exploded into a little yellow and whi
cumulus cloud, scrunchy and delicious. Papa Demetrios too
a twist of paper from his pocket and unwrapped it. It was fu
of coarse grains of grey sea salt, and into this we dipped th
little clouds of corn and scrunched them up with relish.

'I've got something for you,' said the old man at last, wipin
his moustache carefully with a large red and white handke
chief. 'Another one of those terrible animals that you are s
eager to get.'

Stuffing my mouth with the remains of the pop-corn an
wiping my fingers on the grass, I asked him eagerly what
was.

'I'll fetch it,' he said, getting to his feet. 'It's a very curiou
thing. I've never seen one like it before.'

I waited impatiently while he went into the olive pre
and reappeared carrying a battered tin, the neck of which l
had stuffed with leaves.

'There you are,' he said. 'Be careful, because it smells.'

I pulled out the plug of leaves, peered into the tin and di
covered that Papa Demetrios was quite right, it smelt
strongly of garlic as a peasant bus on market day. In th
bottom was crouched a medium size, rather smooth-skinne
greenish-brown toad with enormous amber eyes and a mout
set in a perpetual, rather insane, grin. As I put my hand int
the tin to pick him up, he ducked his head between his for
legs, retracted his protuberant eyes into his skull in the od
way that toads have and uttered a sharp bleating cry rather lik
that of a miniature sheep. I lifted him out of the tin and h
struggled violently, exuding a terrible odour of garlic. I notice
that on each hind foot he had a horny black excrescence, blad

shaped, like a ploughshare. I was delighted with him for I
had spent a considerable amount of time and energy trying to
track down spade-footed toads without success. Thanking
Papa Demetrios profusely, I carried him home triumphantly
and installed him in an aquarium in my bedroom.

I had placed earth and sand to a depth of two or three inches
at the bottom of the aquarium and Augustus, having been
christened and released, immediately set to work to build himself a home. With a curious movement of his hind legs, working backwards, using the blades of his feet as spades, he very
rapidly dug himself a hole and disappeared from view with the
exception of his protuberant eyes and grinning face.

Augustus, I soon discovered, was a remarkably intelligent
beast and had many endearing traits of character which made
themselves apparent as he got tamer. When I went into the
room, he would scuttle out of his hole and make desperate
endeavours to reach me through the glass walls of the aquarium. If I took him out and placed him on the floor, he would
hop round the room after me and then, if I sat down, would
climb laboriously up my leg until he reached my lap, where he
would recline in a variety of undignified attitudes, basking in
the heat of my body, blinking his eyes slowly, grinning up at
me and gulping. It was then that I discovered he liked to lie
on his back and have his stomach gently massaged by my
forefinger, and so from this unusual behaviour he derived the
surname of Tickletummy. He would also, I learnt, sing for his
food. If I held a large, writhing earth worm over the top of the
aquarium, Augustus would go into paroxysms of delight, his
eyes seeming to protrude more and more with excitement,
and he would utter a series of little pig-like grunts and the
strange bleating cry he had given when I first picked him up.
When the worm was finally dropped in front of him, he
would nod his head vigorously as if in thanks, grab one end
of it and stuff it into his mouth with his thumbs. Whenever we
had any guests, they were treated to an Augustus Tickletummy
recital and they all agreed, gravely, that he had the best voice
and repertoire of any toad they had met.

It was round about this time that Larry introduced Donald
and Max into our life. Max was an immensely tall Austrian
with curly blond hair, a blond moustache perched like an

elegant butterfly on his lip and intensely blue and kindly eyes
Donald, on the other hand was short and pale-faced; one of
those Englishmen who give you the first impression of being
not only inarticulate, but completely devoid of personality

Larry had run into this ill-assorted couple in the town and
had lavishly invited them up to have drinks. The fact that they
arrived, mellowed by a variety of alcoholic stimuli, at two
o'clock in the morning did not strike any of us as being par
ticularly curious since, by that time, we were inured, or almost
inured, to Larry's acquaintances.

Mother had gone to bed early with a severe cold and th
rest of the family had also retired to their rooms. I was th
only member of the household awake. The reason for thi
was that I was waiting for Ulysses to return to the bedroom
from his nightly wanderings and devour his supper of mea
and minced liver. As I lay there reading, I heard a dim, blurre
sound echoing through the olive groves. I thought at first
was a party of peasants returning late from a wedding, an
took no notice. Then the cacophony grew closer and close
and from the clop and jingle accompanying it I realised it wa
some late-night revellers passing on the road below in a ca
The song they were singing did not sound particularly Gree
and I wondered who they could be. I got out of bed and lea
out of the window, staring down through the olive tree
At that moment the cab turned off the road and started up th
long drive towards the house. I could see it quite clearly be
cause whoever was sitting in the back had apparently lighted
small bonfire. I watched this, puzzled and intrigued, as
flickered and shook through the trees on its way up to us.

At that moment Ulysses appeared out of the night sky, lil
a silently drifting dandelion clock, and endeavoured to per
on my naked shoulder. I shook him off and went and fetche
his plate of food, which he proceeded to peck and gobble a
uttering tiny throaty noises to himself and blinking his brillia
eyes at me.

By this time the cab had made slow but steady progress an
had entered the forecourt of the house. I leant out of the wi
dow enraptured by the sight.

It was not, as I had thought, a bonfire in the back of t
cab. There were two individuals sitting there, each clasping

138

enormous silver candelabra in which had been stuck some of the great white candles that one normally bought to put in the church of Saint Spiridion. They were singing loudly and untunefully, but with great panache, a song from *The Maid of the Mountains*, endeavouring, wherever possible, to harmonize.

The cab rolled to a halt at the steps that led up to the veranda.

'At seventeen . . .' sighed a very British baritone.

'At seventeen!' intoned the other singer in a rather heavy middle-European accent.

'He falls in love quite madly,' said the baritone, waving his candelabra about wildly, 'with eyes of tender blue.'

'Tender blue,' intoned the middle-European accent, giving lechery to these simple words that had to be heard to be believed.

'At twenty-five,' continued the baritone, 'he thinks he's got badly.'

'Badly,' said the middle-European accent dolefully.

'With eyes of different hue,' said the baritone, making such a wild gesture with his candelabra that the candles sped out of their sockets like rockets and fell sizzling on to the grass.

My bedroom door opened and Margo, clad in yards of lace and what appeared to be butter muslin, came in.

'What on earth's that *noise*?' she said in a hoarse, accusing whisper. 'You *know* Mother's not well.'

I explained that the noise was nothing whatever to do with me, but apparently we had company. Margo leant out of the window and peered down at the cab where the singers had just reached the next verse of their song.

'I say,' she called, in muted tones, 'do you mind not making quite so much noise. My mother's sick.'

Immediate silence enveloped the cab and then a tall gangling figure rose unsteadily to its feet. He held his candelabra aloft and gazed earnestly up at Margo as she leant out of the window.

'Must not, dear lady,' he intoned sepulchrally, 'must not disturb Muzzer.'

'No, by Jove,' agreed the English voice from the interior of the cab.

'Who do you think they are?' Margo whispered to me in agitation.

I said that to me the thing was perfectly clear; they must be friends of Larry's.

'Are you friends of my brother's?' Margo fluted out of the window.

'A noble being,' said the tall figure, waving the candelabra at her. 'He invited us for drinks.'

'Er . . . Just a minute, I'll come down,' said Margo.

'To look you closer would be to fulfil the ambition of a lifetime,' said the tall man, bowing somewhat uncertainly.

'See you closer,' corrected a quiet voice from the back of the cab.

'I'll go downstairs,' said Margo to me, 'and get them inside and keep them quiet. You go and wake Larry.'

I pulled on a pair of shorts, picked up Ulysses unceremoniously (who, with half-closed eyes, was digesting his food) and went to the window and threw him out.

'Extraordinary!' said the tall man, watching Ulysses fly away over the moon-silvered olive tops. 'Dis like the house of Dracula, no, Donald?'

'By Jove, yes,' said Donald.

I pattered down the corridor and burst into Larry's room. It took me some time to shake him awake for, under the impression that Mother had been breathing her cold germs over him, he had taken the precaution of consuming half a bottle of whisky before he went to bed. Eventually he sat up blearily and looked at me.

'What the bloody hell do you want?' he enquired.

I explained about the two characters in the cab and that they said they had been invited to drinks.

'Oh, Christ!' said Larry. 'Just tell them I've gone to Dubrovnik.'

I explained that I could not very well do this as by now Margo would have lured them into the house and that Mother, in her fragile condition, must not be disturbed. Groaning, Larry got out of bed and put on his dressing-gown and slippers, and together we went down the creaking stairs to the drawing-room. Here we found Max, lanky, flamboyant, good-natured, sprawled in a chair waving his candelabra at Margo, all the candles of which had gone out. Donald sat hunched and gloomy in another chair, looking like an undertaker's assistant.

Your eyes, they are tender blue,' said Max, waving a long
ger at Margo. 'Ve vas singing about blue eyes, vere ve
:, Donald?'

We *were* singing about blue eyes,' said Donald.

Dat's what I said,' said Max benevolently.

You said "was",' said Donald.

Max thought about this for a brief moment.

Any vay,' he said, 'de eyes vas blue.'

Were blue,' said Donald.

Oh, there you are,' said Margo, breathlessly, as Larry and
ame in. 'I think these are friends of yours, Larry.'

'Larry!' bellowed Max, lurching up with the ungainly grace
a giraffe, 've have come like you told us.'

How very nice,' said Larry, forcing his sleep-crumpled
tures into something approaching an ingratiating smile.
) you mind keeping your voice down because my mother's
?'

Muzzers,' said Max, with immense conviction, 'are de most
ortant thing in de vorld.'

Ie turned to Donald, laid a long finger across his moustache
I said 'Shush' with such violence that Roger, who had sunk
) a peaceful sleep, immediately leapt to his feet and started
king wildly. Widdle and Puke joined in vociferously.

Damned bad form that,' observed Donald between the
ks. 'Guests should not make his host's dogs bark.'

Max went down on his knees and engulfed the still barking
ger in his long arms, a manoeuvre that I viewed with some
rm, since Roger, I felt, was quite capable of misinterpreting

Hush, Bow-Wow,' said Max, beaming into Roger's bristl-
and belligerent face.

To my astonishment, Roger immediately stopped barking
I started to lick Max's face extravagantly.

Would you . . ., er . . ., like a drink?' said Larry. 'I can't
you to stop long, of course, because unfortunately my
ther's ill.'

Very civil of you,' said Donald. 'Very civil indeed. I must
logise for him. Foreigner, you know.'

Well, I think I'll just go back to bed,' said Margo, edging
atively towards the door.

141

'No you won't,' Larry barked. 'Somebody's got to pour the drinks.'

'Do not,' said Max, reclining on the floor with Roger in arms and gazing at her piteously, 'do not remove doze e from my orbit.'

'Well, I'll go and get the drinks, then,' said Margo brea lessly.

'And I vill help you,' said Max, casting Roger from l and leaping to his feet.

Roger had been under the misguided impression that M had intended to spend the rest of the night cuddling him front of the dying fire, and so was not unnaturally put when he was thrown aside like this. He started barking aga

The door of the drawing-room burst open and Leslie, sta naked except for a shot gun under his arm, made his appe ance.

'What the bloody hell's going on?' he asked truculently.

'Leslie, *do* go and put some clothes on,' said Margo. 'Th are friends of Larry's.'

'Oh, God,' said Leslie, dismally, 'not *more.*'

He turned and made his way back upstairs.

'Drinks!' said Max rapturously, seizing Margo in his ar and waltzing her around to the accompaniment of alm hysterical barks on the part of Roger.

'I do wish you would try to be more quiet,' said Lar 'Max, for Christ's sake.'

'Damned bad form,' said Donald.

'Remember my mother,' said Larry, since this reference l obviously struck a chord in Max's soul.

Immediately he ceased waltzing with the breathless Ma and came to a halt.

'Vere is your muzzer?' he enquired. 'De lady is sick . take me to her dat I may secure her.'

'Succour,' said Donald.

'I'm here,' said Mother in a slightly nasal tone of voice fr the doorway. 'What *is* going on?'

She was clad in her nightie and wearing, for reasons of cold, a voluminous shawl over her shoulders. She carried un one arm the drooping, panting, apathetic figure of Dodo, dog.

'Why, you're just in time, Mother,' said Larry. 'I want you
meet Donald and Max.'

With the first sign of animation that he had shown, Donald
se to his feet, marched swiftly across the room to Mother,
ized her hand and gave a slight bow over it.

'Enchanted,' he said. 'Terribly sorry about the disturbance.
y friend, you know. Continental.'

'How nice to see you,' said Mother, summoning up all her
sources.

At her entrance, Max had thrown his arms wide and was
w gazing upon her with all the devoutness of a Crusader
tching his first sight of Jerusalem.

'Muzzer!' he intoned dramatically. 'You are de muzzer!'

'How do you do,' said Mother, uncertainly.

'You are,' Max asked, getting his facts straight, 'de sick
uzzer?'

'Oh, it's just a bit of a cold,' said Mother, deprecatingly.

'Ve have voked you,' said Max, clasping his breast, his eyes
imming with tears.

'Awoken or woken,' said Donald, sotto voce.

'Come,' said Max, putting his long arms round Mother, and
hered her to a chair near the fire, pressing her into it with the
most delicacy. He took off his coat and spread it gently about
r knees. Then he squatted by her side, took her hand and
ered earnestly into her face.

'Vhat,' he enquired, 'does Muzzer vant?'

'An uninterrupted night's sleep,' said Leslie, who had just
turned, more conventionally garbed in a pair of pyjama
users and sandals.

'Max,' said Donald sternly. 'Stop monopolizing the con-
rsation. Remember what we have come for.'

'Of course,' said Max delightedly. 'Ve have vunderful news,
rry. Donald has decided to become an author.'

'Had to,' murmured Donald modestly. 'Seeing all you chaps
ing in the lap of luxury. Royalties pouring in. Felt I must
' my hand at it.'

'That's jolly good,' said Larry, with a certain lack of enthu-
sm.

'I've just completed,' said Donald, 'the first chapter and so
came out hot foot, as it were, so that I could read it to you.'

'Oh, God,' said Larry horrified. 'No, Donald, really. ▌
critical faculties are completely dehydrated at half past two ▌
the morning. Can't you leave it here and I'll read it ▌
morrow?'

'It's short,' said Donald, taking no notice of Larry and p▌
ducing a small sheet of paper from his pocket, 'but I thi▌
you will find the style interesting.'

Larry gave an exasperated sigh and we all sat back a▌
listened expectantly while Donald cleared his throat.

'Suddenly,' he began in a deep vibrant voice, 'sudden▌
suddenly, suddenly, there he was and then, suddenly, there▌
was, suddenly, suddenly suddenly. And suddenly he looked▌
her, suddenly, suddenly, suddenly, and she suddenly looked▌
him, suddenly. She suddenly opened her arms, suddenly, s▌
denly, and he opened his arms, suddenly. Then suddenly t▌
came together and, suddenly, suddenly, suddenly, he co▌
feel the warmth of her body and suddenly, suddenly she co▌
feel the warmth of his mouth on hers as they suddenly, s▌
denly, suddenly, suddenly fell on the couch together.'

There was a long pause while we waited for Donald to ▌
on. He gulped once or twice as though overcome with emot▌
at his own writing, folded the piece of paper carefully and ▌
it back in his pocket.

'What do you think?' he enquired of Larry.

'Well, it's a bit short,' said Larry, cautiously.

'Ah, but what do you think of the style?' said Donald▌

'Well, it's um, interesting,' said Larry. 'I think you'll ▌
it's been done before, though.'

'Couldn't have been,' explained Donald. 'You see, I o▌
thought of it tonight.'

'I don't think he ought to have any more to drink,' s▌
Leslie loudly.

'Hush, dear,' said Mother. 'What do you intend to call▌
Donald?'

'I thought,' said Donald, owlishly, 'I thought I would cal▌
THE SUDDENLY BOOK.'

'A very trenchant title,' said Larry. 'I feel, however, t▌
your main characters could be padded out a little bit, in de▌
as it were, before you get them all tangled up on the sofa▌

'Yes,' said Donald. 'You could well be right.'

'Well, that *is* interesting,' said Mother, sneezing violen▌

And now I think we really all ought to have a cup of tea.'

'I vill make de tea for you, Muzzer,' said Max, leaping to his
eet and starting all the dogs barking again.

'I will help you,' said Donald.

'Margo, dear, you had better go with them and just make
ure they find everything,' said Mother.

When the three of them had left the room, Mother looked
t Larry.

'And these are the people,' she said coldly, 'you say are not
ccentric.'

'Well, Donald's not eccentric,' said Larry. 'He's just a bit
igh.'

'And suddenly, suddenly, suddenly, suddenly he was drunk,'
toned Leslie, putting some more logs on the fire and kicking
into some semblance of a blaze.

'They are both of them very good chaps,' said Larry.
)onald's already laid half of Corfu by its ears.'

'What do you mean?' said Mother.

'Well, you know how the Corfiots love to worm every
dden secret out of you,' said Larry. 'They're all convinced
at, since he appears to have private means and is so incred-
ly British, he must have a terribly posh background. So he
s been amusing himself by telling them all different stories.
e has so far, I have been assured, been the elder son of a
ke, the cousin of the Bishop of London and the illegitimate
n of Lord Chesterfield. He has been educated at Eton,
arrow, Oxford, Cambridge and, to my delight, this morning
rs Papanopoulos assured me that his formal education had
en undertaken at Girton.'

Just at that moment Margo came back into the drawing-
om, looking slightly distraught.

'I think you had better come and do something with them,
rry,' she said. 'Max has just lit the kitchen fire with a five
und note and Donald has disappeared and keeps shouting
ooee" at us and we can't see where he's gone.'

All of us trooped down to the gigantic stone-flagged kitchen
ere a kettle was starting to sing on one of the charcoal fires
I Max was contemplating, woefully, the charred remains of
ve pound note which he held in one hand.

Really, Max,' said Mother, 'what a silly thing to do.'
Max beamed at her.

'No expense spared for Muzzer,' he said, and then pressi
the remains of the fiver into her hand, 'Keep it, Muzzer, a
souvenir.'

'Cooee,' came a doleful, echoing cry.

'That's Donald,' said Max, proudly.

'Where is he?' said Mother.

'I don't know,' said Max. 'Ven he vants to hide, he vants
hide.'

Leslie strode to the back door and flung it open.

'Donald,' he called, 'are you there?'

'Cooee,' came a quavering cry from Donald with sub
echoing overtones.

'Christ!' said Leslie. 'The silly bastard's fallen down
well.'

In the garden at the back of the kitchen there was a la
well some fifty feet deep with a thick, round, iron pipe runni
right down the shaft. From the echoing qualities of Dona
voice, we were quite sure that Leslie's guess was right. Car
ing a lamp, we made our way hurriedly up to the edge of
well, and peered, in a circle, down into its dark depths. Ha
way down the pipe was Donald, his arms and legs entwir
firmly round it. He gazed up at us.

'Cooee,' he said coyly.

'Donald, don't be a bloody fool,' said Larry exasperated
'Come up out of there. If you fall into that water yo
drown. Not that I worry about that, but you'll pollute
entire water supply.'

'Shan't,' said Donald.

'Donald,' said Max, 'we vant you. Come. It is cold do
dere. Come and have some tea with Muzzer and ve will t
about your book.'

'Do you insist?' asked Donald.

'Yes, yes, we insist,' said Larry impatiently.

Slowly and laboriously Donald climbed up the pipe, wh
we watched him breathlessly. When he was within rea
Max and the entire family leant over the wall, grabbed vari
portions of his anatomy and hauled him to safety. Then
escorted our guests back into the house and plied them w
vast quantities of hot tea until they seemed as sober as th
were likely to be without having slept.

'I think you had better go home now,' said Larry firmly, and we'll meet you in town tomorrow.'

We escorted them out on to the veranda. The cab stood, with the horse drooping forlornly between the shafts. The cab driver was nowhere to be seen.

'Did they have a driver?' Larry asked of me.

I said that, quite honestly, I had been so captivated by the sight of their candelabras that I had not noticed.

'I vill drive,' said Max, 'and Donald shall sing to me.'

Donald arranged himself carefully in the back of the cab with the candelabras and Max took to the driving-seat. He cracked the whip in a most professional manner and the horse roused itself from its comatose condition, gave a sigh and ambled off down the drive.

'Goodnight,' shouted Max, waving his whip.

We waited until they had disappeared from sight behind the olive trees, then trooped back inside the house and, with sighs of heartfelt relief, closed the front door.

'Really, Larry, you shouldn't invite people at this hour of night,' said Mother.

'I didn't invite them at this hour of the night,' said Larry annoyed. 'They just came. I invited them for drinks.'

Just at that moment there was a thunderous knocking on the front door.

'Well, I'm off,' said Mother and scuttled upstairs with considerable alacrity.

Larry opened the front door and there stood the distraught figure of the cab driver.

'Where's my *carrochino*?' he shouted.

'Where were you?' retorted Larry. 'The *kyrios* have taken
.

'They have stolen my *carrochino*?' shouted the man.

'Of course they haven't stolen it, foolish one,' said Larry, now tried beyond endurance. 'Because you weren't waiting here they took it to get back into town. If you run quickly you can catch them up.'

Imploring Saint Spiridion to help him, the man ran off through the olive trees and down towards the road.

Determined not to miss the last act in this drama, I ran to a vantage point where I got a clear view of the entrance to our

147

drive and a stretch of moonlit roadway which led into town.
The cab had just left the drive and arrived on the road at a
brisk walk, Donald and Max singing happily together. At that
moment the cab driver appeared through the olives and,
screaming imprecations, started to run after them.

Max, startled, looked over his shoulder.

'Volves, Donald,' he shouted. 'Hold tight!' He proceeded
to belabour the unfortunate behind of the horse who, startled,
broke into a gallop. But it was the sort of gallop that only a
Corfu cab horse could achieve, just fast enough to keep the
cab owner running at full stretch some ten paces behind the
cab. He was shouting and imploring and almost weeping with
rage. Max, determined to save Donald at all costs, was belabouring the horse unmercifully while Donald leant over the
back of the cab and shouted 'Bang!' at intervals. Thus they
disappeared out of my sight along the Corfu road.

The following morning, at breakfast, all of us felt slightly
jaded, and Mother was lecturing Larry severely for allowing
people to turn up at two o'clock in the morning for drinks.
Just at that moment, Spiro's car drove up to the front of the
house and he waddled on to the veranda where we were sitting,
clasping in his arms an enormous, flat brown paper parcel.

'This is for yous, Mrs Durrells,' he said.

'For me?' said Mother, adjusting her spectacles. 'What on
earth can it be?'

She unwrapped the brown paper cautiously and there, inside, as bright as a rainbow, was the biggest box of chocolates
I had ever seen in my life. Pinned to it was a little white card
on which had been written in a rather shaky hand, 'With
apologies for last night. Donald and Max'.

Owls and Aristocracy

Now winter was upon us. Everything was redolent with the smoke of olive wood fires. The shutters creaked and slapped the sides of the house as the wind caught them, and the birds and leaves were tumbled across a dark lowering sky. The brown mountains of the mainland wore tattered caps of snow and the rain filled the eroded, rocky valleys, turning them into foaming torrents that fled eagerly to the sea, carrying mud and debris with them. Once they reached the sea they spread like yellow veins through the blue water and the surface was dotted with squill bulbs, logs and twisted branches, dead beetles and butterflies, clumps of brown grass and splintered canes. Storms would brew amongst the whitened spikes of the Albanian mountains and then tumble across to us, great black piles of cumulus, spitting a stinging rain, with sheet lightning blooming and dying like yellow ferns across the sky.

It was at the beginning of the winter that I received a letter.

Dear Gerald Durrell,

I understand from our mutual friend, Dr Stephanides, that you are a keen naturalist and possess a number of pets. I was wondering, therefore, if you would care to have a white owl which my workmen found in an old shed they were demolishing? He has, unfortunately, a broken wing, but is otherwise in good health and feeding well.

If you would like him, I suggest you come to lunch on Friday and take him with you when you return home. Perhaps you would be kind enough to let me know. A quarter to one for one o'clock would be suitable.

Yours sincerely,
Countess Mavrodaki

This letter excited me for two reasons. Firstly because I had always wanted a barn owl, for that was what it obviously was, and, secondly, because the whole of Corfu society had been

trying unavailingly for years to get to know the Countess.
She was the recluse *par excellence*. Immensely wealthy, she
lived in a gigantic, rambling Venetian villa deep in the country
and never entertained or saw anybody except the workmen on
her vast estate. Her acquaintance with Theodore was only due
to the fact that he was her medical adviser. The Countess was
reputed to possess a large and valuable library and for this
reason Larry had been most anxious to try and get himself invited to her villa, but without success.

'Dear God,' he said bitterly, when I showed him my invitation, 'Here I've been, trying for months to get that old harpy
to let me see her books and she invites you to lunch—there's
no justice in the world.'

I said that after I had lunched with the Countess, maybe
I could ask her if he could see her books.

'After she's had lunch with you I shouldn't think she would
be willing to show me a copy of *The Times*, let alone her
library,' said Larry witheringly.

However, in spite of my brother's low opinion of my social
graces, I was determined to put in a good word for him if I
saw a suitable opportunity. It was, I felt, an important, even
solemn occasion, and so I dressed with care. My shirt and
shorts were carefully laundered and I had prevailed upon
Mother to buy me a new pair of sandals and a new straw hat.
I rode on Sally—who had a new blanket as a saddle to honour
the occasion—for the Countess's estate was some distance
away.

The day was dark and the ground mushy under foot. It
looked as though we would have a storm, but I hoped this
would not be until after I had arrived, for the rain would spoil
the crisp whiteness of my shirt. As we jogged along through the
olives, the occasional woodcock zooming up from the myrtle
in front of us, I became increasingly nervous. I discovered that
I was ill-prepared for this occasion. To begin with I had forgotten to bring my four-legged chicken in spirits. I had felt
sure that the Countess would want to see this and, in any case,
I felt it would provide a subject of conversation that would
help us in the initial awkward stages of our meeting. Secondly,
I had forgotten to consult anybody on the correct way to
address a countess. 'Your Majesty' would surely be too formal,
I thought, especially as she was giving me an owl? Perhaps

'Highness' would be better, or maybe just a simple 'Ma'am'? Puzzling over the intricacies of protocol, I had left Sally to her own devices and she had promptly fallen into a donkey-doze. Of all the beasts of burden, only the donkey seems capable of falling asleep while still moving. The result was that she ambled close to the ditch at the side of the road, suddenly stumbled and lurched and I, deep in thought, fell off her back into six inches of mud and water. Sally stared down at me with the expression of accusing astonishment that she always wore when she knew she was in the wrong. I was so furious, I could have strangled her. My new sandals oozed, my shorts and shirt—so crisp, so clean, so *well-behaved-looking* a moment before—were now bespattered with mud and bits of decaying water-weeds. I almost wept with rage and frustration. We were too far from home to retrace our footsteps so that I could change; there was nothing for it but to go on, damp and miserable, convinced now that it did not matter how I addressed the Countess. She would, I felt sure, take one look at my gypsy-like condition and order me home. Not only would I lose my owl, but any chance I had of getting Larry in to see her library. I was a fool, I thought bitterly. I should have walked instead of trusting myself to this hopeless creature, who was now trotting along at a brisk pace, her ears pricked like furry arum lilies.

Presently we came to the Countess's villa, lying deep in the olive groves, approached by a drive lined with tall green and pink-trunked eucalyptus trees. The entrance to the drive was guarded by two columns on which were perched a pair of white-winged lions who stared scornfully at Sally and I as we trotted down the drive. The house was immense, built in a hollow square. It had at one time been a lovely rich Venetian red, but this had now faded to a rose pink, the plaster bulged and cracked in places, and I noted that a number of brown tiles were missing from the roof. The eaves had slung under them more swallows' nests—now empty, like small forgotten brown ovens—than I had ever seen congregated in one spot before.

I tied Sally up under a convenient tree and made my way to the archway that led into the central patio. Here a rusty chain hung down and when I pulled it I heard a bell jangle faintly somewhere in the depths of the house. I waited patiently for some time and was just about to ring the bell again when the massive wooden doors were opened. There stood a man who looked at me exactly like a bandit. He was tall and powerful, with a great jutting hawk-nose, sweeping flamboyant white moustache and a mane of curling white hair. He was wearing a scarlet *tarbush*, a loose white blouse beautifully embroidered with scarlet and gold thread, baggy pleated black pants and, on his feet, upturned *charukias* decorated with enormous red and white pom-poms. His brown face cracked into a grin and I saw that all his teeth were gold. It was like looking into a mint.

'*Kyrié* Durrell?' he enquired. 'Welcome.'

I followed him through the patio, full of magnolia trees and forlorn winter flower beds, and into the house. He led me down a long corridor tiled in scarlet and blue, threw open a door and ushered me into a great, gloomy room lined from ceiling to floor with bookshelves. At one end was a large fire-place in which a blaze flapped and hissed and crackled. Over the fire-place was an enormous gold-framed mirror, nearly black with age. Sitting by the fire on a long couch almost obliterated by coloured shawls and cushions, was the Countess.

She was not a bit what I had expected. I had visualised her as tall, gaunt and rather forbidding, but as she rose to her feet and danced across the room to me I saw that she was tiny, very fat and as pink and dimpled as a rose bud. Her honey-coloured hair was piled high on her head in a pompadour style and her eyes, under permanently arched and surprised eyebrows, were as green and shiny as unripe olives. She seized my hand in both her warm little pudgy ones and clasped it to her ample breast.

'How kind, how *kind* of you to come,' she exclaimed in a musical, little girl's voice, exuding an overpowering odour of Parma violets and brandy in equal quantities. 'How very, *very* kind. May I call you Gerry? Of course I may. My friends call me Matilda . . ., it isn't my *real* name, of course. That Stephani Zinia . . ., so uncouth—like a patent medicine. I *much* prefer Matilda, don't you?'

I said, cautiously, that I thought Matilda a very nice name.

'Yes, a comforting *old-fashioned* name. Names are *so* important, don't you think. Now he there,' she said, gesturing

152

the man who had shown me in, '*he* calls himself Demetrios. I call him Mustapha.'

She glanced at the man and then leant forward, nearly asphyxiating me with brandy and Parma violets and hissed suddenly, in Greek.

'He's a misbegotten Turk.'

The man's face grew red and his moustache bristled making him look more like a bandit than ever.

'I am not a Turk,' he snarled. 'You lie.'

'You are a Turk and your name's Mustapha,' she retorted.

'It isn't . . ., I'm not . . ., It isn't . . ., I'm not,' said the man, almost incoherent with rage. 'You are lying.'

'I'm not.'

'You are.'

'I'm not.'

'You are.'

'I'm *not*.'

'You're a damned elderly liar.'

'Elderly,' she squeaked, her face growing red. 'You dare to call me elderly . . ., you . . ., you *Turk* you.'

'You are elderly and you're fat,' said Demetrios-Mustapha coldly.

'That's too much,' she screamed, 'elderly . . ., fat . . . that's too much. You're sacked. Take a month's notice. No, leave this instant, you son of a misbegotten Turk.'

Demetrios-Mustapha drew himself up regally.

'Very well,' he said, 'do you wish me to serve the drinks and lunch before I go?'

'Of course,' she said.

In silence he crossed the room and extracted a bottle of champagne from an ice-bucket behind the sofa. He opened it and then poured equal quantities of brandy and champagne into three large glasses. He handed us one each and lifted the third himself.

'I give you a toast,' he said to me solemnly. 'We will drink the health of a fat, elderly liar.'

I was in a quandary. If I drank the toast it would seem that I was concurring in his opinion of the Countess, and that would scarcely seem polite; and yet, if I did not drink the toast he looked quite capable of doing me an injury. As I hesi-

tated, the Countess, to my astonishment, burst into delighted
giggles, her smooth fat cheeks dimpling charmingly.

'You mustn't tease our guest, Mustapha. But I must admit
the toast was a good touch,' she said, gulping at her drink.

Demetrios-Mustapha grinned at me, his teeth glittering and
winking in the firelight.

'Drink, kyrié,' he said. 'Take no notice of us. She lives for
food, drink and fighting and it is my job to provide all three.'

'Nonsense,' said the Countess seizing my hand and leading
me to the sofa so that I felt as though I was hitched to a small
fat, pink cloud. 'Nonsense, I live for a lot of things, a lot of
things. Now, don't stand there drinking my drink, you drunkard. Go and see to the food.'

Demetrios-Mustapha drained his glass and left the room
while the Countess seated herself on the sofa, clasping my hand
in hers and beaming at me.

'This is cosy,' she said delightedly. 'Just you and I. Tell me
do you always wear mud all over your clothes?'

I hastily and embarrassedly explained about Sally.

'So you came by donkey,' she said, making it sound a very
exotic form of transport. 'How wise of you. I distrust motor
cars myself, noisy, uncontrollable things. Unreliable. I remember we had one when my husband was alive, a big
yellow one. But, my dear, it was a brute. It would obey my
husband, but it would not do a thing I told it to do. One day
it deliberately backed into a large stall containing fruit and
vegetables—in spite of all I was trying to do to stop it—and
then went over the edge of the harbour into the sea. When
came out of hospital, I said to my husband, "Henri," I said—
that was his name—such a nice, bourgeois name, don't you
think? Where was I? Oh yes. Well, "Henri," I said, "the
car's malevolent," I said. "It's possessed of an evil spirit. You
must sell it." And so he did.'

Brandy and champagne on an empty stomach combined
with the fire to make me feel extremely mellow. My head
whirled pleasantly and I nodded and smiled as the Countess
chattered on.

'My husband was a very cultured man, very cultured indeed.
He collected books, you know. Books, paintings, stamps, beer
bottle tops, anything cultural appealed to him. Just before

154

died, he started collecting busts of Napoleon. You would be surprised how many busts they had made of that horrible little Corsican. My husband had five hundred and eighty-two. 'Henri,' I said to him, "Henri, this must stop. Either you give up collecting busts of Napoleon or I will leave you and go to St Helena." I said it as a joke though, only as a joke, and you know what he said? He said he had been thinking about going to St Helena for a holiday—with all his busts. My God, what dedication! It was not to be borne! I believe in a little bit of culture in its place, but not to become *obsessed* with it.'

Demetrios-Mustapha came into the room, refilled our glasses and said,

'Lunch in five minutes.'

'He was what you might call a *compulsive* collector, my dear. The times that I trembled when I saw that fanatical gleam in his eye. At a state fair once he saw a combine harvester, simply immense it was, and I could *see* the gleam in his eyes, but I put my foot down. "Henri," I said to him, "Henri, we are not going to have combine harvesters all over the place. If you must collect, why not something sensible? Jewels, or furs or something?" It may seem harsh, my dear, but what could I do? If I had relaxed for an *instant* he would have had the whole house full of farm machinery.'

Demetrios-Mustapha came into the room again.

'Lunch is ready,' he said.

Still chattering, the Countess led me by the hand out of the room, down the tiled corridor, then down some creaking wooden stairs into a huge kitchen in the cellars. The kitchen at our villa was enormous enough, but this kitchen simply dwarfed it. It was stone-flagged and at one end a positive battery of charcoal fires glowed and winked under the bubbling pots. The walls were covered with a great variety of copper pots, kettles, platters, coffee pots, huge serving dishes and soup tureens. They all glowed with a pinky-red gleam in the firelight, glinting and winking like tiger beetles. In the centre of the floor was a twelve-foot-long dining-table of beautiful polished walnut. This was carefully set for two with snowy-white serviettes and gleaming cutlery. In the centre of the table two giant silver candelabras each held a white forest of lighted candles. The effect of a kitchen and a state dining-room combined was very odd. It was very hot and so redolent with delicious smells that they almost suffocated the Countess's scent.

'I hope you don't mind eating in the kitchen,' said the Countess, making it sound as though it was really the most degrading thing to eat food in such humble surroundings.

I said I thought eating in the kitchen was a most sensible idea, especially in winter as it was warmer.

'Quite right,' said the Countess, seating herself as Demetrios Mustapha held her chair for her. 'And, you see, if we eat upstairs I get complaints from this elderly Turk about how far he has to walk.'

'It isn't the distance I complain of, it's the weight of the food,' said Demetrios-Mustapha, pouring a pale greeny-gold wine into our glasses. 'If you didn't eat so much, it wouldn't be so bad.'

'Oh, stop complaining and get on with serving,' said the Countess plaintively, tucking her serviette carefully under her dimpled chin.

I, filled with champagne and brandy, was now more than a little drunk and ravenously hungry. I viewed with alarm the number of eating utensils that were flanking my plate, for I was not quite sure which to use first. I remembered Mother's maxim that you started on the outside and worked in, but was still uneasy. I decided to wait, see what the Countess used and then follow suit. It was an unwise decision for I soon discovered that she used any and every knife, fork or spoon with a fine lack of discrimination and so, before long, I became so muddled that I was doing the same.

The first course that Demetrios-Mustapha set before us was a fine, clear soup, sequined with tiny golden bubbles of fat, with finger-nail size croutons floating like crisp little rafts on an amber sea. It was delicious and the Countess had two helpings, scrunching up the croutons, the noise like someone walking over crisp leaves. Demetrios-Mustapha filled our glasses with more of the pale, musky wine and placed before us a platter of minute baby fish, each one fried a golden brown. Slices of yellow green lemons in a large dish and a brimming sauce-boat of some exotic sauce unknown to me accompanied it. The Countess piled her plate high with fish, added a lavish flow of sauce and then squeezed lemon juice lavishly over the fish, the table and herself. She beamed at me, her face now a bright rose pink, her forehead slightly beaded with sweat. Her prodigious appetite did not appear to impair her conversational powers one jot, for she talked incessantly.

'Don't you love these little fish? Heavenly! Of course, it's such a pity that they should die so *young*, but there we are. *So* nice to be able to eat *all* of them without worrying about the bones. *Such* a relief! Henri, my husband you know, started to collect skeletons once. My dear, the house looked and smelt like a mortuary. "Henri," I said to him, "Henri, this must stop. This is an unhealthy death wish you have developed. You must go and see a psychiatrist".'

Demetrios-Mustapha removed our empty plates, poured red wine out for us, dark as the heart of a dragon, and then placed before us a dish in which lay snipe, the heads twisted round so that their long beaks could skewer themselves and their empty eye-sockets look at us accusingly. They were plump and brown with cooking, each having its own little square of toast. They were surrounded by thin wafers of fried potatoes like drifts of autumn leaves, pale greeny-white candles of asparagus and small peas.

'I simply cannot understand people who are vegetarians,' said the Countess, banging vigorously at a snipe's skull with her fork so that she might crack it and get to the brain. 'Henri once tried to be a vegetarian. Would you believe it? But I couldn't endure it. "Henri," I said to him, "this must stop. We have enough food in the larder to feed an army, and I can't eat it single-handed." Imagine, my dear, I had just ordered two dozen hares. "Henri," I said, "you will have to give up this foolish fad".'

It struck me that Henri, although obviously a bit of a trial as a husband, had nevertheless led a very frustrated existence. Demetrios-Mustapha cleared away the debris of the snipe and poured out more wine. I was beginning to feel bloated with food and hoped that there was not too much more to come. But there was still an army of knives and forks and spoons, unused, beside my plate, so it was with alarm I saw Demetrios-Mustapha approaching through the gloomy kitchen bearing a huge dish.

'Ah!' said the Countess, holding up her plump hands in excitement. 'The main dish! What is it, Mustapha, what is it?'

'The wild boar that Makroyannis sent,' said Demetrios-Mustapha.

'Oh, the boar! The *boar*!' squeaked the Countess, clasping her fat cheeks in her hands, 'Oh lovely! I had forgotten all about it. You do like wild boar, I hope?'

I said that it was one of my favourite meats, which was true, but could I have a very small helping, please?

'But of course you shall,' she said, leaning over the great brown, gravy-glistening haunch and starting to cut thick, pink slabs of it. She placed three of these on a plate—obviously under the impression that this was, by anyone's standards, a small portion—and then proceeded to surround them with the accoutrements. There were piles of the lovely little golden wild mushrooms, *chanterelles*, with their delicate, almost winy flavour; tiny marrows stuffed with sour cream and capers; potatoes baked in their skins neatly split and annointed with butter; carrots red as a frosty winter sun and great tree trunk of white leeks, poached in cream. I surveyed this dish of food and surreptitiously undid the top three buttons of my shorts.

'We used to get wild boar *such* a lot when Henri was alive. He used to go to Albania and shoot them, you know. But now we seldom have it. What a *treat*! Will you have some more mushrooms? No? *So* good for one. After this, I think we will have a pause. A pause is essential, I always think, for a good digestion,' said the Countess, adding naïvely, 'and it enable you to eat so much *more*.'

The wild boar was fragrant and succulent, having been marinaded well with herb-scented wine and stuffed with garli cloves, but even so I only just managed to finish it. The Count ess had two helpings, both identical in size, and then leant back her face congested to a pale puce colour and mopped the swe from her brow with an inadequate lace handkerchief.

'A pause, eh?' she said thickly, smiling at me. 'A pause marshal our resources.'

I felt that I had not any resources to marshal, but I d not like to say so. I nodded and smiled and undid all the r of the buttons on my shorts.

During the pause, the Countess smoked on a long th cheroot and ate salted peanuts, chatting on interminably abo her husband. The pause did me good. I felt a little less solid and somnolent. When the Countess eventually decided that we had rested our internal organs sufficiently, she called for the next course and Demetrios-Mustapha produced two mercifully small omelets, crisp brown on the outside and liquid and succulent on the inside, stuffed with tiny pink shrimps.

'What have you got for sweet?' enquired the Countess, her mouth full of omelet.

'I didn't make one,' said Demetrios-Mustapha.

The Countess's eyes grew round and fixed.

'You didn't make a sweet?' she said in tones of horror, as though he were confessing to some heinous crime.

'I didn't have time,' said Demetrios-Mustapha. 'You can't expect me to do all this cooking and all the housework.'

'But no *sweet*,' said the Countess, despairingly. 'You can't have a lunch without a sweet.'

'Well, I bought you some meringues,' said Mustapha. 'You'll have to make do with those.'

'Oh, lovely!' said the Countess glowing and happy again. 'Just what's needed.'

It was the last thing I needed. The meringues were large and white and brittle as coral and stuffed to overflowing with cream. I wished fervently that I had brought Roger with me, as he could have sat under the table and accepted half my food, since the Countess was far too occupied with her own plate and her reminiscences really to concentrate on me.

'Now,' she said at last, swallowing the last mouthful of meringue and brushing the white crumbs from her chin. 'Now, do you feel replete? Or would you care for a little something more? Some fruit perhaps? Not that there's very much at this time of the year.'

I said no, thank you very much, I had had quite sufficient. The Countess sighed and looked at me soulfully. I think nothing would have pleased her more than to ply me with another two or three courses.

'You don't eat enough,' she said. 'A growing boy like you should eat more. You're far too thin for your age. Does your mother feed you properly?'

I could imagine Mother's wrath if she had heard this innuendo. I said yes, Mother was an excellent cook and we all fed like lords.

'I'm glad to hear it,' said the Countess. 'But you still look a
little peaky to me.'

I could not say so, but the reason I was beginning to look
peaky was that the assault of food upon my stomach was beginning to make itself felt. I said, as politely as I could, that I
thought I ought to be getting back.

'But of course, dear,' said the Countess. 'Dear me, a quarter
past four already. How time flies.'

She sighed at the thought, then brightened perceptibly.

'However, it's nearly time for tea. Are you sure you
wouldn't like to stay and have something?'

I said no, that Mother would be worried about me.

'Now, let me see,' said the Countess. 'What did you come
for? Oh, yes, the owl. Mustapha, bring the boy his owl and
bring me some coffee and some of those nice Turkish delight
up in the lounge.'

Mustapha appeared with a cardboard box done up with
string and handed it to me.

'I wouldn't open it until you get home,' he said. 'That's a
wild one, that.'

I was overcome with the terrifying thought that, if I did not
hurry my departure, the Countess would ask me to partake of
Turkish delight with her. So I thanked them both sincerely
for my owl, and made my way to the front door.

'Well,' said the Countess, 'it has been enchanting having
you, *absolutely enchanting*. You must come again. You must
come in the spring or the summer when we have got more
choice of fruit and vegetables. Mustapha's got a way of cooking octopus which makes it simply melt in your mouth.'

I said I would love to come again, making a mental vow
that, if I did, I would starve for three days in advance.

'Here,' said the Countess pressing an orange into my pocket,
'take this. You might feel peckish on the way home.'

As I mounted Sally and trotted off down the drive, she
called, 'Drive carefully.'

Grim-faced I sat there with the owl clasped to my bosom till
we were outside the gates of the Countess's estate. Then the
jogging I was subjected to on Sally's back was too much. I
dismounted, went behind an olive tree and was deliciously and
flamboyantly sick.

When I got home, I carried the owl up to my bedroom, untied the box and lifted him, struggling and beak-clicking out on to the floor. The dogs, who had gathered round in a circle to view the new addition, backed away hurriedly. They knew what Ulysses could do when he was in a bad temper, and this owl was three times his size. He was, I thought, one of the most beautiful birds I had ever seen. The feathers on his back and wings were honey-comb golden, smudged with pale ash grey; his breast was a spotless cream white and the mask of white feathers round his dark, strangely Oriental-looking eyes, was as crisp and as starched-looking as any Elizabethan's ruff. His wing was not as bad as I had feared. It was a clean break and after half an hour's struggle, during which he managed to draw blood on several occasions, I had it splinted up to my satisfaction. The owl, which I had decided to call Lampadusa, simply because the name appealed to me, seemed to be belligerently scared of the dogs, totally unwilling to make friends with Ulysses and viewed Augustus Tickletummy with undisguised loathing. I felt he might be happier, till he settled down, in a dark, secluded place, so I carried him up to the attics. One of the attic rooms was very tiny and lit by one small window which was so covered with cobwebs and dust that it allowed little light to penetrate. It was quiet and as dim as a cave, and I thought that here Lampadusa would enjoy his convalescence. I put him on the floor with a large saucer of chopped meat and locked the door carefully so that he would not be disturbed. That evening, when I went to visit him, taking him a dead mouse by way of a present, he seemed very much improved. He had eaten most of his meat and now hissed and beak-clicked at me with outspread wings and blazing eyes as he teeter-pattered about the floor. Encouraged by his obvious progress, I left him with his mouse, and went to bed.

Some hours later I was woken by the sound of voices emanating from Mother's room. Wondering, sleepily, what on earth the family could be doing at that hour, I got out of bed and stuck my head out of the bedroom door to listen.

'I tell you,' Larry was saying, 'it's a damned great poltergeist.'

'It can't be a poltergeist, dear,' said Mother. 'Poltergeists throw things.'

'Well, whatever it is, it's up there clanking its chains,' sa[i]
Larry, 'and I want it exorcised. You and Margo are suppose[d]
to be the experts on the after-life. You go up and do it.'

'I'm not going up there,' said Margo tremulously. 'It mig[ht]
be anything. It might be a malignant spirit.'

'It's bloody malignant all right,' said Larry. 'It's been keepin[g]
me awake for the last hour.'

'Are you sure it isn't the wind or something, dear?' ask[ed]
Mother.

'I know the difference between wind and a damned gho[st]
playing around with balls and chains,' said Larry.

'Perhaps it's burglars,' said Margo, more to give hers[elf]
confidence than anything else. 'Perhaps it's burglars and [we]
ought to wake Leslie.'

Half-asleep and still bee-drowsy from the liquor I had co[n-]
sumed that day, I could not think what the family were talki[ng]
about. It sounded as intriguing as any of the other crises th[at]
they were capable of evoking at the most unexpected hours [of]
the day or night, so I went to Mother's door and peered in[to]
the room. Larry was marching up and down, his dressin[g]
gown swishing imperially.

'Something's got to be done,' he said. 'I can't sleep w[ith]
rattling chains over my head, and if I can't sleep I can't writ[e.]'

'I don't see what you expect *us* to do about it, dear,' sa[id]
Mother. 'I'm sure it must be the wind.'

'Yes, you can't expect us to go up there,' said Mar[go.]
'You're a man, *you* go.'

'Look,' said Larry, 'you are the one who came back fr[om]
London covered with ectoplasm and talking about the infin[ite.]
It's probably some hellish thing you've conjured up from [one]
of your seances that's followed you here. That makes it y[our]
pet. You go and deal with it.'

The word 'pet' penetrated. Surely it could not be Lam[b-]
dusa? Like all owls, barn owls have wings as soft and as si[lent]
as dandelion clocks. Surely he could not be responsible [for]
making a noise like a ball and chain?

I went into the room and enquired what they were all ta[lk-]
ing about.

'It's only a ghost, dear,' said Mother, soothingly. 'Lar[ry's]
found a ghost.'

'It's in the attic,' said Margo, excitedly. 'Larry thinks it followed me from England. I wonder if it's Mawake?'

'We're not going to start *that* all over again,' said Mother firmly.

'I don't care who it is,' said Larry. 'Which one of your disembodied friends. I want it removed.'

I said I thought there was just the faintest possibility that it might be Lampadusa.

'What's that?' enquired Mother.

I explained that it was the owl the Countess had given me.

'I might have known it,' said Larry. 'I might have known. Why it didn't occur to me instantly, I don't know.'

'Now, now, dear,' said Mother. 'It's only an owl.'

'Only an owl!' said Larry. 'It sounds like a battalion of tanks crashing about up there. Tell him to get it out of the loft.'

I said I could not understand why Lampadusa was making noise since owls were the quietest of things . . ., I said they drifted through the night on silent wings like flakes of ash . . .

'This one hasn't got silent wings,' said Larry. 'It sounds like one owl jazz band. Go and get it *out*!'

Hurriedly I took a lamp and made my way up to the attic. When I opened the door I saw at once what the trouble was. Lampadusa had devoured his mouse and then discovered that there was a long shred of meat still lying in his saucer. This, during the course of the long, hot day, had solidified and become welded to the surface of the saucer. Lampadusa, feeling that this shred of meat would do well as a light snack to keep body and soul together until dawn, had endeavoured to pick it off the plate. The curve of his sharp amber beak had gone through the meat, but the meat had refused to part company with the saucer, so that there he was, effectively trapped, flopping ineffectually around the floor, banging and clattering the saucer against the wooden boards in an effort to disentangle it from his beak. So I extricated him from this predicament and carried him down to my bedroom where I shut him in his carboard box for safe keeping.

PART IV

Criseda

This place is wonderfully lovely. I wish you could see it; if you came I could put you up beautifully, and feed you on Ginger-beer and claret and prawns and figs.

EDWARD LEAR

Hedgehogs and Sea Dogs

When spring came, we moved to a new villa, an elegant, snow-white one shaded by a huge magnolia tree, that lay in the olive groves not far from where our very first villa had been. It was on a hillside overlooking a great flat area marked out like a gigantic chess board by irrigation ditches, which I knew as the fields. They were in fact the old Venetian salt pans used long ago for collecting the brine that floated into the channels from the big salt-water lake on whose shores they lay. The lake had long since silted up and the channels, now flooded by fresh water from the hills, provided a grid-work of lush fields. This was an area overflowing with wildlife and so it was one of my happiest hunting-grounds.

Spring in Corfu was never half-hearted. Almost overnight, it seemed, the winter winds had blown the skies clean of cloud so that they shone a clear delphinium-blue and overnight the winter rains had flooded the valleys with wild flowers; the pink of pyramid orchids, yellow of crocus, tall pale spikes of the asphodels, the blue eyes of the grape hyacinths peering at you from the grass, and the wine-dipped anemones that bowed in the slightest breeze. The olive groves were alive and rustling with the newly arrived birds; the hoopoes, salmon pink and black with surprised crests, probed their long curved beaks at the soft earth between the clumps of emerald grass; goldfinches, chiming and wheezing, danced merrily from twig to twig, their plumage glowing gold and scarlet and black. In the irrigation ditches the waters became green with weed, interlaced with the strings of toad spawn, like black pearl necklaces; emerald-green frogs croaked at each other, and the water tortoises, their shells as black as ebony, crawled up the banks to dig their holes and lay their eggs. Steel-blue dragonflies, slender as threads, hatched and drifted like smoke through the undergrowth, moving in a curious stiff flight. Now was the time when the banks at night were lit by the throbbing, green-white light of a thousand

glow worms and, in the day time, by the glint of wild straw-
berries hanging like scarlet lanterns in the shade. It was an
exciting time, a time for explorations and new discoveries, a
time when an overturned log might reveal almost anything
from a field vole's nest to a wriggling glitter of baby slow
worms, looking as though they were cast in burnished bronze.

I was down in the fields one day, trying to catch some of the
brown water snakes that inhabited the irrigation ditches, when
an old woman, whom I knew slightly, called me from some
six fields away. She had been digging up the ground with her
short-handled, broad-bladed hoe, standing up to her ankles in
the rich loam, wearing the thick, ungainly sheep's wool
stockings the peasants put on for this operation.

'I've found you something,' she called. 'Come quickly.'

It was impossible for me to get there quickly, for each field
was surrounded by an irrigation ditch on all four sides and so
finding the bridges across these was like finding your way
through a maze.

'Quickly! Quickly!' screamed the old woman. 'They are
running away. Quickly!'

I ran and leapt and scuttled, almost falling into the ditches,
racing across the rickety plank bridges, until, panting, I reached
her side.

'There,' she said, pointing. 'There. Mind they don't bite
you.'

I saw that she had dug up a bundle of leaves from under the
earth in which something white was moving. Gingerly I
parted the leaves with the handle of my butterfly net and saw
to my delight four fat, newly-born baby hedgehogs, pink as
cyclamen, with soft, snow-white spines. They were still blind
and they wriggled and nosed at each other like a litter of tiny
pigs. I picked them up and put them carefully inside my shirt,
thanked the old woman and made my way homewards. I was
excited about my new pets principally because they were so
young. I already had two adult hedgehogs, called Itch and
Scratch due to the vast quantities of fleas that they harboured,
but they were not really tame. These babies, I thought, would
grow up differently. I would be, as far as they were concerned,
their mother. I visualized myself walking proudly through the
olive groves, preceded by the dogs, Ulysses and my two mag-

ies and, trotting at my heels, four tame hedgehogs, all of which I would have taught to do tricks.

The family were arranged on the veranda under the grape vine, all occupied with their own affairs. Mother was knitting, counting the stitches audibly at intervals to herself and saying 'damn' periodically when she went wrong. Leslie was squatting on the flagstones, carefully weighing gunpowder and little piles of silver shot as he filled shiny red cartridge cases. Larry was reading a massive tome and occasionally glancing irritably at Margo who was clattering away at her machine, making some diaphanous garment, and singing, if key, the only line she knew of her favourite song of the moment.

'She wore her little jacket of blue,' she warbled. 'She wore her little jacket of blue. She wore her little jacket of blue. She wore her little jacket of blue.'

'The only remarkable thing about your singing is your tenacity,' said Larry. 'Anybody else, faced with the fact that they could not carry a tune and couldn't remember the simplest lyric, would have given up, defeated, a long time ago.'

He threw his cigarette butt down on the flagstones and this produced a roar of rage from Leslie.

'Watch the gunpowder,' he shouted.

'Leslie, dear,' said Mother, 'I do wish you wouldn't shout like that, you've made me lose count.'

I produced my hedgehogs proudly and showed them to Mother.

'Aren't they sweet,' she said, peering at them benignly through her spectacles.

'Oh God! He hasn't got something new, has he?' asked Larry. He peered with distaste at my pink progeny in their white fur coats.

'What are they?' he enquired.

I explained that they were baby hedgehogs.

'They can't be,' he said. 'Hedgehogs are all brown.'

My family's ignorance of the world they lived in was always a source of worry to me and I never lost an opportunity of imparting information. I explained that female hedgehogs could not, without suffering the most refined tor-

ture, give birth to babies covered with hard spines, and
they were born with these little rubbery white spines whi
could be bent between the fingers as easily as a feather. Lat
as they grew, the spines would darken and harden.

'How are you going to feed them, dear? They've got su
tiny mouths,' said Mother, 'and they must still be drinki
milk, surely?'

I said that I had seen, in a shop in the town, a compl
do-it-yourself baby outfit for children. It consisted of seve
worthless items, such as a celluloid doll, nappies, a potty a
so forth, but one article had caught my attention; a miniat
feeding bottle with a supply of tiny red teats. This, I sa
would be ideal for feeding the baby hedgehogs, while t
potty, doll and other accoutrements could be given to so
deserving peasant child. There was only one slight snag, a
that was that I had had some rather heavy expenses to m
recently (such as the wire for the magpie cage) and so h
over-spent on my pocket money.

'Well, dear,' said Mother doubtfully, 'if it isn't too expens
I suppose I could buy it for you.'

I said it was not expensive at all, when you considered t
it was more like an investment, for not only would you
getting an invaluable feeding bottle which would come in u
ful for other animals, but you would be rearing four ta
hedgehogs and getting a grateful peasant child into the barga
What finer way, I asked, of spending money? So the outfit v
purchased. A young peasant girl, whom I rathed fancied,
ceived with the most satisfactory joy the doll, potty and ot
rubbish and I went about the stern task of rearing my bab

They lived under my bed in a large cardboard box, f
of cotton wool, and at night, in order to keep them warm
placed their box on top of a hot water bottle. I had wanted
have them sleeping in the bed with me, but Mother poin
out that this was not only unhygienic, but that I risked roll
on them in the night and killing them. I found they thri
best on watered cow's milk and fed them assiduously th
times a day and once in the middle of the night. The night f
proved to be a little difficult, for in order to make sure t
I woke up I had borrowed a large tin alarm clock from Sp
This used to go off like a rattle of musketry and, unfortunat
woke not only me but the entire family as well. Eventually

ciferous were the family in their complaints, that Mother
ggested I gave them an extra feed late at night when I went
bed, in lieu of the feed at two o'clock in the morning that
ke everybody up. This I did and the hedgehogs thrived
d grew. Their eyes opened and their spines turned from
ow-white to grey and became firmer. They had now, as I
ticipated, convinced themselves that I was their mother, and
uld come scrambling on to the edge of the box when I
ened it, jostling and pushing for first suck at the bottle,
ering tiny wheezy squeaks and grunts. I was immensely
oud of them and looked forward happily to the day when
y would trot at my heels through the olive groves.

Then Mother and I were invited to spend a week-end with
ne friends in the extreme south of the island, and I found
self in a quandary. I longed to go, for the sandy, shallow
asts of the south were a fine place for finding heart urchins
ich, in fact, looked not unlike baby hedgehogs. Heart
aped, they were covered with soft spines which formed a
ted tail at one end and a spiky Red Indian-like head-dress
ong the back. I had only found one of these, and that had
en crushed by the sea and was scarcely recognisable, but I
ew from Theodore that they were found in abundance two
three inches under the sand in the south of the island. How-
r, I had my brood of hedgehogs to consider, for I could not
ry well take them with me and, as Mother was coming too,
re was nobody I really trusted to look after them.

'I'll look after them,' offered Margo. 'Dear little things.'

I was doubtful. Did she realise, I asked, the intricacies of
oking after the hedgehogs? The fact that, for example, the
ton wool in their box had to be changed three times a day?
at they must only have diluted cow's milk? That the milk
d to be warmed to blood heat and no more? And, most im-
rtant of all, that they were only allowed half a bottle of
lk each at every feed? For I had very soon found out that,
you let them, they would drink themselves comatose at every
al, with the most dire results that entailed the changing of
 cotton wool even more frequently.

'Don't be silly,' said Margo. 'Of course I can look after
m. I know about babies and things. You just write down on
iece of paper what I am supposed to do, and they'll be
te all right.'

171

CRISEDA

Margo grew so indignant at my doubting her, that eventually, reluctantly, I gave in. I had prevailed upon Larry, who happened to be in a good mood, to type out a detailed list of dos and don'ts for hedgehog rearers and I gave Margo a practical course in bottle warming and cotton wool changing.

'They seem awfully hungry,' she said as she lifted each writhing, squeaking baby out of the box and pushed the end of the teat into its groping, eager mouth.

I said that they were always like that. One should take no notice of it. They were just naturally greedy.

'Poor little things,' said Margo.

I should have been warned.

I spent an exhilarating week-end. I got myself badly sunburnt, for the fragile spring sun was deceptive, but came back triumphant, with eight heart urchins, four shells new to my collection and a baby sparrow that had fallen out of its nest. At the villa, after I had suffered the barks and licks and nibbles of greeting that the dogs always bestowed upon you if you had been away for more than two hours, I asked Margo eagerly how my baby hedgehogs were.

'They're doing all right now,' she said. 'But really, Gerry, I do think you ill-treat your pets. You were starving those poor little things to death. They were so hungry. You've no idea.'

With a sinking feeling in the pit of my stomach, I listened to my sister.

'Ravenous, poor little dears. Do you know, they've been taking two bottles each at every feed?'

Horrified, I rushed up to my bedroom and pulled the cardboard box out from under my bed. In it lay my four hedgehogs, bloated beyond belief. Their stomachs were so large that they could only paw feebly with their legs without making any progress. They had degenerated into pink sacks full of milk, frosted with spines. They all died that night and Margo wept copiously over their balloon-like corpses. But her grief did not give me any pleasure, for never would my hedgehogs trot obediently at my heels through the olive groves. As a punishment to my over-indulgent sister, I dug four little graves and erected four little crosses in the garden as a permanent reminder, and for four days I did not speak to her.

My grief over the death of my hedgehogs was, however, short lived, for at that time Donald and Max reappeared in

172

island, triumphantly, with a thirty-foot yacht, and Larry introduced into our midst Captain Creech.

Mother and I had spent a very pleasant afternoon in the olive groves, she collecting wild flowers and herbs and I newly emerged butterflies. Tired but happy, we made our way back to the villa for tea. When we came in sight of the villa she came to a sudden halt.

'Who's that man sitting on the veranda?' she asked.

I had been busy throwing sticks for the dogs, so was not really concentrating. Now I saw, stretched out on the veranda, a strange figure in crumpled white ducks.

'Who is he? Can you see?' asked Mother, agitatedly.

At that time she was suffering under the delusion that the manager of our bank in England was liable, at any moment, to pay a flying visit to Corfu, for the express purpose of discussing our overdraft, so this unknown figure on the veranda tormented her fears.

I examined the stranger carefully. He was old, almost completely bald, and what little hair he had adhering to the back of his skull was long and as white and wispy as late summer thistle-down. He had an equally unkempt white beard and moustache. I assured Mother that, as far as I could see, he bore no resemblance to the bank manager.

'Oh dear,' said Mother, annoyed. 'He would arrive now. I've got absolutely nothing for tea. I wonder who he is?'

As we got nearer, the stranger, who had been dozing peacefully, suddenly woke up and spotted us.

'Ahoy!' he shouted, so loudly and suddenly that Mother stopped and almost fell down. 'Ahoy! You must be Mother Durrell, and the boy, of course. Larry told me all about you. Welcome aboard.'

'Oh dear,' whispered Mother to me. 'It's another one of Larry's.'

As we got closer, I could see that our guest had a most extraordinary face, pink and as carunculated as a walnut. The cartilage of his nose had obviously received, at one time or other, so many severe blows that it twisted down his face like a snake. His jaw too had suffered the same fate and was now twisted to one side, as though hitched up to his right ear lobe by an invisible thread.

'Delighted to meet you,' he said, as though he owned the

173

villa, his rheumy eyes beaming. 'My, you're a better lookin
wench than your son described.'

Mother stiffened and dropped an anemone from the bunc
of flowers she carried. 'I,' she said with frigid dignity, 'am M
Durrell, and this is my son Gerald.'

'My name's Creech,' said the old man. 'Captain Patric
Creech.' He paused and spat accurately and copiously over th
veranda rail into mother's favourite bed of zinnias. 'Welcom
aboard,' he said again, exuding bonhomie. 'Glad to know yo

Mother cleared her throat nervously.

'Is my son Lawrence here?' she enquired, adopting h
fruity, aristocratic voice, which she only did in moments
extreme stress.

'No, no,' said Captain Creech. 'I left him in town. He to
me to come out here for tea. He said he would be aboa
shortly.'

'Well,' said Mother, making the best of a bad job, 'do
down. If you will excuse me a moment I'll just go and ma
some scones.'

'Scones, eh?' said Captain Creech, eyeing Mother wi
such lasciviousness that she dropped two more wild flowers.
like scones, and I like a woman that's handy in the galley

'Gerry,' said Mother frostily, 'you entertain Captain Cree
while I get the tea.'

She made a hurried and slightly undignified exit and I w
left to cope with Captain Creech.

He had re-slumped himself in his chair and was staring at r
with watery eyes from under his tattered white eyebrov
His stare was so fixed that I became slightly unnerved. Co
scious of my duties as host, however, I offered him a box f
of cigarettes. He peered into it, as though it was a well, h
jaw moving to and fro like a ventriloquist's dummy.

'Death!' he shouted so suddenly and so vigorously that
almost dropped the cigarettes. He lay back in his chair a
fixed me with his blue eyes.

'Cigarettes are death, boyo,' he said. He felt in the pocket
his white ducks and produced a stubby pipe as blackened a
gnarled as a piece of charcoal. He stuck it between his tee
which made his jaw look more lopsided than ever.

'Never forget,' he said, 'a man's best friend is his pipe.'

He laughed uproariously at his own joke and dutifully

174

ughed too. He got up, spat copiously over the veranda rail
nd then flopped back into his chair. I searched my mind for
topic of conversation. Nothing seemed to present itself. He
ould surely not be interested in the fact that today I had
eard the first cicada, nor that Agathi's chicken laid six eggs
e size of hazel nuts? Since he was nautically inclined, I
ondered whether the exciting news that Taki, who could not
ford a boat, had been night-fishing (holding a light above his
ead with one hand and a trident in the other) and had success-
lly driven the trident through his own foot, imagining it was
a exotic form of fish? But Captain Creech, peering at me
om behind the oily fumes of his pipe, started the conversation
mself.

'You're wondering about my face, aren't you, boyo?' he
id accusingly, and I noticed that the skin on his cheeks
ecame pinker and more shiny, like satin, as he said it. Before
could voice a denial, he went on.

'Windjammers, that's what did it. Windjammers. Going
und the Horn. Tearing wind, straight out of the arsehole of
e earth. I fell, see? The canvas flapping and roaring like
od's thunder. The rope slipped through my fingers like an
led snake. Straight on to the deck. They did what they could
ith it . . . of course, we hadn't got a doctor on board.' He
used and felt his jaw meditatively. I sat riveted in my chair,
scinated. 'By the time we got round to Chile the whole thing
d set as hard as Portland,' he said, still fondling his jaw.
was sixteen years old.'

I wondered whether to commiserate with him or not, but
e had fallen into a reverie, his blue eyes blank. Mother came
a to the veranda and paused, struck by our immobility.

'Chile,' said the Captain with relish. 'Chile. That was the
st time I got gonorrhoea.'

Mother started and then cleared her throat loudly.

'Gerry, come and help me bring out the tea,' she said.

Together we brought out the tea pot, milk jug and cups
nd the plates with golden yellow scones and toast that
[M]other had prepared.

'Tucker,' said Captain Creech, filling his mouth with scone.
tops your belly rumbling.'

'Are you, um, staying here long?' asked Mother, obviously
pping that he was not.

'Might retire here,' said Captain Creech indistinctly, wipi
scone crumbs off his moustache. 'Looks a pretty little pla
Might go to anchor here.'

He was forced, because of his jaw, to slurp his tea noisily
could see Mother getting increasingly alarmed.

'Don't you, um, have a ship?' she asked.

'No bloody fear,' said Captain Creech, seizing anoth
scone. 'Retired, that's me. Got time now to look a little mo
closely at the wenches.'

He eyed Mother meditatively as he spoke, masticating
scone with great vigour.

'A bed without a woman is like a ship without a hold,'
observed.

Mercifully Mother was saved from having to reply by t
arrival of the car containing the rest of the family and Don:
and Max.

'Muzzer, we have come,' announced Max, beaming at
and embracing her tenderly. 'And I see we are in time for t
Strumpets! How lovely! Donald, we have strumpets for te:

'Crumpets,' corrected Donald.

'They're scones,' said Mother.

'I remember a strumpet in Montevideo,' said Capt.
Creech. 'Marvellous bitch. Kept the whole ship entertair
for two days. They don't breed them with stamina like t
nowadays.'

'Who is this disgusting old man?' asked Mother, as soon
she had an opportunity of backing Larry into a corner aw
from the tea party, which was now in full swing.

'He's called Creech,' said Larry.

'I know *that*,' said Mother, 'but what did you bring him h
for?'

'He's an interesting old boy,' said Larry, 'and I don't th
he's got a lot of money. He's come here to retire on a min
pension, I think.'

'Well, he's not going to retire on us,' said Mother firm
'Don't invite him again.'

'I thought you'd like him,' said Larry. 'He's travelled
over the world. He's even been to India. He's full of the m
fascinating stories.'

'As far as I am concerned he can go on travelling,' s

lother. 'The stories he's been telling up to now aren't what
call fascinating.'

Captain Creech, once having discovered our 'anchorage', as
e put it, became a frequent visitor. He would arrive gener-
ly, we noticed, just in time for a meal, shouting 'Ahoy there!
an I come aboard and have a chin-wag?' As he had obviously
alked two and a half miles through the olive groves to reach
, it was difficult to deny him this privilege, and so Mother,
uttering evilly, would rush into the kitchen, water the soup
d bisect the sausages so that Captain Creech could join us.
e would regale us with tales of his life at sea and the names
the places that he had visited. Names that I only knew from
aps would slide enticingly out of his disjointed mouth. Trin-
malee, Darwin and Durban, Buenos Aires, Wellington and
lcutta, the Galapagos, the Seychelles and the Friendly
ands. It seemed that there was no corner of the globe to
ich he had not penetrated. He would intersperse these
ries with prolonged and exceptionally vulgar sea shanties
d limericks of such biological complexity that, fortunately,
ther could not understand them.

Then came the never to be forgotten day when Captain
eech arrived, uninvited, for tea as we were entertaining the
al English minister and his wife, more out of a sense of
y than of religion. To our amazement, Captain Creech be-
ved remarkably well. He exchanged views on sea serpents
l the height of tidal waves with the padre and explained the
erence between longitude and latitude to the padre's wife.
manners were exemplary and we were quite proud of him,
towards the end of tea the padre's wife, with extreme
ning, managed to steer the conversation on to her children.
s subject was all-absorbing to her; you would have thought
not only was she the only woman in the world to have
en birth, but that they had been immaculately conceived
vell. Having treated us to a ten minute monologue on the
edible perspicacity of her offspring, she paused moment-
y to drink her tea.

'm a bit too old to have babies,' said Captain Creech.
he padre's wife choked.
But,' he went on with satisfaction, 'I have a lot of fun
ng.'

The tea party was not a success.

Shortly after this, Donald and Max turned up one day [at] the villa.

'Muzzer,' said Max, 'we are going to carry you away.'

'Yacht party,' said Donald. 'Fabulous idea. Max's idea [of] course.'

'Yacht party where?' enquired Mother.

'Round ze island,' said Max, throwing out his long arm[s in] an all-embracing gesture.

'But I thought you didn't know how to sail her,' said Les[lie.]

'No, no. We don't sail her. Larry sails her,' said M[ax] triumphantly.

'Larry?' said Leslie incredulously. 'But Larry doesn't kn[ow] the first thing about boats.'

'Oh no,' said Donald earnestly. 'Oh no. He's quite an exp[ert.] He's been taking lessons from Captain Creech. The Capta[in's] coming along too, as crew.'

'Well, that settles it then,' said Mother. 'I'm not com[ing] on a yacht with that disgusting old man, apart from the da[nger] involved if Larry's going to sail it.'

They did their best to persuade her, but Mother [was] adamant. The most she would concede was that the res[t of] the family, with Theodore, would drive across the island [and] rendezvous with them at a certain bay where we could pi[cnic] and, if it was warm enough, bathe.

It was a bright, clean morning when we set off and it loo[ked] as though it was going to be ideal for both sailing and picn[ick]ing, but by the time we reached the other side of the is[land] and had unpacked the picnic things, it began to look as tho[ugh] we were in for a sirocco. Theodore and I made our way d[own] through the trees to the edge of the bay. The sea had tu[rned] a cold steel-grey and the wind had stretched and starch[ed a] number of white clouds across the blue sky. Suddenly a[long] the rim of the sea, three water spouts appeared, loping a[long] the horizon like the huge undulating necks of some prehis[toric] monsters. Bowing and swaying, graceful as swans they da[nced] along the horizon and disappeared.

'Aha,' said Theodore, who had been watching this phe[no]menon interestedly, 'I have never seen *three* of them tog[ether.] Very curious. Did you notice how they moved tog[ether]

ost as if they were . . ., er . . ., you know, animals in a
d?'

said that I wished they had been closer.

Um,' said Theodore rasping his beard with his thumb. 'I
't think water spouts are things one wants to get on . . .,
. . ., um . . ., intimate terms with. I remember once I
ted a place in Macedonia where one had . . ., er . . ., you
w, come ashore. It had left a trail of damage about two
dred yards wide and a quarter of a mile long, that is to say
nd. Even quite big olive trees had been, er, you know,
naged and the smaller ones were broken up like match
od. And, of course, at the point where the water spout
lly broke up, the ground was saturated by tons of salt
er and so it was . . ., you know . . ., completely unsuitable
agriculture.'

I say, did you see those bloody great water spouts?' asked
lie, joining us.

Yes, very curious,' said Theodore.

Mother's in a panic,' said Leslie. 'She's convinced they're
ding straight for Larry.'

I don't think there's any danger of that,' said Theodore.
ey look too far out to me.'

By the time we had installed ourselves in the olive groves at
edge of the bay, it was obvious that we were in for one of
se sudden and exceedingly sharp siroccos which blew up
hat time of the year. The wind lashed the olive trees and
rned up the bay to white-capped rollers.

We might as well go home,' said Leslie. 'It isn't going to be
ch fun picnicking in this.'

We can't, dear,' said Mother. 'We promised to meet Larry
e.'

If they've got any sense, they'll have put in somewhere else,'
l Leslie.

I can't say I envy them being out in this,' said Theodore,
ing at the waves pounding the rocks.

Oh dear, I do hope they will be all right,' said Mother.
rry really is foolish.'

Ve waited an hour with Mother getting increasingly pan-
with each passing moment. Then Leslie, who had climbed
a neighbouring headland, came back with the news that
could see them.

179

'I must say I think it's surprising they got this far,' s
Leslie. 'The boom's swinging about all over the place a
they're tacking practically in circles.'

Presently the yacht headed into the narrow mouth of
bay and we could see Donald and Max dodging about, pull
at ropes and canvas, while Larry and Captain Creech clung
the tiller and were obviously shouting instructions.
watched their progress with interest.

'I hope they remember that reef,' said Leslie.

'What reef?' said Mother in alarm.

'There's a damn' great reef just there where that white wa
is,' said Leslie.

Spiro had been standing gazing out to sea like a bro
gargoyle, his face scowling.

'I don't likes it, Master Leslies,' he said in a hoarse whisp
'They don't looks as though they knows how to sails.'

'Oh dear,' said Mother. 'Why ever did I agree to this?'

At that moment (owing to the fact, we discovered la
that Donald and Max misinterpreted their instructions a
hauled up a length of canvas instead of taking it down) seve
things happened simultaneously. The yacht's sails were s
denly caught by an errant gust of wind. They puffed
The boom came over with a splintering crash that one co
hear quite clearly on shore and knocked Max overboard. '
yacht turned almost on her side and, propelled by the gus
wind, ran with a remarkably loud scrunching noise strai
on to the reef, where she remained upright for a brief mom
and then, as if despairing of the yachtsmen on board, lay dc
languidly on her side. Immediately all was confusion.

Mother shouting 'Oh my God! Oh my God!' had to
down hurriedly on an olive root. Margo burst into te
waved her hands and screamed, 'They'll drown! The
drown!' Spiro, Leslie and I made our way to the edge of
bay. There was not much we could do as there was no b
available to launch as a rescue vessel. But presently we
the four expert sailors swimming away from the wreck of
yacht, Larry and Donald apparently propelling Capt
Creech through the water. Leslie and I and Spiro stripped
our clothes hurredly and plunged into the sea. The wa
was icy cold and the waves had considerably more force
them than I gave them credit for.

'Are you all right?' shouted Leslie as the flotilla of ship-wrecked mariners came towards us.

'Yes,' said Max. 'Right as rain.'

He had a four inch gash on his forehead and the blood was running down his face and into his moustache. Larry had one eye bruised and scraped and rapidly swelling. Captain Creech's face, bobbing between Larry's and Donald's had achieved an extraordinary mauve colour, rather like the bloom of a plum.

'Give us a hand with the Captain,' said Larry. 'Silly old bastard only told me as we went over that he couldn't swim.'

Spiro, Leslie and I laid hands upon Captain Creech and re-lieved the panting Donald and Larry on their rescue work. We must have made an arresting tableau as we staggered gasping through the shallows and out on to the shore. Leslie and Spiro were supporting Captain Creech, one on each side of him, as his legs seemed in imminent danger of buckling.

'Ahoy there!' he called to Mother. 'Ahoy there, my wench.'

'Look at Max's head!' screamed Margo. 'He'll bleed to death!'

We staggered up into the shelter of the olive groves and while Mother, Margo and Theodore did hasty first aid on Max's head and Larry's eye, we laid Captain Creech under an olive tree, since he seemed incapable of standing up.

'Port at last,' he said with satisfaction. 'Port at last, I'll make sailors of you lads yet.'

It became obvious, now that we had time to concentrate, that Captain Creech was extremely drunk.

'Really, Larry, you do make me cross,' said Mother. 'You might all have been drowned.'

'It wasn't my fault,' said Larry aggrievedly. 'We were doing what the Captain told us to. Donald and Max went and pulled the wrong ropes.'

'How can you take instructions from him?' said Mother. 'He's drunk.'

'He wasn't drunk when he started,' said Larry. 'He must have had a secret supply somewhere on board. He did seem to pop down to the cabin rather a lot, now I come to think about —'

'Do not trust him, gentle maiden,' sang Captain Creech in a wavering baritone. 'Though his heart be pure as gold, he'll have you one fine morning, with a cargo in your hold.'

181

'Disgusting old brute,' said Mother. 'Really, Larry, I'm
extremely cross with you.'

'A drink, me boyos,' called Captain Creech hoarsely, gestur
ing at the dishevelled Max and Donald. 'You can't sail withou
a drink.'

At length we had dried ourselves as best we could and
wrung the water out of everybody's clothes, then we made
our way, shivering, up the hill to the car.

'What are we going to do about the yacht?' said Leslie
since Donald and Max, as the owners, appeared unperturbed
by her fate.

'We'll stops at the next village,' said Spiro. 'I know
fishermans there. He'll fix it.'

'I think, you know,' said Theodore, 'if we've got any stimu
lant with us, it would be an idea to give some to Max. He may
possibly suffer from concussion after a blow like that.'

'Yes, we've got some brandy,' said Mother, delving into th
car.

She produced a bottle and a cup.

'Darling girl,' said Captain Creech, fixing his wavering ey
upon the bottle. 'Just what the doctor ordered.'

'You're not having any of this,' said Mother firmly. 'Thi
is for Max.'

We had to dispose ourselves in the car as best we could
sitting on each other's laps and trying to give as much spac
as possible to Max, who had now gone a very nasty leade
colour and was shivering violently. To Mother's annoyanc
she found herself, willy nilly, wedged in alongside Captai
Creech.

'Sit on my lap,' said the Captain hospitably. 'Sit on my la
and we can have a little cuddle to keep warm.'

'Certainly not,' said Mother primly. 'I'd rather sit o
Donald's lap.'

As we drove back across the island to town, the Captai
regaled us with his version of some sea shanties. The famil
argued acrimoniously.

'I do wish you'd stop him singing these songs, Larry,' sai
Mother.

'How can I stop him? You're in the back. You stop him

'He's your friend,' said Mother.

'Ain't it a pity, she's only one titty to feed the baby on. The poor little bugger will never play rugger and grow up big and strong.'

'Might have killed you all, filthy old brute,' said Mother.

'Actually, most of it was Larry's fault,' said Leslie.

'It was not,' said Larry indignantly. 'You weren't there, so you don't know. It's extremely difficult when someone shouts at you to luff your helm, or whatever it is, when there's a howling gale blowing.'

'There was a young lady from Chichester,' observed Captain Creech with relish, 'Who made all the saints in their niches stir.'

'The one I'm sorry for is poor Max,' said Margo looking at him commiseratingly.

'I don't know why he should get the sympathy,' said Larry, whose eye had now almost completely disappeared and was a rich shiny black. 'He's the fool who caused it all. I had the boat under perfect control till he hauled up that sail.'

'Well, I can't call you a sailor,' said Margo. 'If you'd been sailor you wouldn't have told him to haul it up.'

'That's just the point,' snarled Larry. 'I didn't tell him to haul it up. He hauled it up on his own.'

'It was the good ship Venus,' began the Captain, whose repertoire appeared to be inexhaustible.

'Don't argue about it, dear,' said Mother. 'I've got a severe headache. The sooner we get into town the better.'

We got to town eventually, dropped Donald and Max at their hotel and the still carolling Captain Creech at his, and drove home, wet, cold and acrimonious.

The following morning we were sitting, all feeling slightly jilted, finishing our breakfast on the veranda. Larry's eye had now achieved sunset hues which could only have been captured by the brush of Turner. Spiro drove up honking his horn, the dogs racing in front of the car snarling and trying to bite the heels.

'I do wish Spiro wouldn't make quite so much noise when he arrives,' said Larry.

Spiro stumped up to the veranda and went through his normal morning routine.

'Morning, Mrs Durrells; morning, Missy Margo; morning,

Master Larrys; morning, Master Leslies; morning, Master Gerrys. How's your eyes, Master Larrys?' he said, screwing up his face into a commiserating scowl.

'At the moment I feel as if I shall probably be going round with a white stick for the rest of my days,' said Larry.

'I've got a letter for you,' said Spiro to Mother.

Mother put on her glasses and opened it. We waited expectantly. Her face went red.

'The impertinence! The insolence! Disgusting old *brute*! Really, I have never heard anything like it.'

'What on earth's the matter?' asked Larry.

'That revolting old Creech creature,' said Mother, waving the letter at him. '—It's your fault, you introduced him to the house.

'What have I done now?' asked Larry, bewildered.

'That filthy old brute has written and proposed to me,' said Mother.

There was a moment's stunned silence while we took in this remarkable information.

'Proposal?' said Larry cautiously. 'An indecent proposal, I presume?'

'No, no,' said Mother. 'He says he wants to marry me. What a fine little woman I am and a lot of sentimental twaddle like that.'

The family, united for once, sat back and laughed until tears came.

'It's no laughing matter,' said Mother stamping about the veranda angrily. 'You've got to do something about it.'

'Oh,' said Larry, mopping his eyes. 'Oh, this is the best thing that's happened for ages. I suppose he thinks since he took his trousers off in front of you yesterday to wring them out, he must make an honest woman of you.'

'Do stop laughing,' said Mother angrily. 'It isn't funny.'

'I can see it all,' said Larry unctuously. 'You in white muslin, Leslie and me in toppers to give you away, Margo as your bridesmaid and Gerry as your page. It will be a very affecting scene. I expect the church will be full of jaded ladies pleasure, all waiting to forbid the banns.'

Mother glared at him.

'When there's a real crisis,' she said angrily, 'you children are of absolutely no use whatsoever.'

184

'But I think you would look lovely in white,' said Margo,
gling.

Where have you decided on for your honeymoon?' asked
rry. 'They say Capri is awfully nice at this time of year.'

3ut Mother was not listening. She turned to Spiro, register-
determination from top to toe.

Spiro, you are to tell the Captain the answer is no, and
t I never want him to set foot in this house again.'

Oh, come now, Mother,' protested Larry. 'What we chil-
n *want* is a father.'

And you all,' said Mother, rounding on us in a fury, 'are
to tell anybody about this. I will not have my name linked
h that disgusting . . ., disgusting *reprobate*.'

And so that was the last we saw of Captain Creech. But
at we all referred to as Mother's great romance made an
spicious start to the year.

The Talking Head

Summer gaped upon the island like the mouth of a great ov
Even in the shade of the olive groves it was not cool and t
incessant, penetrating cries of the cicadas seemed to swell a
become more insistent with each hot, blue noon. The wa
in the ponds and ditches shrank and the mud at the edges b
came jigsawed, cracked and curled by the sun. The sea lay
breathless and still as a bale of silk, the shallow waters t
warm to be refreshing. You had to row the boat out into de
water, you and your reflection the only moving things, a
dive over the side to get cool. It was like diving into the s

Now was the time for butterflies and moths. In the day,
the hillsides where it seemed sucked free of every drop
moisture by the beating sun, you would get the great lang
Swallow Tails, flapping elegantly and erratically from b
to bush; Fritillaries, glowing almost as hot and angry as a
coal, skittered quickly and efficiently from flower to flow
Cabbage Whites; Clouded Yellows and the lemon-yellow a
orange Brimstones bumbled to and fro on untidy win
Among the grasses the skippers, like little brown furry ae
planes, would skim and purr, and on glittering slabs of gyps
the Red Admirals, as flamboyant as a cluster of Woolwort
jewellery, would sit opening and closing their wings as thou
expiring from the heat. At night the lamps would becom
teeming metropolis of moths, and the pink geckos on the c
ing, big-eyed and splay-footed, would gorge until they co
hardly move. Oleander Hawk Moths, green and silver, wo
zoom into the room from nowhere, and, in a frenzy of lo
dive at the lamp, hitting it with such force that the gl
shattered. Death's Head Hawk Moths, mottled ginger a
black, with the macabre skull and crossbones embroidered
the plush fur of their thoraxes, would come tumbling down
chimney to lie fluttering and twitching in the grate, squeak
like mice.

Up on the hillsides where the great beds of heather w
burnt crisp and warm by the sun, the tortoises, lizards a

186

akes would prowl and the praying mantis would hang
nongst the green leaves of the myrtle, swaying slowly and
illy from side to side. The afternoon was the best time to
vestigate life on the hills, but it was also the hottest. The sun
ayed a tattoo on your skull, and the baked ground was as hot
a griddle under your sandalled feet. Widdle and Puke were
wards about the sun and would never accompany me in the
ernoons, but Roger, that indefatigable student of natural
story, would always be with me, panting vigorously, swal-
ving his drooling saliva in great gulps.

Together we shared many adventures. There was the time
en we watched, entranced, two hedgehogs, drunk as lords
the fallen and semi-fermented grapes they had eaten from
der the vines, staggering in circles, snapping at each other
ligerently, uttering high-pitched screams and hiccups. There
s a time we watched a fox cub, red as an autumn leaf,
cover his first tortoise amongst the heather. The tortoise, in
phlegmatic way that they have, folded himself up in his
ll, tightly closed as a portmanteau. But the fox had seen
novement and, prick-eared, it moved around him cautiously.
en, for it was still only a puppy, it dabbed quickly at the
toise's shell with its paw and jumped away, expecting re-
ation. Then it lay down and examined the tortoise for
eral minutes, its head between its paws. Finally it went for-
d rather gingerly and after several unsuccessful attempts
naged to pick the tortoise up with its jaws and, with head
l high, trotted off proudly through the heather. It was on
se hills that we watched the baby tortoises hatching out of
r papery-shelled eggs, each one looking as wizened and as
kled as though it were a thousand years old at the moment
irth, and it was here that I witnessed for the first time the
ing dance of the snakes.

oger and I were sitting under a large clump of myrtles
ch offered a small patch of shade and some concealment.
had disturbed a hawk in a cypress tree nearby and were
ing patiently for him to return so that we could identify
. Suddenly, some ten feet from where we crouched, I saw
snakes weaving their way out of a brown web of heather
ks. Roger, who was frightened of snakes, uttered an uneasy
whine and put his ears back. I shushed him violently and
hed to see what the snakes would do. One appeared to

187

be following close on the heels of the other. Was he, I won
dered, perhaps in pursuit of it in order to eat it? They slid ou
of the heather and into some clumps of sun-whitened grass an
I lost sight of them. Cursing my luck, I was just about to shi
my position in the hopes of seeing them again when they r
appeared on a comparatively open piece of ground.

Here the one that was leading paused and the one that ha
been following slid alongside. They lay like this for a momer
or so and then the pursuer started to nose tentatively at t
other one's head. I decided that the first snake was a fema
and that her follower was her mate. He continued butting h
head at her throat until eventually he had raised her head ar
neck slightly off the ground. She froze in that position and t
male, backing away a few inches, raised his head also. Th
stayed like that, immobile, staring at each other for some co
siderable time. Then, slowly, the male slid forward and twin
himself round the female's body and they both rose as hi
as they could without overbalancing, entwined like a co
volvulus. Again they remained motionless for a time and th
started to sway, like two wrestlers pushing against each oth
in the ring, their tails curling and grasping at the grass roo
around them to give themselves better purchase. Sudder
they flopped sideways, the hinder ends of their bodies met a
they mated lying there in the sun, as entangled as streamers
a carnival.

At this moment Roger, who had viewed with increas
distress my interest in the snakes, got to his feet and sho
himself before I could stop him, indicating that, as far as
was concerned, it would be far better if we moved on. T
snakes unfortunately saw his movement. They convulsed i
tangled heap for a moment, their skins gleaming in the s
and then the female disentangled herself and sped rapidly
wards the sanctuary of the heather, dragging the male, s
fastened to her, helplessly behind her. Roger looked at r
gave a small sneeze of pleasure and wagged his stumpy t
But I was annoyed with him and told him so in no uncert
terms. After all, as I pointed out to him, on the numer
occasions when he was latched to a bitch how would *he*
to be overtaken by some danger and dragged so ignominiou
from the field of love?

With the summer came the bands of gypsies to the island to help harvest the crops and steal what they could while they were there. Sloe-eyed, their dusky skins burnt almost black by the sun, their hair unkempt and their clothing in rags, you would see them moving in family groups along the white, dusty roads, riding on donkeys or on lithe little ponies, shiny as chestnuts. Their encampments were always a squalid enchantment, with a dozen pots bubbling with different ingredients over the fires, the old women squatting in the shadow of their grubby lean-tos with the heads of the younger children in their laps, carefully searching them for lice, while the older children, tattered as dandelion leaves, rolled and creamed and played in the dust. Those of the men who had a side-line would be busy with it. One would be twisting and tying multi-coloured balloons together, so that they screeched a protest, making strange animal shapes. Another, perhaps, who was the proud possessor of a Karaghiozi shadow show, would be refurbishing the highly coloured cut-out figures and practising some of Karaghiozi's vulgarities and innuendoes to the giggling delight of the handsome young women who stirred the cooking-pots, or knitted in the shade.

I had always wanted to get on intimate terms with the gypsies, but they were a shy and hostile people, barely tolerating the Greeks. My mop of hair, bleached almost white by the sun, and my blue eyes, made me automatically suspect and though they would allow me to visit their camps, they were never forthcoming, in the way that the peasants were, in telling me about their private lives and their aspirations. It was, nevertheless, the gypsies who were indirectly responsible for an uproar in the family. For once I was entirely innocent.

It was the tail-end of an exceptionally hot summer's afternoon. Roger and I had been having an exhausting time pursuing a large and indignant king snake along a length of dry stone wall. No sooner had we dismantled one section of it than the snake would ease himself fluidly along into the next section, and by the time we had re-built the section we had pulled down, it would take half an hour or so to locate him again in the jigsaw of rocks. Finally we had to concede defeat and were now making our way home to tea, thirsty, sweating and covered with dust. As we rounded an elbow of the road, I glanced into a small valley, and saw what, at first glance, I took to be a man with an exceptionally large dog. A closer look, however, and I realised, incredulously, that it was a man with a bear. I was so astonished that I cried out involuntarily. The bear stood up on its hind legs and turned to look up at me, as did the man. They stared at me for a moment and then the man waved his hand in casual greeting and turned back to the task of spreading his belongings under the olive tree, while the bear got down again on its haunches and squatted, watching him with interest. I made my way hurriedly down the hillside, filled with excitement. I had heard that there were dancing bears in Greece, but I had never actually seen one. This was an opportunity too good to be missed. As I drew near, I called a greeting to the man and he turned from his jumble of possessions and replied courteously enough. I saw that he was indeed a gypsy, with the dark, wild eyes and the blue-black hair, but he was infinitely more prosperous looking than most of them, for his suit was in good repair and he wore shoes, a mark of distinction, in those days, even among the landed peasantry of the island.

I asked whether it was safe to approach, for the bear, although wearing a leather muzzle, was untethered.

'Yes, come,' called the man. 'Pavlo won't hurt you, but leave your dog.'

I turned to Roger and I could see that, brave though he was, he did not like the look of the bear and was only staying by me out of a sense of duty. When I told him to go home, he gave me a grateful look and trotted off up the hillside, trying to pretend that he was ignorant of the whole scene. In spite of the man's assurances that Pavlo was harmless, I approached with caution for, although it was only a youngster, the bear, when it reared on to its hind legs, was a good foot or so taller than I was and possessed on each broad, furry paw a formidable and very serviceable array of glittering claws. It squatted on its haunches and peered at me out of tiny, twinkling brown eyes, panting gently. It looked like a large pile of animated, unkempt sea-weed. To me it was the most desirable animal I had ever set eyes on and I walked round it, viewing its excellence from every possible vantage point.

I plied the man with eager questions. How old was it? Where did he get it? What was he doing with it?

'He dances for his and my living,' said the man, obviously
ınused by my enthusiasm. 'Here, I'll show you.'
He picked up a stick with a small hook at the end and slid
into a ring set into the leather muzzle the bear wore.
'Come, dance with your papa.'
In one swift movement the bear rose on to its hind legs.
he man clicked his fingers and whistled a plaintive tune,
arting to shuffle his feet in time to the music and the bear
llowed suit. Together they shuffled in a slow, stately minuet
nong the electric blue thistles and the dried asphodel stalks.
could have watched them for ever. When the man reached
e end of his tune, the bear, as of habit, got down on all fours
ain and sneezed.
'Bravo!' said the man softly. 'Bravo!'
I clapped enthusiastically. Never, I said earnestly, had I seen
ch a fine dance, nor such an accomplished performer as
vlo. Could I, perhaps, pat him?
'You can do what you like with him,' said the man, chuck-
ıg, as he unhooked his stick from the bear's muzzle. 'He's a
ol, this one. He wouldn't even hurt a bandit who was robb-
g him of his food.'
To prove it he started scratching the bear's back and the
ar, pointing its head up into the sky, uttered throaty wheezy
ırmurings of pleasure and sank gradually down on to the
ound in ecstasy, until he was spread out looking almost, I
ought, like a bear-skin rug.
'He likes to be tickled,' said the man. 'Come and tickle him.'
The next half hour was pure delight for me. I tickled the
ar while he crooned with delight. I examined his great
ıws and his ears and his tiny bright eyes and he lay there and
fered me as though he were asleep. Then I leant against his
rm bulk and talked to his owner. A plan was forming in
mind. The bear, I decided, had got to become mine. The
gs and my other animals would soon get used to it and to-
her we could go waltzing over the hillsides. I convinced
self that the family would be overjoyed at my acquisition
such an intelligent pet. But first I had to get the man into
uitable frame of mind for bargaining. With the peasants,
gaining was a loud, protracted and difficult business. But
s man was a gypsy and what they did not know about bar-
ning would fit conveniently into an acorn cup. The man

191

CRISEDA

seemed much less taciturn and reticent than the other gypsi
I had come into contact with and I took this as a good sig
I asked him where he had come from.

'Way beyond, way beyond,' he said, covering his possessio
with a shabby tarpaulin and shaking out some threadba
blankets which were obviously going to serve as his be
'Landed at Lefkimi last night and we've been walking ev
since, Pavlo, the Head and I. You see, they wouldn't tal
Pavlo on the buses; they were frightened of him. So we g
no sleep last night, but tonight we'll sleep here and then t
morrow we'll reach the town.'

Intrigued, I asked him what he meant by 'he, Pavlo, a
the Head' walking up from Lefkimi.

'My Head, of course,' he said. 'My little talking Hea
And he picked up the bear stick and slapped it on a pile
goods under the tarpaulin, grinning at me.

I had unearthed the battered remains of a bar of chocola
from the pocket of my shorts and I was busy feeding this
the bear, who received each fragment with great moans a
slobberings of satisfaction. I said to the man that I did n
understand what he was talking about. He squatted on I
haunches in front of me and lit a cigarette, peering at me o
of dark eyes, as inimical as a lizard's.

'I have a Head,' he said jerking his thumb towards his p
of belongings, 'a living Head. It talks and answers questions.
is without doubt the most remarkable thing in the world.'

I was puzzled. Did he mean, I asked, a head without
body?

'Of course without a body. Just a Head,' and he cupped I
hands in front of him, as though holding a coconut. 'It sits
a little stick and talks to you. Nothing like it has ever be
seen in the world.'

But how, I enquired, if the head were a disembodied hea
could it live?

'Magic,' said the man solemnly. 'Magic that my gre
great-grandfather passed down to me.'

I felt sure that he was pulling my leg, but, intriguing thou
the discussion on talking heads was, I felt we were wanderi
away from my main objective, which was to acquire the i
mediate freehold of Pavlo, now sucking in through his muzz

th wheezy sighs of satisfaction, my last bit of chocolate. I
idied the man carefully as he squatted dreamy-eyed, his head
veloped in a cloud of smoke. I decided that with him the
ld approach was the best. I asked him bluntly whether he
uld consider selling the bear and for how much?

'Sell Pavlo?' he said. 'Never! He's like my own son.'

Surely, I said, if he went to a good home? Somewhere
ere he was loved and allowed to dance, surely then he
ght be tempted to sell? The man looked at me meditatively
ffing on his cigarette.

'Twenty million drachmas?' he enquired, and then laughed
my look of consternation. 'Men who have fields must have
nkeys to work them,' he said. 'They don't part with them
sily. Pavlo is my donkey. He dances for his living and he
nces for mine, and until he is too old to dance, I will not part
th him.'

I was bitterly disappointed, but I could see that he was
amant. I rose from my recumbent position on the broad,
rm, faintly snoring back of Pavlo and dusted myself down.
ell, I said, there was nothing more I could do. I understood
wanting to keep the bear, but if he changed his mind, would
get in touch with me? He nodded gravely. And if he was
rforming in town, could he possibly let me know where, so
t I could attend?

'Of course,' he said, 'but I think people will tell you where
m, for my Head is extraordinary.'

I nodded and shook his hand. Pavlo got to his feet and I
tted his head.

When I reached the top of the valley I looked back. They
re both standing side by side. The man waved briefly and
vlo, swaying on his hind legs, had his muzzle in the air,
esting after me with his nose. I liked to feel it was a gesture
farewell.

I walked slowly home thinking about the man and his
king Head and the wonderful Pavlo. Would it be possible,
ondered, for me to get a bear cub from somewhere and
r it? Perhaps if I advertised in a newspaper in Athens it
ght bring results?

The family were in the drawing-room having tea and I
ided to put my problem to them. As I entered the room,

however, a startling change came over what had been a plac
scene. Margo uttered a piercing scream, Larry dropped a cu
full of tea into his lap and then leapt up and took refug
behind the table, while Leslie picked up a chair and Moth
gaped at me with a look of horror on her face. I had neve
known my presence to provoke quite such a positive reactio
on the part of the family.

'Get it out of here,' roared Larry.

'Yes, get the bloody thing out,' said Leslie.

'It'll kill us all!' screamed Margo.

'Get a gun,' said Mother faintly, 'Get a gun and sav
Gerry.'

I couldn't, for the life of me, think what was the matter wit
them. They were all staring at something behind me. I turne
and looked and there, standing in the doorway, sniffing hope
fully towards the tea table, was Pavlo. I went up to him an
caught hold of his muzzle. He nuzzled at me affectionately.
explained to the family that it was only Pavlo.

'I am not *having* it,' said Larry throatily. 'I am not *having* i
Birds and dogs and hedgehogs all over the house and now
bear. What does he think this is, for Christ's sake? A blood
Roman arena?'

'Gerry, dear, do be careful,' said Mother quaveringly. '
looks rather fierce.'

'It will kill us all,' quavered Margo with conviction.

'I can't get past it to get to my guns,' said Leslie.

'You are *not* going to have it. I forbid it,' said Larry. 'I wi
not have the place turned into a bear pit.'

'Where did you get it, dear?' asked Mother.

'I don't care where he got it,' said Larry. 'He's to take
back this instant, quickly, before it rips us to pieces. The boy
got no sense of responsibility. I am not going to be turned int
an early Christian martyr at my time of life.'

Pavlo got up on to his hind legs and uttered a long wheezin
moan which I took to mean that he desired to join us in wha
ever delicacies were on the tea table. The family interpreted
differently.

'Ow!' screeched Margo, as though she had been bitte
'It's attacking.'

'Gerry, do be careful,' said Mother.

'I'll not be responsible for what I do to that boy,' said
Larry.

'If you survive,' said Leslie. 'Do shut up, Margo, you're only
making matters worse. You'll provoke the bloody thing.'

'I can scream if I want to,' said Margo indignantly.

So raucous in their fear were the family that they had not
given me a chance to explain. Now I attempted to. I said that,
first of all, Pavlo was not mine, and secondly he was as tame
as a dog and would not hurt a fly.

'Two statements I refuse to believe,' said Larry. 'You
pinched it from some flaming circus. Not only are we to be
disembowelled, but arrested for harbouring stolen goods as
well.'

'Now, now, dear,' said Mother, 'let Gerry explain.'

'Explain?' said Larry. 'Explain? How do you explain a
bloody great bear in the drawing-room?'

I said that the bear belonged to a gypsy who had a talking
head.

'What do you mean, a talking head?' asked Margo.

I said that it was a disembodied head that talked.

'The boy's mad,' said Larry with conviction. 'The sooner we
have him certified the better.'

The family had now all backed away to the farthest corner
of the room in a trembling group. I said, indignantly, that my
story was perfectly true and that, to prove it, I'd make Pavlo
dance. I seized a piece of cake from the table, hooked my
finger into the ring on his muzzle and uttered the same com-
mands as his master had done. His eyes fixed greedily on the
cake, Pavlo reared up and danced with me.

'Oo, look!' said Margo. 'Look! It's dancing!'

'I don't care if it's behaving like a whole *corps de ballet*,'
said Larry. 'I want the damn' thing out of here.'

I shovelled the cake in through Pavlo's muzzle and he
licked it down greedily.

'He really is rather sweet,' said Mother, adjusting her spectacles and staring at him with interest. 'I remember my brother
had a bear in India once. She was a very nice pet.'

'No!' said Larry and Leslie simultaneously. 'He's not having

I said I could not have it anyway, because the man did not
want to sell it.

'A jolly good thing too,' said Larry.

'Why don't you now return it to him, if you have quite finished doing a cabaret act all over the tea table?'

Getting another slice of cake as a bribe, I hooked my finger once more in the ring on Pavlo's muzzle and led him out of the house. Half way back to the olive grove, I met the distraught owner.

'There he is! There he is! The wicked one. I couldn't think where he had got to. He never leaves my side normally, that's why I don't keep him tied up. He must have taken a great fancy to you.'

Honesty made me admit that I thought the only reason Pavlo had followed me was because he viewed me in the light of a purveyor of chocolates.

'Phew!' said the man. 'It is a relief to me. I thought he might have gone down to the village and that would have got me into trouble with the police.'

Reluctantly, I handed Pavlo over to his owner and watched them make their way back to their camp under the trees. And then, in some trepidation, I went back to face the family. Although it had not been my fault that Pavlo had followed me, my activities in the past stood against me and the family took a lot of convincing that, on this occasion, the guilt was not mine.

The following morning, my head still filled with thoughts of Pavlo, I dutifully went into town—as I did every morning—to the house of my tutor, Richard Kralefsky. Kralefsky was a little gnome of a man with a slightly humped back and great earnest amber eyes who suffered from real tortures in his unsuccessful attempts to educate me. He had two most endearing qualities; one, a deep love for natural history (the whole attic of his house was devoted to an enormous variety of canaries and other birds), the other that, for at least a part of the time he lived in a dream world where he was always the hero. These adventures he would relate to me. He was inevitably accompanied in them by a heroine who was never named, but known simply as 'a Lady'.

The first half of the morning was devoted to mathematics and, with my head full of thoughts of Pavlo, I proved to be even duller than usual, to the consternation of Kralefsky who

ı hitherto been under the impression that he had plumbed
: depths of my ignorance.

My dear boy, you simply aren't concentrating this morn-
:,' he said earnestly. 'You don't seem able to grasp the
aplest fact. Perhaps you are a trifle overtired? We'll have a
ırt rest from it, shall we?'

Kralefsky enjoyed these short rests as much as I did. He
ıld potter out into the kitchen and bring back two cups of
fee and some biscuits, and we would sit companionably
ile he told me highly coloured stories of his imaginary
ventures. But this particular morning he did not get a
ınce. As soon as we were sitting comfortably, sipping our
fee, I told him all about Pavlo and the man with the talking
ad and the bear.

Quite extraordinary!' he said. 'Not the sort of thing that
: expects to find in an olive grove. It must have surprised
ı, I'll be bound?'

Then his eyes glazed and he fell into a reverie, staring at the
ling, tipping his cup of coffee so that it slopped into the
cer. It was obvious that my interest in the bear had set off
rain of thought in his mind. It was several days since I had
ı an instalment of his memoirs and I waited eagerly to see
at the result would be.

When I was a young man,' began Kralefsky, glancing at me
nestly to see whether I was listening. 'When I was a young
n I'm afraid I was a bit of a harum scarum. Always getting
ɔ trouble, you know.'

Ie chuckled reminiscently and brushed a few biscuit crumbs
m his waistcoat. With his delicately manicured hands and
large, gentle eyes it was difficult to imagine him as a harum
rum, but I tried dutifully.

I thought at one time I would even join a circus,' he said,
h the air of one confessing to infanticide. 'I remember a
ge circus came to the village where we were living and I
ended every performance. Every single performance. I got
know the circus folk quite well, and they even taught me
ıe of their tricks. They said I was excellent on the trapeze.'
glanced at me, shyly, to see how I would take this. I nodded
ously, as though there was nothing ludicrous in the
ught of Kralefsky, in a pair of spangled tights, on a trapeze.

'Have another biscuit?' he enquired. 'Yes? That's ⸻
ticket! I think I'll have one, too.'

Munching my biscuit, I waited patiently for him to resur⸻

'Well,' he continued, 'the week simply flew past and ⸻
evening came for the final performance. I wouldn't have miss⸻
it for the world. I was accompanied by a Lady, a young frie⸻
of mine, who was desirous of seeing the performance. H⸻
she laughed at the clowns! *And* admired the horses. She lit⸻
knew of the horror that was soon to strike.'

He took out his delicately scented handkerchief and patt⸻
his moist brow with it. He always tended to get a trifle ov⸻
excited as he reached the climax of a story.

'The final act,' he said, 'was the lion tamer.' He paused ⸻
that the full portent of this statement could sink in. 'Five bea⸻
he had. Huge Nubian lions with black manes, fresh from ⸻
jungle so he told me. The Lady and I were sitting in the fr⸻
row where we could obtain the best possible view of the ri⸻
You know the sort of cage affair that they put up in the ri⸻
for the lion act? Well, in the middle of the act, one of t⸻
sections, which had not been securely bolted, fell inwards. ⸻
our horror, we saw it fall on the lion tamer, knocking him ⸻
conscious.' He paused, took a nervous sip of coffee, and wip⸻
his brow once more.

'What was to be done?' he enquired, rhetorically. 'Th⸻
were five huge, snarling lions and I had a Lady by my si⸻
My thoughts worked fast. If the Lady was to be saved, the⸻
was only one thing I could do. Seizing my walking-stick⸻
leapt into the ring and marched into the cage.'

I made just audible sounds, indicative of admiration.

'During the week when I had been visiting the circus, I h⸻
studied the lion tamer's method with great care, and n⸻
I thanked my lucky stars for it. The snarling beasts on th⸻
pedestals towered over me, but I looked them straight in t⸻
eye. The human eye, you know, has great power over t⸻
animal world. Slowly, fixing them with a piercing gaze a⸻
pointing my walking-stick at them, I got them under cont⸻
and drove them inch by inch out of the ring and back in⸻
their cage. A dreadful tragedy had been averted.'

I said that the Lady must have been grateful to him.

'She was indeed. She was indeed,' said Kralefsky, pleased⸻

he even went so far as to say that I gave a better performance
an the lion tamer himself.'

Had he, I wondered, during his circus days, ever had any-
ing to do with dancing bears?

'All sorts of animals,' said Kralefsky lavishly. 'Elephants,
als, performing dogs, bears. They were all there.'

In that case, I said tentatively, would he not like to come
d see the dancing bear. It was only just down the road and,
though it was not exactly a circus, I felt it might interest him.

'By Jove, that's an idea,' said Kralefsky. He pulled his watch
t of his waistcoat pocket and consulted it. 'Ten minutes, eh?
ll help blow the cobwebs away.'

He got his hat and stick and together we made our way
gerly through the narrow, crowded streets of the town,
dolent with the smell of fruit and vegetables, drains and
shly baked bread. By dint of questioning several small boys,
discovered where Pavlo's owner was holding his show.
was a large, dim barn at the back of a shop in the centre of
vn. On the way there I borrowed some money off Kralefsky
d purchased a bar of sticky nougat, for I felt that I could not
to see Pavlo without taking him a present.

Ah, Pavlo's friend! Welcome,' said the gypsy as we
peared in the doorway of the barn.

To my delight, Pavlo recognised me and came shuffling
ward, uttering little grunts, and then reared up on his hind
s in front of me. Kralefsky backed away, rather hurriedly,
ought, for one of his circus training, and took a firmer grip
his stick.

Do be careful, my boy,' he said.

fed the nougat to Pavlo and when finally he had squelched
last sticky lump off his back teeth and swallowed it, he
e a contented sigh and lay down with his head between his
vs.

Do you want to see the Head?' asked the gypsy. He ges-
d towards the back of the barn where there was a plain
l table on which was a square box, apparently made out of
h.

Wait,' he said, 'and I'll light the candles.'

Ie had a dozen or so large candles soldered to the top of
ox on their own wax, and these he now lit so that they

flickered and quivered and made the shadows dance. Then
went forward to the table and rapped on it with his bear sti
'Head, are you ready?' he asked.
I waited with a delicate prickle of apprehension in my spi
Then from the interior of the cloth box a clear treble vo
said,
'Yes, I'm ready.'
The man lifted the cloth at one side of the box and I s
that the box was formed of slender laths on which thin cl
had been loosely tacked. The box was about three feet squa
In the centre of it was a small pedestal with a flattened top a
on it, looking macabre in the flickering light of the candl
was the head of a seven-year-old boy.
'By Jove!' said Kralefsky in admiration. 'That is clever!
What astonished me was that the head was alive. It w
obviously the head of a young gypsy lad, made up rat
crudely with black grease paint to look like a Negro. It sta
at us and blinked its eyes.
'Are you ready to answer questions now?' said the gyp
looking, with obvious satisfaction, at the entranced Kralefs
The Head licked its lips and then said, 'Yes, I am ready.
'How old are you?' asked the gypsy.
'Over a thousand years old,' said the Head.
'Where do you come from?'
'I come from Africa and my name is Ngo.'
The gypsy droned on with his questions and the H
answered them, but I was not interested in that. What I wan
to know was how the trick was done. When he at first told
about the Head, I had expected something carved out of we
or plaster which, by ventriloquism, could be made to spe
but this was a living head perched on a little wooden pedes
the circumference of a candle. I had no doubt that the H
was alive for its eyes wandered to and fro as it answered
questions automatically, and once, when Pavlo got up a
shook himself, a look of apprehension came over its face
'There,' said the gypsy proudly, when he had finished
questioning. 'I told you, didn't I? It's the most remarka
thing in the world.'
I asked him whether I could examine the whole thing m
closely. I had suddenly remembered that Theodore had t

e of a similar illusion which was created with the aid of
.irrors. I did not see where it was possible to conceal the body
at obviously belonged to the head, but I felt that the table
d the box needed investigation.

'Certainly,' said the gypsy, somewhat to my surprise. 'Here,
ke my stick. But all I ask is that you don't touch the Head
self.'

Carefully, with the aid of the stick I poked all round the
destal to see if there were any concealed mirrors or wires,
d the Head watched me with a slightly amused expression
its black eyes. The sides of the box were definitely only of
oth and the floor of the box was, in fact, the top of the table
a which it stood. I walked round the back of it and I could
e nothing. I even crawled under the table, but there was
thing there and certainly no room to conceal a body. I was
mpletely mystified.

'Ah,' said the gypsy in triumph. 'You didn't expect that,
d you? You thought I had a boy concealed in there, didn't
u?'

I admitted the charge humbly and begged him to tell me
w it was done.

'Oh, no. I can't tell you,' he said. 'It's magic. If I told you,
e Head would disappear in a puff of smoke.'

I examined both the box and the table for a second time,
t, even bringing a candle closer to aid my investigations, I
ll could not see how it was possible.

'Come,' said the gypsy. 'Enough of the Head. Come and
nce with Pavlo.'

He hooked the stick into the bear's muzzle and Pavlo rose
to his hind legs. The gypsy handed the stick to me and then
cked up a small wooden flute and started to play and Pavlo
d I did a solemn dance together.

'Excellent, by Jove! Excellent!' said Kralefsky, clapping his
nds with enthusiasm. I suggested that he might like to dance
th Pavlo too, since he had such vast circus experience.

'Well, now,' said Kralefsky. 'I wonder whether it would be
ogether wise? The animal, you see, is not familiar with me.'

'Oh, he'll be all right,' said the gypsy. 'He's tame with any-
e.'

'Well,' said Kralefsky reluctantly, 'if you're sure. If you
sist.'

201

He took the bear stick gingerly from me and stood facing Pavlo, looking extremely apprehensive.

'And now,' said the gypsy, 'you will dance.'

And he started to play a lilting little tune on his pipe.

I stood enchanted by the sight. The yellow, flickering light of the candles showing the shadows of Kralefsky's little hump backed figure and the shaggy form of the bear on the wall as they pirouetted round and round and, squatting on its pedestal in the box, the Head watched them, grinning and chuckling to itself.

The Angry Barrels

At the tail end of the summer came the grape harvest. Throughout the year you had been aware of the vineyards as part of the scenery, but it was only when the grape harvest came that you remembered the sequence of events that led up to it; the vineyards in winter, when the vines looked dead, like so many pieces of drift-wood stuck in lines in the soil; and then the day in spring, when you first noticed a green sheen on each vine as the delicate, frilly little leaves uncurled. And then the leaves grew larger and hung on the vines, like green hands warming themselves in the heat of the sun. After that the grapes started to appear, tiny nodules on a branched stem, which gradually grew and plumped themselves in the sunlight until they looked like the jade eggs of some strange sea monster. Then was the time for the washing of the vines. The lime and copper sulphate in big barrels would be dragged to the vineyards in little wooden carts pulled by the ever-patient donkeys. The sprayers would appear in their uniform that made them look like visitors from another planet: goggles and masks, a great canister strapped on their backs from which led a rubber pipe, as mobile as an elephant's trunk, through which the liquid would run. This mixture was of a blue that put the sky and the sea to shame. It was the distilled blueness of everything blue in the world. Tanks would be filled and the sprayers would move through the frilly groves of vine, covering each leaf, wrapping each bunch of green grapes in a delicate web of Madonna blue. Under this protective blue mantle, the grapes swelled and ripened until at last in the hot dog-days of summer, they were ready to be plucked and eased of their juice. The grape harvest was so important that it naturally became a time of visiting, a time of picnics and of celebrations, a time when you brought out last year's wine and mused over it. We had been invited to attend a wine harvest by a Mr Stavrodakis, a tiny, kindly wizened little man with a face like a half-starved tortoise, who owned a villa and some big vine-

yards towards the north of the island. He was a man who lived
for his wine, who thought that wine was the most important
thing in the world, and so his invitation was delivered with all
the solemnity befitting such an occasion and received with
equal solemnity by the family. In his note of invitation, written
in bold copper plate, embellished with little frills and flourishes
so that it looked like wrought iron tracery, he had said 'Do
please feel free to bring those of your friends that you think
might enjoy this'.

'Wonderful,' said Larry. 'He's supposed to have the best
cellar in Corfu.'

'Well, I suppose we can go if you want to,' said Mother
doubtfully.

'Of course I want to,' said Larry. 'Think of all that wine.
tell you what, we'll hire a *benzina* and make up a party.'

'Oh yes,' said Margo eagerly. 'He's got that marvellou
beach on his estate. We must get in some more swimmin
before the summer ends.'

'We can invite Sven,' said Larry. 'He should be back b
then. And we'll ask Donald and Max to come along.'

'And Theodore,' said Leslie.

'Larry, dear,' said Mother, 'the man's only invited us t
watch his grapes being pressed or whatever it is they do
you can't take a whole assortment of people along wit
you.'

'He says in his letter to bring any of our friends we want to
said Larry.

'Yes, but you can't take a whole circus,' said Mother. 'How
the poor man going to feed us all?'

'Well, that's easily solved,' said Larry. 'Write and tell hi
that we'll bring our own food.'

'I suppose that means I'll have to cook it?' said Mother.

'Nonsense,' said Larry vaguely, 'we'll just take a few cho
or something and grill them over an open fire.'

'I know what *that* means,' said Mother.

'Well, surely you can organize it somehow,' said Larr
'After all, it seems to me a perfectly simple thing to do.'

'Well,' said Mother reluctantly, 'I'll have a word with Spi
in the morning and see what can be done.'

The result was that Mother penned a careful note to M
Stavrodakis saying that we would be delighted to accept h

tation and bring a few friends. We would bring our own
d and picnic on the beach. Mr Stavrodakis sent back an-
er piece of copper-plate topiary expressing himself over-
lmed at our kindness in accepting his invitation and saying
he looked forward to seeing us. He added, 'Do please
ne undressed as we are in the family way.' The phrase
zled us all considerably—since he was a bachelor of long
ding—until we realised he had translated it literally from
French.

he party finally consisted of Donald and Max, Theodore,
lefsky, Sven, who had turned up in the nick of time from
ens, Spiro and the family. We assembled at six-thirty in
morning at the sunken steps behind the king's palace in
town, where a dumpy, freshly painted *benzina* waited,
bing a greeting to us on the tiny ripples. Getting on board
us quite some time. There were the numerous hampers
ood and wine, the cooking utensils and Mother's enormous
rella which she refused to travel without during the
mer months. Then Kralefsky, bowing and beaming, had
o through the performance of handing Mother and Margo
board.

ently now. Don't stumble. That's the ticket!' he said as
scorted them on to the boat with all the courtesy of a
handing his latest mistress into a gondola.

ortunately,' said Theodore, peering up at the blue sky
tratingly from under the brim of his Homburg, 'for-
tely it looks as though it's going to be er . . . , um . . .,
know, a fine day. I'm glad of that, for, as you know, the
test motion upsets me.'

ven missed his footing as he was getting on board and
st dropped his precious accordion into the sea, but it was
eved from a watery death by Max's long arm. Eventually
vere all on board. The *benzina* was pushed out, the engine
started and we were off. In the pale, pearly, early morning
haze, the town looked like a child's town, built out of
ling bricks. The façades of tall, elderly Venetian houses,
bling gently, coloured in pale shades of cream and
vn and white and cyclamen pink, were blurred by the heat
so they looked like a smudged pastel drawing.

life on the ocean wave!' said Kralefsky inhaling the
n, still air dramatically. 'That's the ticket!'

'Although the sea *looks* so calm,' observed Theodore, 'th
is, I think, a slight—almost imperceptible—motion.'

'What rubbish, Theodore,' said Larry. 'You could la
spirit level on this sea and you wouldn't get a wink out of
bubble.'

'Is Muzzer comfortable?' enquired Max lovingly of Mot

'Oh yes, dear, thank you, quite comfortable,' she said, '
I'm a little bit worried. I'm not sure whether Spiro rem
bered the garlic.'

'Don't yous worries, Mrs Durrells,' said Spiro, who
overheard the remark. 'I gots all the things that you tells m
get.'

Sven, having examined his accordion with the utmost c
to make sure that it had come to no harm, now lashe
round himself and ran an experimental series of fingers up
keyboard.

'A rousing sea shanty,' said Donald. 'That's what we n
Yo, ho, ho, and a bottle of rum.'

I left them and made my way up into the bows of the *M
zina* where I lay, staring down over the prow as it sheared
way through the glassy, blue sea. Occasionally little flock
flying fish would break the surface ahead of us, glittering t
and moon-silver in the sun, as they burst from the water
skimmed along the surface, like insect-gleaning sum
swallows across a blue meadow.

We reached our destination at eight o'clock: a half-m
long beach that lay under the flanks of Pandokrator. Here
olive grove came almost to the sea, only separated from it t
wide strip of shingle. As we approached the shore, the en
was switched off and we drifted in gently under our c
momentum. Now there was no engine noise we could t
the cries of the cicadas welcoming us to land. The *benz*
with an enormous sigh, pressed its bow into the pebbles of
shallows. The lithe, brown boy, whose boat it was, came
ward from the engine and leapt from the bows with the anc
which he lodged firmly in the shingle. Then he pile
collection of boxes alongside the bows of the *benzina* t
sort of tottering staircase down which Mother and Margo v
escorted by Kralefsky. He bowed elegantly as each one rea
the shingle, and somewhat marred the effect by inadverte
stepping backward into six inches of sea water and irretu

y ruining the crease of his elegant trousering. Eventually,
and all of our goods and chattels were ashore and, leaving
possessions under the olive trees, strewn haphazardly like
ething from a wrecked ship that had been disgorged
the sea, we made our way up the hill to Stavrodakis'
a.

he villa was large and square, faded red with green shutters
built up high so that the lower floor formed a spacious
ar. Streams of peasant girls were walking up the drive
rying baskets of grapes on their heads, moving with the
e gracefulness of cats. Stavrodakis came scuttling among
m to greet us.

So kind, so kind! Really so kind!' he kept repeating, as
h introduction was made.

Ie seated us all on his veranda under a great carnival red
of bougainvillea and opened several bottles of his best
e. It was heavy and sharp and glowed a sullen red as
ugh he were pouring garnets into our glasses. When we
e fortified and slightly light-headed, he led us, skittering
ad like an amiable black beetle, down to his cellars.

he cellars were so big that their dimmest recesses had to
lit by oil lamps, little flickering wicks floating in pots of
ber oil. The cellar was divided into two parts and he led
irst to where the treading was taking place. Looming over
rything else in the dim light were three gigantic barrels.
e of them was being filled with grapes by a constant pro-
sion of peasant women. The other two were occupied by
treaders. In the corner, seated on an upturned keg, was a
y, fragile-looking old man who, with great solemnity, was
ving on a fiddle.

hat's Taki and that's Yani,' said Stavrodakis, pointing to
two wine treaders.

aki's head could only just be seen above the rim of the
el, whereas Yani's head and shoulders were still visible.

aki's been treading since last night,' said Stavrodakis,
cing nervously at Mother and Margo, 'so I'm afraid
a little bit inebriated.'

deed, from where we stood we could smell the heady
es of the grape pulp and they were intoxicating enough, so
r force must have been trebled when concentrated in
warm depths of the barrel. From the base of the barrel the

crude young wine dribbled out into a trough where it
smouldering with patches of froth on top as pink as alm
blossom. From here it was syphoned off into barrels.

'This is, of course, the end of the harvest,' Stavrodakis
explaining. 'These are the last of the red grapes. They co
from a little vineyard high up and produce, I venture to thi
one of the better wines of Corfu.'

Taki momentarily stopped his jig on the grapes, hoo
his arms over the side of the barrel and hung there lik
drunken swallow on its nest, his arms and hands stained w
wine and covered with a crust of grape skins and seeds.

'It's time I came out,' he said thickly, 'or I shall be dr
as a lord.'

'Yes, yes, in a minute, my Taki,' said Stavrodakis look
around him nervously. 'In a minute Costos will be here
relieve you.'

'One must pee,' Taki explained, aggrievedly. 'A man c
work unless he pees.'

The old man put down his fiddle and, presumably by way
compensation, handed Taki a lump of coarse bread which
ate wolfishly.

Theodore was giving Sven an erudite lecture on vi
pointing at both treaders and the barrels with his walking-s
as though they had been objects in a museum.

'Who was it?' said Max to Larry, 'that drownded in a
of Malmsey?'

'One of Shakespeare's more sensible heroes,' said Larry.

'I remember once,' Kralefsky said to Donald, 'taking a L
round one of the biggest cellars in France. Half way round
cellar I began to feel uneasy. I had a premonition of dar
and so I escorted the Lady out and at that moment four
of the barrels burst with a roar like cannons . . .'

'Here, as you have seen, we do the treading,' said Sta
dakis. 'Now if you will just follow me this way, I'll show
where the wine is stored.'

He led us through an archway into the other gloomy sec
of the cellar. Here rank after rank of barrels lay on their si
The noise was incredible. At first I thought it must have s
outside source, until I realised that it emanated from
barrels. As the wine fermented in their brown bellies,
barrels gurgled and squeaked and growled at each other

1 angry mob. The sound was fascinating, but slightly horrific. was as though in each barrel there was incarcerated some ightful demon mouthing incomprehensible abuse.

'The peasants say,' said Theodore, with macabre relish, tapp-g one of the barrels lightly with his stick, 'the peasants say at it sounds like a drowning man.'

'Malmsey!' said Max excitedly. 'Barrels and barrels of almsey! Larry, we'll get drownded together!'

'Drowned,' said Donald.

'Most interesting,' Mother was saying insincerely to Stavro-akis, 'but if you will excuse us, I think Margo and I had better back to the beach and see about lunch.'

'I wonder what force it generates in there?' said Leslie, ancing round moodily. 'I mean if it generated sufficient force push one of those bungs out, I wonder what power it would ave?'

'Quite considerable,' said Theodore. 'I remember once see-g a man quite badly injured by the bung from a barrel.' As to demonstrate this, he tapped a barrel sharply with his stick d we all jumped.

'Yes, well, if you will excuse us,' said Mother nervously, 'I ink Margo and I had better be going.'

'But the rest of you, the rest of you will come up to the use and have some wine?' pleaded Stavrodakis.

'Of course we will,' said Larry as though he was doing him favour.

'Malmsey!' said Max rolling his eyes in ecstasy. 'We will ve Malmsey!'

So while Margo and Mother went back to the beach to help iro in the preparations for lunch, Stavrodakis fussily hurried back on to the veranda and plied us with wine so that when was time for us to go back to the beach, we were mellow, rm and flushed.

'I dreamt,' carolled Max as we walked through the olives, king a delighted Stavrodakis with us to share our lunch, 'I eamt that I dwelt in marble halls with vessels and turfs by y side.'

'He does it to annoy me,' Donald confided to Theodore. e knows that song perfectly well.'

Under the trees at the edge of the sea, three charcoal fires d been lighted. They glowed, shuddered and smoked gently

209

and over them popped and sizzled a variety of foods. Marg
had laid a great cloth in the shade and was putting cutlery an
glasses on it, singing untunefully to herself, while Mother an
Spiro crouched like witches over the fires, larding the brow
sizzling carcass of a kid with oil and squeezed garlic an
anointing the great body of a fish—its skin bubbled an
crisped enticingly by the heat of the fire—with lemon juic

Lunch we ate in a leisurely fashion sprawled round th
bright cloth, the glasses glowing with wine. The mouthfuls
kid were rich and succulent, woven with herbs, and the se
tions of fish melted like snowflakes in your mouth. The co
versation drifted and sprang up and then coiled languidly aga
as the smoke from the fires.

'You have to be in love with a piece of stone,' said Sve
solemnly. 'You see a dozen pieces of stone. You say, Pa
That's not for me, and then you see a piece, delicate and el
gant, and you fall in love with it. It's like women. But the
comes marriage and that can be terrible. You fight with
and you find that the stone is hard. You are in despair, the
suddenly, like wax, it melts under your hands and you crea
a shape.'

'I remember,' said Theodore, 'being asked by Berlincourt
you know, that French painter who lives over at Paleocastrit
—being asked by him to go and look at his work. He said,
you know, quite distinctly, "come and see my *paintings*". So
went one afternoon and he was most hospitable. He gave m
um, you know, little cakes and tea and then I said I would li
to see his paintings and he pointed to one large canvas whic
was on the, um, what is it, that thing that painters use? Ah ye
easel. It was quite a pretty painting really. It showed the bay
Paleocastritsa with the monastery quite clearly and when I h
admired it I looked round to see where the rest of his wor
was, but there didn't appear to be any. So I, um, asked hi
where the *rest* of his paintings were and he pointed to the eas
and said, um, "under there." It appeared that he couldn
afford canvases and so he painted one picture on top
another.'

'Great artists have to suffer,' said Sven lugubriously.

'When winter comes, I'll take you over to the Butrin
marshes,' said Leslie with enthusiasm. 'Masses of duck the
and damned great wild boars up in the hills,'

'Ducks I like, but wild board I think are a bit big for me,' id Max, with the conviction of one who knows his limi- tions.

'I don't think Max is up to it,' said Donald. 'He'd probably it and run at a crucial moment. He's a foreigner, you iow.'

'And then,' said Mother to Kralefsky, 'you put your bay leaf d sorrel in just *before* it starts to simmer.'

'So I says to him, Misses Margos, I says I don't care if he is e French Ambassador, he's a bastard.'

'Then, at the edge of the marsh—it's a bit difficult walking, course, because the ground's so mushy—you can get wood- ck and snipe.'

'I remember once I visited a village in Macedonia where they d very curious, um, you know, wood sculptures.'

'I knew a Lady once who used to make it without the bay af, but with a pinch of mint.'

It was the hottest hour of the day when even the cicadas em to slow down and falter occasionally in their song. The ack ants moved busily across the cloth, gathering the crumbs our food. A horse fly, its eyes gleaming like malevolent neralds, settled for a brief moment on Theodore's beard and en zoomed away.

Slowly, full of food and wine, I got up and made my way wn to the sea. 'And sometimes,' I could hear Stavrodakis y to Margo, 'sometimes the barrels really shout. They make noise as if they were fighting. It keeps me awake.'

'Oh don't,' said Margo shuddering. 'It makes me creepy st to think of it.'

The sea was still and warm, looking as though it had been rnished, with just a tiny ripple patting languidly at the shore. he shingle scrunched and shifted, hot under my bare feet. he rocks and pebbles that made up this beach were incredible shape and colour, moulded by the waves and the gentle bbing and polishing, one against the other. They had been ilptured into a million shapes: arrow-heads, sickles, cock- ls, horses, dragons and starfish. Their colouring was as zarre as their shapes, for they had been patterned by the rth's juices millions of years before and now their decora- ns had been buffed and polished by the sea. White with gold red filigree, blood red with white spots, green, blue and

211

pale fawn, hen's egg-brown with a deep rusty red pattern li
a fern, pink as a peony with white Egyptian hieroglyphi
forming a mysterious, indecipherable message across them.
was like a vast treasure trove of jewels spread along the ri
of the sea.

I waded into the warm shallows and then dived and swa
out to cooler water. Here, if you held your breath and let you
self sink to the bottom, the soft velvety blanket of the s
momentarily stunned and crippled your ears. Then, after
moment, they became attuned to the underwater symphon
The distant throb of a boat engine, soft as a heart beat, t
gentle whisper of the sand as the sea's movement shuffled a
rearranged it and, above all, the musical clink of the pebbl
on the shore's edge. To hear the sea at work on its great sto
of pebbles, rubbing and polishing them lovingly, I swam fro
the deep waters into the shallows. I anchored myself with
handful of multi-coloured stones and then, ducking my he
below the surface, listened to the beach singing under t
gentle touch of the small waves. If walnuts could sing, I
flected, they would sound like this. Scrunch, tinkle, squea
mumble, cough (silence while the wave retreats) and then t
whole thing in different keys repeated with the next wa
The sea played on the beach as though it were an instrument
lay and dozed for a time in the warm shallows and then, hea
with sleep, made my way back into the olive groves.

Everyone lay about disjointedly, sleeping around the ru
of our meal. It looked like the aftermath of some terri
battle. I curled up like a dormouse in the protective roots
a great olive and drifted off to sleep myself.

I woke to the gentle clinking of tea cups as Margo a
Mother laid the cloth for tea. Spiro brooded with immer
concentration over a fire on which he had set a kettle. A
watched drowsily, the kettle lifted its lid and waved pertly
him, hissing steam. He seized it in one massive hand a
poured the contents into a tea pot, then, turning, scowled
our recumbent bodies.

'Teas,' he roared thunderously. 'Teas is readys.'

Everybody started and woke.

'Dear God! Must you yell like that, Spiro?' said La
plaintively, his voice thickened by sleep.

'Tea,' said Kralefsky, waking up and peering around hi

king like a dishevelled moth. 'Tea, by Jove. Excellent.
at's the ticket.'

'God, my head aches,' said Leslie. 'It must be that wine. It's
t a kick like a mule.'

'Yes, I'm feeling a bit fragile myself,' said Larry, yawning
d stretching.

'I feel as though I've been drowned,' said Max with con-
ction. 'Drowned in Malmsey and then brought back by arti-
ial inspiration.'

'Must you always massacre the English tongue?' said Donald
itably. 'God knows it's bad enough having thousands of
glishmen doing it, without you foreigners starting.'

'I remember reading somewhere,' began Theodore, who
d woken up instantly, like a cat, and who, having slept like
e, looked as immaculate as though he had not been to sleep
all. 'I remember reading once that there's a tribe up in the
untains of Ceylon that speaks a language that nobody can
derstand. I mean to say, not even expert linguists have been
le to understand it.'

'It sounds just like Max's English,' said Donald.

Under the influence of tea, buttered toast, salt biscuits,
ter-cress sandwiches and an enormous fruit cake as damp,
fragile and as rich-smelling as loam, we started to wake up.
esently we went down to the sea and swam in the warm
ters until the sun sank and pushed the mountain's shadow
er the beach, making it look cold and drained of colour.
en we went up to Stavrodakis's villa and sat under the
ugainvillea, watching the sunset colours blur and mingle
er the sea. We left Stavrodakis, who insisted on giving us a
zen great jars of his best wine to commemorate our visit,
d made our way back to the *benzina*.

As we headed out to sea we left the shadow of the moun-
n and came into the warm glow of the sun again, which was
king, smudged blood-red behind the bulk of Pandokrator,
sting a shimmering reflection across the water like a flaming
press tree. A few tiny clouds turned pink and wine-yellow,
n the sun dipped behind the mountain and the sky turned
m blue to pale green and the smooth surface of the sea be-
ne for a brief moment all the magical colours of a fire opal.
e engine throbbed as we edged our way back towards the
vn, unrolling a white bale of lace wake behind us. Sven

213

played the opening of *The Almond Tree* very softly a
everyone started to sing.

> 'She shook the flowering almond tree
>   one sunny day
> With her soft little hands,
> The snowy blossoms on her breast and
>   shoulders lay
> And in her hair's dark strands,
> The snowy blossoms on her breast and
>   shoulders lay
> And in her hair's dark strands.'

Spiro's voice, deep, rich and smooth as black velvet, h
monizing with Theodore's pleasant baritone and Larry's ten
Two flying fish skimmed up from the blue depths beneath c
bows, skittered along the water and were lost in the twili
sea.

Now it was getting dark enough to see the tiny green cor
cations of phosphorus as our bow slid through the wat
The dark wine glugged pleasantly from the earthenw
pitchers into the glasses, the red wine that, last year, had l
snarling to itself in the brown barrels. A tiny wind, warm a
soft as a kitten's paw, stroked the boat. Kralefsky, his he
thrown back, his large eyes full of tears, sang at the velvet b
sky, shuddering with stars. The sea crisped along the sides
the boat with the sound of winter leaves, wind-lifted, rubb
themselves affectionately against the trunks of the trees t
gave them birth.

> 'But when I saw my darling thus in snow
>   arrayed,
> To her sweet side I sped.
> I brushed the gleaming petals from each
>   lock and braid,
> I kissed her and I said:
> I brushed the gleaming petals from each
>   lock and braid,
> I kissed her and I said:'

Far out in the channel between Corfu and the mainla

darkness was speckled and picked out with the lights of the
ing-boats. It was as though a small section of the Milky
y had fallen into the sea. Slowly the moon edged up over
carapace of the Albanian mountains, at first red like the
, then fading to copper, to yellow, and at last to white. The
y wind-shimmers on the sea glinted like a thousand fish
les.

he warm air, the wine and the melancholy beauty of the
ht filled me with a delicious sadness. It would always be
this, I thought. The brilliant, friendly island, full of secrets,
family and my animals around me and, for good measure,
friends. Theodore's bearded head outlined against the
on, wanting only horns to make him Pan; Kralefsky crying
shamedly now, like a black gnome weeping over his banish-
nt from fairyland; Spiro with his scowling brown face, his
ce as richly vibrant as a million summer bees; Donald and
x, frowning as they endeavoured to remember the words
the song and harmonize at the same time; Sven, like a great
y white baby, gently squeezing the soulful trickle of music
m his ungainly instrument.

> 'Oh, foolish one, to deck your hair so soon
> with snow,
> Long may you have to wait;
> The dreary winter days when chilling north
> winds blow
> Do not anticipate!
> The dreary winter days when chilling north
> winds blow
> Do not anticipate!'

w, I thought, we were edging into winter, but soon it
ld be spring again, burnished, glittering, bright as a gold-
h; and then it would be summer, the long, hot, daffodil
ow days,

> 'Oh, foolish one, to deck your hair so soon
> with snow,
> Long may you have to wait;
> The dreary winter days when chilling north
> winds blow

215

Do not anticipate!
The dreary winter days when chilling north
    winds blow
Do not anticipate!'

Lulled by the wine and the throbbing heart of the boat
engine, lulled by the warm night and the singing, I fell asleep
while the boat carried us back across the warm, smooth water
to our island and the brilliant days that were not to be.

Epilogue

Corfu is of such importance to me that its loss would deal a fatal blow to my projects.
Remember this: in the present state of Europe, the greatest misfortune which could befall me is the loss of Corfu.

NAPOLEON

Mail

Letter
Dear Mrs Durrell,

It seems at last war can no longer be avoided and I think perhaps you were wise to leave Corfu. One can only hope that we can all meet in happier times when mankind has regained its senses. I will look forward to that.

Should you wish to reach me, my address is c/o The Ionian Bank, Athens.

I wish you and your family the very best of luck in the future.

Love to you all,
  Yours,
  Theodore

Post Card
Mother,

Have moved to Athens, so keep in touch. Place marvellous. Acropolis like pink flesh in the sun. Have sent my things to you. In a trunk marked '3' you will find book called *An Evaluation of Marlowe*. Can you send it to me? Everyone here wearing tin hats and looking like war. Am buying myself large spear.

Love,
  Larry

Letter
Dear Mother,

I have had all my travellers' cheques pinched by some bloody Italian. They nearly arrested me because I punched him in the snoot. Give me the Greeks any day.

Can you send some more money to me at the Magnifica Hotel, Plaza de Contina, Milan? Will be home soon. Don't worry.

Love,
  Les

s. It looks like war, doesn't it?

Letter

Darling Mother,

Just a hurried note to tell you I'm leaving on the bo[a]
on Monday so I should be in England in about three week[s]

Things here are rather hectic, but what can you expe[ct]
It never rains but it snows. I think it's simply disgustin[g]
the way the Germans are carrying on. If I had my way I[']
tell them.

Will see you soon,

Love to you,

Margo

P.S. I enclose a letter from Spiro. Most odd.

Letter

Dear Missy Margo,

This is to tell you that war has been declared. Don['t]
tell a soul.

Spiro.

Have you heard about The Jersey Wildlife Preservation Trust?

A special appeal by Gerald Durrell

If you have read my books with pleasure, may I point out that those books would never have been written if it had not been for the wildlife of the world. Now, all over the world, many of these same animals are in a desperate plight and unless they are helped they will vanish for ever.

I am trying to do what I can and I want you to help me. If you have enjoyed my writing, if the animals I have described have amused or interested you, then please join my Trust and help in a cause which I believe to be of the utmost importance and urgency.

We need money to create ideal surroundings for the breeding colonies we will establish . . . to provide scientific laboratories so that the animals can be carefully studied . . . to extend and increase the Veterinary Department so that the animals can have the best possible treatment.

You have unfailingly supported me as a writer on wildlife—please support me now in my efforts to save it.

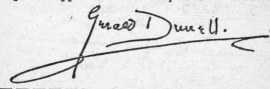

- - - - - - - - - - - - - - - -

Jersey Wildlife Preservation Trust
Les Augrès Manor, Trinity, Jersey, Channel Islands.
Hon. Director: Gerald Durrell

Please send me details of how I may become a member of the Trust.

NAME (Block letters) _____

ADDRESS _____
_____
_____

Animal Books in Fontana

JOY ADAMSON
Born Free (illus.)
Forever Free (illus.)
Living Free (illus.)

PHILIP BROWN
Uncle Whiskers

PHIL DRABBLE
Badgers at My Window (illus.)
Of Pedigree Unknown (illus.)
My Beloved Wilderness (illus.)
Phil Drabble's Book of Pets (illus.)

GERALD DURRELL
Beasts in My Belfry
Birds, Beasts and Relatives
Catch Me a Colobus (illus.)
Fillets of Plaice
Rosy is My Relative
The Stationary Ark (illus.)
Two in the Bush

JACQUIE DURRELL
Beasts in My Bed (illus.)
Intimate Relations (illus.)

HUGO VAN LAWICK
Solo (illus.)

More Animal Books in Fontana

JANE VAN LAWICK GOODALL
In the Shadow of Man (illus.)

B. and M. GRZIMEK
Serengeti Shall Not Die (illus.)

SUSANNE HART
Vet in the Wild (illus.)

BUSTER LLOYD-JONES
The Animals Came in One by One
Come into My World
Love on a Lead (illus.)

EVE PALMER
The Plains of Camdeboo (illus.)

DAPHNE SHELDRICK
Orphans of Tsavo (illus.)

GERALD SUMMERS
The Lure of the Falcon
Owned by an Eagle (illus.)

ERIC VARLEY
The Judy Story (illus.)

PHILIP WAYRE
The River People

Fontana Books

Fontana is a leading paperback publisher of fiction an non-fiction, with authors ranging from Alistair MacLean Agatha Christie and Desmond Bagley to Solzhenitsyn an Pasternak, from Gerald Durrell and Joy Adamson to th famous Modern Masters series.

In addition to a wide-ranging collection of international popular writers of fiction, Fontana also has an outstandin reputation for history, natural history, military histor psychology, psychiatry, politics, economics, religion an the social sciences.

All Fontana books are available at your bookshop newsagent; or can be ordered direct. Just fill in the for and list the titles you want.

FONTANA BOOKS, Cash Sales Department, G.P.O. B 29, Douglas, Isle of Man, British Isles. Please send purcha price, plus 8p per book. Customers outside the U.K. se purchase price, plus 10p per book. Cheque, postal or mon order. No currency.

NAME (Block letters)

ADDRESS

While every effort is made to keep prices low, it is sometimes necessar increase prices on short notice. Fontana Books reserve the right to show retail prices on covers which may differ from those previously advertised in text or elsewhere.